Materials developed just for the Upper Level SSAT:

Success on the Upper Level SSAT
- Strategies for each section of the test
- Reading and vocabulary drills
- In-depth math content instruction with practice sets
- 1 full-length practice test

The Best Unofficial Practice Tests for the Upper Level SSAT
- 2 additional full-length practice tests

30 Days to Acing the Upper Level SSAT
- Strategies for each section of the test
- Fifteen workouts, each providing practice problems and detailed explanations for every section of the test
- Perfect for additional practice or homework

30 More Days to Acing the Upper Level SSAT - NEW
- Fifteen more workouts, focused on the most challenging questions
- Recommended as additional practice for students who have already mastered the basics

Are you an educator?

Incorporate materials from Test Prep Works into your test prep program

- Use the materials developed specifically for the test and level your students are taking

- Customize our books to fit your program

    - Choose content modules from any of our books – even from multiple books
    - Add your branding to the cover and title page
    - Greet your students with an introductory message
    - Create custom books with a one-time setup fee*, then order the copies you want with no minimum quantities

- Volume discounts available for bulk orders of 30+ copies

You provide the expertise – let us provide the materials

Contact *sales@testprepworks.com* for more info

* - Setup fees start at $199 per title, which includes branding of the cover and title page and a customer-provided introductory page. Additional customization will incur additional setup fees.

30 More DAYS
to Acing the
Upper Level SSAT

Reaching for the 99th Percentile

Christa Abbott, M.Ed.

Copyright © 2019 Abbott Learning, LLC. All rights reserved. Except as permitted under the Copyright Act of 1976, no part of this publication may be reproduced or distributed in any forms or by any means, or stored in a data base or retrieval system, without the prior written permission of the publisher.

Published by:
Test Prep Works
PO Box 100572
Arlington, VA 22210
www.TestPrepWorks.com

For information about buying this title in bulk, or for editions with customized covers or content, please contact the publisher at sales@testprepworks.com or (703) 944-6727.

The SSAT is a registered trademark of The Enrollment Management Association, which has neither endorsed nor associated itself in any way with this book.

Neither the author nor the publisher of this book claims responsibility for the accuracy of this book or the outcome of students who use these materials.

ISBN: 978-1-68059-014-2

Contents

About the Author 7
How to Use This Book 8
Workouts 11
   Workout #1. 12
   Workout #2. 27
   Workout #3. 45
   Workout #4. 60
   Workout #5. 74
   Workout #6. 92
   Workout #7. 106
   Workout #8. 120
   Workout #9. 133
   Workout #10 147
   Workout #11 160
   Workout #12 174
   Workout #13 189
   Workout #14 203
   Workout #15 218
Appendix – Tips for the Writing Sample 232

About the Author

Christa Abbott has been a private test prep tutor for over a decade. She has worked with students who have been admitted to and attended some of the top independent schools in the country. Over the years, she has developed materials for each test that truly make the difference.

Christa is a graduate of Middlebury College and received her Master's in Education from the University of Virginia, a program nationally known for its excellence. Her background in education allows her to develop materials based on the latest research about how we learn so that preparation can be an effective and efficient use of time. Her materials are also designed to be developmentally appropriate for the ages of the students taking the tests. In her free time, she enjoys hiking, tennis, Scrabble, and reading. Her greatest joy is spending time with her husband and three children.

About Test Prep Works, LLC

Test Prep Works, LLC, was founded to provide effective materials for test preparation. Its founder, Christa Abbott, spent years looking for effective materials for the private school entrance exams but came up empty-handed. The books available combined several different tests and while there are overlaps, they are not the same test. Christa found this to be very overwhelming for students who were in elementary and middle school, and that just didn't seem necessary. Christa developed her own materials to use with students that are specific for each level of the test and are not just adapted from other books. For the first time, these materials are available to the general public as well as other tutors. Our titles include the *Success* series of complete coursebooks, the *30 Days* series of practice books, and the *Best Unofficial Practice Tests* series with additional full-length practice tests. Please visit *www.testprepworks.com* to view all of our offerings.

How to Use This Book

This book is designed to help students who are already scoring well on the SSAT move to the next level. The book starts with a brief introduction. After that, there is a series of "workouts." Each of these workouts should take about 30 minutes, although that can vary widely since we are working on just the hard problems in this book.

Since this book is designed for students who are already scoring well on the SSAT, we have included just the very hardest questions and vocabulary that they are likely to need to work on. Rest assured, the entire test will NOT be this difficult! We wrote this book for the students who don't want to wade through the easier questions that they are already answering correctly.

- This book contains ONLY the hard questions; the entire test is NOT this difficult

Within each workout, I have included practice for each section so that you get a "balanced diet" leading up to test day. You will notice some repetition – this is by design! In particular, you may see vocabulary words or words with the same roots repeated. This is to ensure that you don't forget the vocabulary that you have already studied. After you complete each workout, be sure to check your answers and figure out WHY you missed the questions that you did. The analysis is as important as the answers themselves.

I have spent years studying the test and analyzing the different question types, content, and the types of answers that test writers prefer. Now you can benefit from my hard work!

P.S.: I chose not to go into the nitty-gritty details in this book about how to register and what to bring on test day because I want you to focus on practice for now. Make sure to visit *www.ssat.org* to get all of the current details on registration and other procedures.

P.P.S.: If you are looking for additional Upper Level SSAT resources such as practice tests or content instruction, please visit *www.testprepworks.com* for more information on our other materials, including *Success on the Upper Level SSAT: A Complete Course* and *The Best Unofficial Practice Tests for the Upper Level SSAT*.

Game Plan for Success

Step 1: Set up a study routine.

The questions in this book are difficult and you will need the time and space to focus. Find a quiet place to work. These are also the most difficult problems, so you might need to build in breaks as you work. For example, each math section practice section has 10-11 questions. There will NOT be 10-11 really difficult math questions in a row on the actual test, so taking breaks as you work is fine.

Step 2: Complete the workouts.

When you miss a question, take the time to understand WHY you missed it before you move on to the next workout. Make flashcards for words or roots that you don't know and study them as you go. Rework math problems that you have missed.

Step 3: Read the appendix.

It gives advice on how to tackle the writing sample.

Step 4: Take practice tests.

Order the book *The Official Guide to the Upper Level SSAT*. (Please note that the ONLY place you can get this book is from *www.ssat.org*.) Take the Upper Level practice tests using the strategies that you have learned. Understand why you missed the questions that you did.

Other practice tests are available in addition to the ones in the official guide, including three that Test Prep Works has developed. Two are found in *The Best Unofficial Practice Tests for the Upper Level SSAT*, and a third is included at the back of *Success on the Upper Level SSAT: A Complete Course*.

Step 5: Rock the SSAT!

Basics You Need to Know

How the scoring works

On the Upper Level SSAT, if you answer a question correctly, then you are given one point. If you answer a question incorrectly, then a quarter point is deducted. If you don't answer at all, then you don't get a point added to your raw score, but nothing is deducted either.

You might be asking why they use this crazy system. The thinking behind it is that on a regular test, you would get ahead by guessing. You would answer some of the questions that you guessed on correctly and therefore your score would be higher for blindly guessing. Chances are that you would answer one-fifth of the questions correctly if you blindly guessed, because there are five answer choices for each question. By taking off a quarter point for the four-fifths of the questions that you miss, the test writers are making sure that you don't get ahead for blindly guessing.

When to guess

You should only guess if you can rule out at least one answer choice.

The percentile score

You will receive a raw score for the SSAT based upon how many questions you answered correctly or incorrectly. This raw score will then be converted into a scaled score. Neither of these scores is what schools are really looking at. They are looking for your percentile scores and, in particular, the percentile scores that compare you to other students applying to independent schools.

- Percentile score is what schools are really looking at

You will receive one percentile score that compares you to other students who are in your grade. For example, let's say that you are in eighth grade and scored in the 70th percentile. This means that you scored better than 70 out of 100 students in your grade. In addition, the SSAT provides a percentile score that compares you to students of the same gender in your grade.

The Most Important Strategy You Need to Know

Use the process of elimination, or "ruling out"

If you remember nothing else on test day, remember to use the process of elimination. This is a multiple-choice test, and there are often answers that don't even make sense.

When you read a question, you should read all of the answer choices before selecting one. You need to keep in mind that the test will ask you to choose the answer choice that "best" answers the question. Best is a relative word, so how can you know which answer choice best answers the question if you don't read them all?

- After you read the question, read ALL of the answer choices

- Look for the "best" answer, which may be the least wrong answer choice

After you have read all of the answer choices, rule them out in order from most wrong to least wrong. Sometimes, the "best" answer choice is not a great fit, but it is better than the others. This process will also clarify your thinking so that by the time you get down to only two answer choices, you have a better idea of what makes answer choices right or wrong.

- Rule out in order from most wrong to least wrong

Above all else, remember that you are playing the odds on this test. To increase your score, you need to answer questions even when you are not positive of which answer is correct.

Now that you know the basics, it is time to head to the workouts! Keep in mind that the questions on these workouts are ALL hard. On the real test, this is not the case. We are giving you just the difficult questions because this book is designed for students who are already doing well but aiming for the 99th percentile.

The format of each workout is very predictable so that you can focus on the material and not the directions. Here is what you should look for:

- Vocabulary
    - Each vocabulary section introduces 20 words. Learn these words before you move on to the verbal practice.

- Practice for the verbal section
    - Each workout has 10 synonym and 5 analogy questions.
    - Words from previous workouts will show up again; the point is not to complete a workout and then forget the words!

- Practice for the reading section
    - Each workout has one reading passage.
    - The passages in this book are the passage types that students most struggle with: workouts #1-4 have primary documents, workouts #5-8 have poems, workouts #9-12 have philosophical essays, and workouts #13-15 have fiction passages.

- Practice for the math sections
    - The focus here is to practice the hard math content.
    - Workouts #1-11 each have 10 math questions that are related to an individual topic.
    - Workouts #12-15 each have 11 questions. Why 11 questions? Because there is one question related to each topic of the first 11 workouts. The topics of these questions are in the same sequence as the topics of the first 11 workouts. For example, if you struggle with question #3 in any of these last four workouts, you can go back to workout #3 to review more questions related to the same topic.

There are also explanations. Be sure to review the questions that you miss. Make flashcards for the words you don't know. Rework the math questions that you missed. Remember, we are aiming for the top!

Go get 'em!

Workout #1

Words to Learn

Below are the words used in Workout 1. Refer back to this list as needed as you move through the lesson.

Words that mean to make something better

Allay:	soothe
Bolster:	support
Buttress:	support
Embellish:	to beautify or enhance
Rectify:	to correct
Ratify:	approve

Words with a positive meaning

Benevolent:	kind
Deft:	nimble
Diligent:	persevering
Dogged:	persistent
Exuberant:	enthusiastic or energetic
Invincible:	undefeatable
Prudent:	wise
Reputable:	respectable
Ardor:	passion
Allure:	attraction
Unerring:	perfect
Impartial:	unprejudiced
Proficient:	experienced
Timely:	well-timed

Synonyms Practice

1. EMBELLISH:
   - (A) support
   - (B) inject
   - (C) adorn
   - (D) limit
   - (E) shun

2. PRUDENT:
   - (A) humble
   - (B) wise
   - (C) impartial
   - (D) passionate
   - (E) lavish

3. BOLSTER:
   - (A) rectify
   - (B) ponder
   - (C) approach
   - (D) censor
   - (E) buttress

4. UNERRING:
   - (A) flawless
   - (B) respectable
   - (C) casual
   - (D) peaceful
   - (E) belligerent

5. RATIFY:
   - (A) attract
   - (B) paddle
   - (C) triumph
   - (D) approve
   - (E) calculate

6. DEFT:
   - (A) capable
   - (B) agile
   - (C) vivid
   - (D) strenuous
   - (E) invincible

7. BENEVOLENT:
   - (A) persistent
   - (B) notable
   - (C) kind
   - (D) grumpy
   - (E) enthusiastic

8. RECTIFY:
   - (A) fix
   - (B) insist
   - (C) stumble
   - (D) throw
   - (E) avenge

9. DILIGENT:
   - (A) timely
   - (B) certain
   - (C) resigned
   - (D) embellished
   - (E) conscientious

10. EXUBERANT:
    - (A) wise
    - (B) lively
    - (C) proficient
    - (D) practical
    - (E) deft

Analogies Practice

1. Allay is to fear as
   - (A) bolster is to strength
   - (B) bustle is to contribution
   - (C) thrive is to obstacle
   - (D) muffle is to noise
   - (E) silence is to concert

2. Deft is to clumsy as
   - (A) reputable is to dishonorable
   - (B) spectacular is to righteous
   - (C) flimsy is to floppy
   - (D) exuberant is to joyful
   - (E) homely is to lanky

3. Impartial is to bias as
   - (A) indefinite is to eternity
   - (B) invincible is to vulnerability
   - (C) impulsive is to chaos
   - (D) influential is to laziness
   - (E) intellectual is to academic

4. Affection is to ardor as
   - (A) timely is to dated
   - (B) reckless is to prudent
   - (C) diligent is to dogged
   - (D) frail is to robust
   - (E) buttress is to support

5. Proficient is to unable as
   - (A) attempt is to endeavor
   - (B) quick is to frantic
   - (C) civilized is to routine
   - (D) powerful is to meek
   - (E) alluring is to timely

Reading Practice

The following speech was given by President John F. Kennedy in 1961.

No man can fully grasp how far and how fast we have come, but condense, if you will, the 50,000 years of man's recorded history in a time span of but a half-century. Stated in these terms, we know very little about the first 40 years, except at the end of them advanced man had learned to use the skins of animals to cover them. Then about 10 years ago, under this standard, man emerged from his caves to construct other kinds of shelter. Only five years ago man learned to write and use a cart with wheels. Christianity began less than two years ago. The printing press came this year, and then less than two months ago, during this whole 50-year span of human history, the steam engine provided a new source of power. Newton explored the meaning of gravity. Last month electric lights and telephones and automobiles and airplanes became available. Only last week did we develop penicillin and television and nuclear power, and now if America's new spacecraft succeeds in reaching Venus, we will have literally reached the stars before midnight tonight.

This is a breathtaking pace, and such a pace cannot help but create new ills as it dispels old, new ignorance, new problems, new dangers. Surely the opening vistas of space promise high costs and hardships, as well as high reward.

So it is not surprising that some would have us stay where we are a little longer to rest, to wait. But this city of Houston, this state of Texas, this country of the United States was not built by those who waited and rested and wished to look behind them. This country was conquered by those who moved forward–and so will space.

William Bradford, speaking in 1630 of the founding of the Plymouth Bay Colony, said that all great and honorable actions are accompanied with great difficulties, and both must be enterprised and overcome with answerable courage.

If this capsule history of our progress teaches us anything, it is that man, in his quest for knowledge and progress, is determined and cannot be deterred. The exploration of space will go ahead, whether we join in it or not, and it is one of the great adventures of all time, and no nation which expects to be the leader of other nations can expect to stay behind in this race for space.

1. In the first paragraph, President Kennedy condenses recorded human history into 50 years in order to

    (A) show the importance of considering historical events.
    (B) illustrate how quickly the pace of technological advances has accelerated.
    (C) demonstrate that progress has always happened quickly.
    (D) provide the reader with a brief history of the technological advances of man.
    (E) encourage the reader to take action quickly.

2. President Kennedy mentions that in the first 40 years advanced man learned to cover themselves in animal skins to highlight

    (A) how slow progress can be.
    (B) that even small changes can have a large impact.
    (C) the importance of studying how humans solved problems in the past.
    (D) the lack of courage that humans exhibited in their early history.
    (E) how unimportant this advance was.

3. As used in line 12, the word "dispels" most nearly means

    (A) challenges
    (B) produces
    (C) finds
    (D) trades
    (E) alleviates

4. President Kennedy's tone when describing the space program can best be described as

    (A) ambivalent
    (B) ironic
    (C) admiring
    (D) critical
    (E) sentimental

5. Which of the following best expresses the main idea of the passage?

    (A) It is important that another country not beat the United States in the race to explore space.
    (B) Technological advances are happening more rapidly now than at any other time in history.
    (C) Americans must show determination in overcoming difficulties.
    (D) Americans should invest their resources in developing a space exploration program.
    (E) Technological advances have both advantages and disadvantages.

Math Practice

The first types of questions that we will cover are counting and probability. Counting questions require you to figure out how many possibilities there are. Probability builds on counting – the probability of an event occurring is the number of possibilities that include the desired event over the total number of possibilities.

Here are examples of counting questions on the SSAT:

1. Ramon is packing for a trip. He wants to pack 2 shirts, 1 pair of pants, 2 pairs of shoes, and 1 belt. He can choose from 10 shirts, 5 pairs of pants, 4 pairs of shoes, and 2 belts. How many different combinations can Ramon choose from?

    (A) 21
    (B) 69
    (C) 2,700
    (D) 10,800
    (E) 16,000

2. There are 6 runners in a race: Darnell, Van, Opal, Carlton, Brittany, and Ramon. If either Brittany or Van finished first, in how many unique orders could the runners finish?

    (A) 17
    (B) 120
    (C) 240
    (D) 720
    (E) 1,080

3. Tammy, Conrad, Geneva, Matt, and Justin are being seated at a round table with 5 seats. If Geneva and Matt are seated next to each other and Tammy and Justin are not seated next to each other, how many possibilities are there for the person sitting on Matt's right side?

    (A) 3
    (B) 5
    (C) 6
    (D) 60
    (E) 120

4. Tina wants to order a pizza that has 3 toppings. She can choose from 9 different toppings. How many unique 3-topping pizzas can she create from those 9 toppings?

    (A) 42
    (B) 84
    (C) 168
    (D) 504
    (E) 729

5. A homebuilding company sends teams out on jobs that are made up of 2 experienced carpenters and 3 apprentice carpenters. The company can choose from 6 experienced carpenters and 8 apprentice carpenters to create these teams. How many unique teams can the company create?

(A) 14
(B) 48
(C) 84
(D) 840
(E) 10,080

Here are some examples of difficult probability questions:

6. Cards labeled 3-39 are placed in a hat. If a card is to be selected at random, what is the probability that it is a multiple of 3 but not a multiple of 4?

(A) $\dfrac{2}{9}$

(B) $\dfrac{9}{37}$

(C) $\dfrac{1}{4}$

(D) $\dfrac{10}{37}$

(E) $\dfrac{1}{3}$

7. A random number generator that prints the numbers 0-9 is going to print two numbers. What is the probability that the first number will be even and the second number will be 2?

(A) $\dfrac{1}{20}$

(B) $\dfrac{1}{5}$

(C) $\dfrac{1}{4}$

(D) $\dfrac{1}{2}$

(E) $\dfrac{3}{5}$

Workout #1

8. A bag contains 6 red marbles, 4 green marbles, and 8 black marbles. Anne is going to randomly choose 2 marbles from the bag, without replacing the first marble before picking the second marble. What is the probability that she will choose one red marble and then one marble that is not red?

   (A) $\frac{1}{9}$

   (B) $\frac{2}{9}$

   (C) $\frac{4}{17}$

   (D) $\frac{1}{4}$

   (E) 1

9. Events X, Y, and Z are mutually exclusive and independent. If $P(X) = 0.3$, $P(Y) = 0.4$, and $P(Z) = 0.2$, what is $P(X \text{ and } Y)$?

   (A) 0.07
   (B) 0.12
   (C) 0.24
   (D) 0.60
   (E) 0.70

10. Hannah's basketball team can win, lose, or tie each game, and $P(\text{win}) = 0.55$, $P(\text{loss}) = 0.40$, and $P(\text{tie}) = 0.05$. Her team has 2 games remaining in the season and must win 1 game and not lose the second game in order to win the championship for the league. What is the probability Hannah's team will win the championship?

    (A) 0.25
    (B) 0.30
    (C) 0.33
    (D) 0.55
    (E) 0.60

Workout #1 Answers

Synonyms Practice

As you might have noticed as you went through the synonyms sections, the definition given was not always the one that was listed in the "Words to Learn" section. This is because there is often more than one synonym for a word and on test day, you may get a synonym other than the one listed.

When you check your work, if there are words that you do not know the meaning of, make flashcards for them and then study these flashcards after you complete each workout.

1. C — The word list states that *embellish* means "beautify" or "enhance." This is a positive meaning. We can eliminate choice B because *inject* is neither positive nor negative, and choices D and E because *limit* and *shun* (snub or reject) are negative. We are down to *support* or *adorn*. *Adorn* means "to decorate," which is like *beautify* or *enhance*, so choice C is the best answer, and choice A is not correct.

2. B — The word list states that *prudent* means "wise." Answer choice B is the correct answer. *Wise* is not a synonym for *humble* (modest), *impartial* (not biased), *passionate*, or *lavish* (excessive), so choices A, C, D, and E are not correct.

3. E — The word list states that *bolster* and *buttress* both mean "to support." Therefore, they are synonyms for each other, and choice E is correct. To *rectify* (correct), *ponder* (consider or think about), *approach*, or *censor* (ban) would not be to support, so choices A, B, C, and D are not correct.

4. A — To *err* is to make an error, or a mistake. The prefix *un-* means "not." Therefore, *unerring* means "to NOT make a mistake," or to be flawless. Answer choice A is correct. *Unerring* is a positive word, so we can easily rule out *casual* (choice C) because it is neither positive nor negative, and *belligerent* (choice E) because *belligerent* means "looking for a fight." *Respectable* and *peaceful* are both positive but do not get at the meaning of being without error, so choices B and D are also not correct.

5. D — The word list states that *ratify* means "to approve," so choice D is the correct answer. To *attract* (pull towards), *paddle*, *triumph* (win), and *calculate* do not mean to approve, so choices A, B, C, and E are not correct.

6. B — The word list states that *deft* means "nimble." *Nimble* describes a person who is quick and light in movement or thinking, or able to adjust quickly on the move. *Agile* has the same meaning, so choice B is the correct answer. *Capable* (able to do something), *vivid* (intense), *strenuous* (requiring hard work), and *invincible* (not able to be defeated) do not mean to be quick and light, so choices A, C, D, and E are not correct.

7. C — The word list states that *benevolent* means kind, so choice C is the correct answer. If you have trouble remembering this, the root *bene* means "good," so someone who is benevolent does good. To be *persistent* (not giving up), *notable* (well-known), *grumpy*, or *enthusiastic* does not mean to be kind, so choices A, B, D, and E are not correct.

8. A — The word list states that *rectify* means "to correct." Notice that both *rectify* and *correct* have the root *rect* which means "to guide" or "to make straight." Since *fix* is a synonym for *correct*, answer choice A is the best answer. *Insist* (demand), *stumble* (slip), *throw*, or *avenge* (take revenge) do not mean to correct, so choices B, C, D, and E are not correct.

9. E — The word list states that *diligent* means to be persevering. To be persevering is to follow through on a goal until it is completed, and to be conscientious means the same thing (think of following your conscience when you have committed to something). Answer choice E is correct. To follow through on completing a goal would not describe behavior that is *timely* (well-timed), *certain*, *resigned* (given up), or *embellished* (enhanced), so choices A, B, C, and D are not correct.

10. B — The word list describes the word *exuberant* as "enthusiastic" or "energetic." If you need help remembering this, the words *exuberant* and *excited* start the same way. Since *lively* is another word for *energetic*, choice B is the correct answer. To be *wise*, *proficient* (experienced), *practical* (useful), or *deft* (nimble) does not describe someone who is enthusiastic or energetic, so choices A, C, D, and E are not correct.

Analogies Practice

1. D — The relationship in this question is *to reduce*: to allay is to reduce fear. To *bolster* is to increase *strength*, and not reduce it, so choice A is not correct. *Bustle* (hurry) is not related to *contribution*, so choice B can be ruled out. To *thrive* is to overcome an *obstacle*, but not necessarily to reduce the obstacle, so choice C is not the best answer. To *muffle* is to reduce *noise* (think of a muffler on a car as reducing the noise that the engine makes), so choice D is the correct answer. To *silence* is not to reduce a *concert*, so choice E is not correct.

2. A — The relationship in this question is *opposites*: *deft* is the opposite of *clumsy*. *Reputable* (having a good reputation) is the opposite of *dishonorable* (lacking honor), so choice A is the correct answer. *Spectacular* (impressive) is not the opposite of *righteous* (honorable), *flimsy* and *floppy* are synonyms, *exuberant* and *joyful* are similar in meaning, and *homely* (unattractive) is not related to *lanky* (tall and lean), so choices B, C, D, and E are not correct.

3. B — The relationship in this question is *means without*: *impartial* means "without *bias*." *Indefinite* (without end) does not mean "without *eternity*" (going on forever), so choice A can be ruled out. *Invincible* (unable to be defeated) does mean "without *vulnerability*" (weakness), so choice B is the best answer. *Impulsive* (acting without thought) can lead to *chaos*, and does not mean "without *chaos*," so choice C can be eliminated. *Influential* (having influence) is not

related to *laziness*, so choice D can be ruled out, and *intellectual* and *academic* are similar in meaning, so choice E is not correct.

4. C — The relationship in this question is *degree*: *affection* is a mild fondness, and *ardor* is a strong love, so a stronger *affection* is *ardor*. *Timely* and *dated* (out of date) as well as *reckless* and *prudent* are opposites, so choices A and B are not correct. *Diligent* is to stick with what you have committed to doing, while *dogged* is to never give up. Therefore, to be really diligent is to be dogged, and choice C is the correct answer. *Frail* and *robust* are opposites, so choice D can be eliminated. *Buttress* and *support* are similar in meaning, but *support* is not more extreme than *buttress*, so choice E can be ruled out.

5. D — The relationship in this question is *opposites*: to be *proficient* is the opposite of being *unable* to do something. To *attempt* is the same thing as to *endeavor* (try), so choice A is not correct. *Quick* and *frantic* are also similar in meaning (and not opposites), so choice B can be ruled out. *Civilized* (refined) is not related to *routine* (ordinary), so choice C can be eliminated. *Powerful* is the opposite of *meek* (weak), so choice D is the correct answer. Finally, *alluring* (attractive) and *timely* are not related, so choice E is not correct.

Reading Practice

1. B — This question asks why President Kennedy chose to compare all of human history to a 50-year time span. When he does this, he begins by pointing out that in the first 40 years, very few known advances were made. Then in the last 10 years, he gives advances where the time span between each advance becomes shorter and shorter. Therefore, he is showing how the pace of advances has increased, and choice B is correct. Choices A and C are not correct because the examples given don't show the importance of considering historical events or that progress always has been rapid. While the time scale does give some technological advances, it is not included in order to show the advances themselves, so choice D is not correct. Finally, nowhere in the description of the first 50 years does President Kennedy recommend that the reader take action, so choice E can be eliminated.

2. A — This question also asks us why a piece of information is included. President Kennedy mentions that it would have taken 40 years for humans to cover themselves in animal skins in order to show contrast to more recent events. It shows that progress can at times be very slow. Answer choice A is correct. The passage does not indicate that this small change made a big impact, so choice B can be ruled out. The passage also does not mention the importance of studying how past problems were solved — its focus is looking forward — so choice C is not correct. There is also no evidence that President Kennedy found early man lacking courage or that he considered this advance unimportant, so we can eliminate choices D and E.

3. E — The passage states, "such a pace cannot help but create new ills as it dispels old." The sentence is contrasting creating new ills with dispelling old ones. Therefore, *dispel* is the opposite of *create*. We are looking for something that means "to reduce or do away with." To *challenge* (question), *produce* (make), *find*, or *trade* would not be to reduce or do away with.

Workout #1

Choices A, B, C, and D are not correct. To *alleviate* is to make trouble go away, so choice E is the correct answer.

4. C — President Kennedy's tone is definitely positive about the space program — he is encouraging it. We can eliminate *ambivalent* (undecided) and *critical* because they are not positive words. Choices A and D are not correct. His tone is also not *ironic* (pointing out how the reality is opposite from what is expected). Choice B can be ruled out. His tone is also not *sentimental*, or looking back on the past fondly, so choice E is not correct. We are left with choice C, and since President Kennedy is talking about the positive aspects of the space program, his tone is *admiring*. Choice C is correct.

5. D — To find the main idea of a passage on this test, it is often helpful to reread the last sentence. The last sentence of this passage is telling the audience that no nation can afford to fall behind in the race to space. President Kennedy is making the case that the nation should invest in space exploration, so choice D is the best answer. Answer choice A is tempting but it is too extreme — the passage does not explicitly state that the United States must beat all other countries in the race to space. Choice A is not correct. Choice B is also tempting because it summarizes the first paragraph of the passage but it does not summarize the main idea of the entire passage, so we can rule it out. Answer choices C and E are both mentioned in the passage but are not what the passage is primarily about, so they can be ruled out.

Math Practice

1. C — To figure out the total number of combinations, we need to multiply the total number of possibilities for each choice being made. There are 10 possibilities for the first shirt that he chooses. There are then only 9 possible choices for the second shirt since he has already chosen one. He has 5 choices for the pair of pants. He then has 4 choices for the first pair of shoes and 3 choices for the second pair of shoes. Finally, he has 2 choices for the belt. This gives us $10 \times 9 \times 5 \times 4 \times 3 \times 2$ possible combinations. If we do the math, this results in 10,800 choices. However, some of these choices are repeats. For example, if he chose red pants and then blue pants, that is the same as choosing blue pants and then red pants. There are 2 items this could happen with, shirts and shoes. Since he is choosing 2 shirts and 2 pairs of shoes, we need to divide the total possibilities by 2!2! (2! is 2 factorial and tells us to multiply 2×1) and 2!2! is equal to $2 \times 1 \times 2 \times 1$ or 4. Since 10,800 divided by 4 is 2,700, choice C is the correct answer.

2. C — To answer this question, we need to figure out how many possible choices there are for places 1-6 in the race. In 1st place, there are only 2 options: Brittany or Van. In 2nd place, we have 5 options left since either Brittany or Van had already finished the race. In 3rd place, there are 4 options left since 2 people have already finished. In 4th place, there are only 3 options since 3 people already finished the race. In 5th place, we have 2 options and in 6th place, there is only 1 option left. If we multiply the possibilities for each place, we get $2 \times 5 \times 4 \times 3 \times 2 \times 1$, which results in 240 possibilities. Answer choice C is correct. Note that we didn't have to

divide by anything because if one person finished first and another person finished second, that would not be the same as if the order was reversed. If the order matters in how things are selected, we don't divide by a factorial of options that could be repeats like we had to in the last problem.

3. A — To answer this question, we need to think through the possibilities. The first possibility is that Geneva is sitting on Matt's right side. However, the problem simply says that Matt must sit next to Geneva, but Geneva could be sitting on Matt's left side. This leaves the seat on his right side open. The other restriction given in the problem is that Tammy and Justin are not seated next to each other. Since Matt and Geneva are next to each other, that only leaves Tammy, Justin, and Conrad to be seated. In order for Tammy and Justin not to be next to each other, Conrad would need to be seated in between them. This means that either Justin or Tammy could sit to Matt's right but Conrad could not. This gives us another 2 possibilities for a total of 3 combinations. Answer choice A is correct.

4. B — Tina is choosing 3 toppings and we need to multiply the number of possibilities for each topping. For the first topping, she has 9 choices. For the second topping, she has only 8 choices since the toppings need to be unique and she already used one of the possibilities for the first topping. For the third topping, she has 7 choices since she has already used 2 toppings. If we multiply these options together, we get $9 \times 8 \times 7 = 504$ possible combinations. The problem is that we have repeats in these possibilities since the order in which the toppings are chosen does not matter. For example, this list could include pepperoni, onions, and mushrooms as well as onions, mushrooms, and pepperoni, and these would not be unique combinations. There are 3 choices that could be repeats, so we divide 504 by 3! or $3 \times 2 \times 1 = 6$. Since 504 divided by 6 is 84, choice B is correct.

5. D — For this question, we can first find the number of possibilities for the experienced carpenter portion of each team. There are 2 experienced carpenters that can be chosen from a total of 6 experienced carpenters. Therefore, we have 6 choices for the 1st experienced carpenter, but then only 5 choices for the 2nd experienced carpenter. If we multiply these together, we get a total of 30 teams. However, they aren't all unique. For example, if we chose Bob then Jane, that would be the same as choosing Jane and then Bob. There are 2 choices that could be repeats, so we divide 30 by 2! or $2 \times 1 = 2$. Since 30 divided by 2 is 15, there are 15 combinations for the experienced carpenter portion of the team. Now we can do the apprentice portion of the teams. There are 3 apprentices chosen for each team from a total of 8 apprentices. For the 1st apprentice, there are 8 options, for the 2nd apprentice, there are only 7 options remaining, and for the 3rd apprentice, there are only 6 options left. If we multiply $8 \times 7 \times 6$, we find that there are 336 options. However, they are again not all unique. There are 3 choices that could be repeated, so we divide 336 by 3! or $3 \times 2 \times 1 = 6$. Since 336 divided by 6 is 56, there are 56 options for the apprentice portion of the teams. Now, to find the total possible combinations, we multiply the number of experienced carpenter possibilities by the number of the apprentice carpenter possibilities. Since $15 \times 56 = 840$, there are 840 unique teams that can be created, so choice D is the correct answer.

Workout #1
———

6. D — One approach is to begin by listing out the multiples of 3 between 3 and 39 inclusive. They are 3, 6, 9, 12, 15, 18, 21, 24, 27, 30, 33, 36, and 39. However, the question states that the list shouldn't include multiples of 4. Since 12, 24, and 36 are multiples of 4, we remove them from the list and are left with 3, 6, 9, 15, 18, 21, 27, 30, 33, 39. There are a total of 10 numbers that work. Now we just have to figure out how many total cards there are. This is a little tricky. If we subtract 3 from 39, we get 36 as an answer. However, since the list includes both 3 and 39, we need to add 1 more and get that there are 37 total cards (don't be afraid to list out and then count the total possibilities for this type of question — they are super tricky). There are 10 cards that fit the criteria out of a total of 37 cards, so the probability of choosing one of them is $\frac{10}{37}$. Answer choice D is correct.

7. A — This question asks us to find the probability of 2 events both occurring. We do this by multiplying the probabilities that each individual event will occur. Since half of the numbers 0-9 are even, the probability of choosing an even number the first time is $\frac{1}{2}$. The probability of choosing 2 the second time is $\frac{1}{10}$ since only one card is labeled 2 and there are 10 total cards. If we multiply these together, we find that the probability of both events occurring is $\frac{1}{2} \times \frac{1}{10}$, or $\frac{1}{20}$. Choice A is correct.

8. C — The key to this question is that it states the first marble is NOT replaced before a second marble is selected. When the first marble is drawn, there are 6 red marbles out of a total of 18 marbles. Therefore, the probability of choosing a red marble the first time is $\frac{6}{18}$, which simplifies to $\frac{1}{3}$. When the second marble is chosen, however, there are now only 17 marbles, and 5 of them are red since we already removed one red marble. Therefore, the probability of choosing a marble that is NOT red is $\frac{12}{17}$. Now we can multiply the probabilities of the 2 events: $\frac{1}{3} \times \frac{12}{17}$. To make the math easier, however, we can factor the numerator and then divided both the numerator and denominator by 3: $\frac{1 \times 3 \times 4}{3 \times 17} = \frac{4}{17}$. Choice C is correct.

9. B — The beginning of this problem has some fancy math talk, but we need to not let that confuse us. It is just telling us that the events are mutually exclusive and independent so that we know that the probability of 1 event occurring will not change the probability of any other event occurring. The question is asking us what the probability is of both event X and event Y occurring. We need to multiply the probability of each event occurring. Since the probability of event X occurring is 0.3 and the probability of event Y occurring is 0.4, we multiply 0.3×0.4 and find that the probability of both events occurring is 0.12. Choice B is correct.

———

10. C — This question asks us to find the probability that 2 events are occurring: that the team will win one game and not lose the other. The probability that the team will win 1 game is 0.55. However, since there can be a tie, the probability that the team will not lose 1 game is $1 - P(loss)$ or $1 - 0.40 = 0.60$. We can multiply the probability of both events occurring and find $0.55 \times 0.6 = 0.33$. Answer choice C is correct.

Workout #2

Words to Learn

Below are the words used in Workout 2. Refer back to this list as needed as you move through the lesson.

Words that mean to make something worse

- Affront: offend
- Depreciate: lose value
- Defile: pollute
- Taint: pollute
- Rend: divide

Words with a negative meaning

- Callous: insensitive
- Hapless: unlucky
- Cynical: pessimistic
- Humdrum: boring
- Laborious: arduous or difficult
- Qualm: apprehension
- Quandary: predicament
- Somber: gloomy
- Rue: regret
- Skeptical: doubtful

Words with a very negative meaning

- Appalling: horrific
- Atrocious: dreadful
- Bane: curse
- Bedlam: chaos
- Ire: anger
- Chagrin: disappointment
- Contemptible: despicable
- Despondent: hopeless
- Disreputable: dishonorable
- Havoc: devastation
- Morbid: gruesome
- Impertinent: insulting

Synonyms Practice

1. RUE:
   - (A) soothe
   - (B) idolize
   - (C) taint
   - (D) regret
   - (E) correct

2. DOGGED:
   - (A) contemptible
   - (B) persistent
   - (C) efficient
   - (D) reputable
   - (E) impatient

3. QUANDARY:
   - (A) chaos
   - (B) leadership
   - (C) anger
   - (D) restraint
   - (E) dilemma

4. LABORIOUS:
   - (A) alluring
   - (B) callous
   - (C) difficult
   - (D) nimble
   - (E) probable

5. IMPERTINENT:
   - (A) insulting
   - (B) incapable
   - (C) immense
   - (D) illogical
   - (E) unerring

6. QUALM:
   - (A) skepticism
   - (B) bedlam
   - (C) junction
   - (D) extension
   - (E) misgiving

7. CHAGRIN:
   - (A) ardor
   - (B) disappointment
   - (C) dwelling
   - (D) possessiveness
   - (E) hopelessness

8. HAVOC:
   - (A) objection
   - (B) curse
   - (C) souvenir
   - (D) catastrophe
   - (E) predicament

9. SOMBER:
   - (A) impertinent
   - (B) deft
   - (C) gloomy
   - (D) passionate
   - (E) hapless

10. DEFILE:
    - (A) taint
    - (B) insult
    - (C) rue
    - (D) buttress
    - (E) rend

Analogies Practice

1. Affront is to allay as

    (A) ratify is to approve
    (B) defile is to surrender
    (C) bolster is to depreciate
    (D) stifle is to rue
    (E) rend is to embellish

2. Bane is to blessing as

    (A) havoc is to chaos
    (B) confusion is to ire
    (C) revision is to qualm
    (D) proclamation is to contempt
    (E) tranquility is to bedlam

3. Cynical is to skeptical as

    (A) cursed is to hapless
    (B) impartial is to invincible
    (C) excited is to exuberant
    (D) able is to proficient
    (E) laborious is to benevolent

4. Callous is to contemptible as

    (A) timely is to diligent
    (B) unhappy is to miserable
    (C) respected is to disreputable
    (D) morbid is to impertinent
    (E) dramatic is to humane

5. Benevolent is to atrocious as

    (A) somber is to gloomy
    (B) embarrassed is to chagrined
    (C) humdrum is to fascinating
    (D) prudent is to unerring
    (E) appalling is to despondent

Reading Practice

> *The following speech was given by Emmeline Pankhurst in 1913.*
>
> If I were a man and I said to you, "I come from a country which professes to have representative institutions and yet denies me, a taxpayer, an inhabitant of the country, representative rights," you would at once understand that that human being, being a man, was justified in the adoption of revolutionary methods to get representative institutions. But since I am a woman it is necessary in
> Line 5 the twentieth century to explain why women have adopted revolutionary methods in order to win the rights of citizenship.
>   You see, in spite of a good deal that we hear about revolutionary methods not being necessary for American women, because American women are so well off, most of the men of the United States quite calmly acquiesce in the fact that half of the community are deprived absolutely of
> 10 citizen rights, and we women, in trying to make our case clear, always have to make as part of our argument, and urge upon men in our audience the fact — a very simple fact — that women are human beings. It is quite evident you do not all realize we are human beings or it would not be necessary to argue with you that women may, suffering from intolerable injustice, be driven to adopt revolutionary methods. We have, first of all to convince you we are human beings, and I hope
> 15 to be able to do that in the course of the evening before I sit down, but before doing that, I want to put a few political arguments before you — not arguments for the suffrage, because I said when I opened, I didn't mean to do that — but arguments for the adoption of militant methods in order to win political rights.

1. Emmeline Pankhurst's tone in the first paragraph (lines 1-6) can best be described as

    (A) indignant
    (B) resigned
    (C) forgiving
    (D) indifferent
    (E) pleasant

2. The author mentions men in the first paragraph for which of the following reasons?

    (A) To call upon men to join with women in fighting for women's rights.
    (B) To point out how men and women are no different in deserving human rights.
    (C) To highlight the different reactions that men and women receive when they adopt revolutionary methods.
    (D) To insist that men are justified when they use revolutionary methods to fight injustice.
    (E) To describe the importance of representative rights for all humans.

Workout #2

3. The word "acquiesce" (line 9) most nearly means

    (A) fight vehemently.
    (B) go along with.
    (C) actively encourage.
    (D) quietly undermine.
    (E) stop suddenly.

4. According to the passage, why does Emmeline Pankhurst think that women have to argue for the right to use revolutionary methods?

    (A) Methods traditionally used in the women's suffrage movement are not effective.
    (B) Men have a long history of using revolutionary methods successfully.
    (C) Political arguments are not a useful tool for women.
    (D) Men have acted as the leaders of society and now women must do the same.
    (E) Women are not viewed as human beings that should revolt when denied rights.

5. The primary purpose of Emmeline Pankhurst's speech was to

    (A) point out the ways in which women are treated as lesser in society.
    (B) advocate for a particular approach for women to gain political rights.
    (C) outline the reasons that women should receive voting rights.
    (D) prove that the only way for women to receive voting rights is to engage in armed combat.
    (E) give a brief history of the methods used by the women's suffrage movement.

Math Practice

In this workout, we will be covering three types of geometry problems:

1. Perimeter, Area, and Volume
2. Angles and Shapes
3. Pythagorean Theorem problems not using the coordinate grid (these problems are covered in workout #5)

Perimeter, area, and volume questions on the SSAT often require you to apply more than one of these concepts within the same problem. The key is to keep straight what is given and what is asked for.

Here are some examples of difficult questions testing these concepts:

1. In the figure, X is the center of the circle. If the area of the circle is 64π units^2, what is the area of the shaded region, in units^2?

   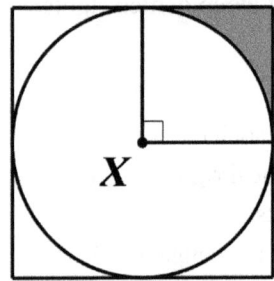

   (A) $64 - 16\pi$
   (B) $64 - 8\pi$
   (C) $32 - 4\pi$
   (D) $64\pi - 32$
   (E) $64\pi - 16$

2. A rectangular swimming pool is 20 feet wide, 30 feet long, and is filled with water that is 6 feet deep throughout the pool. When it is drained, the volume of the remaining water can be found by using the function $v(m) = 3{,}600 - 600m$, where v is the volume in cubic feet, and m is the number of minutes that the pool has been draining. Based on this equation, after the pool is drained for one minute, how deep would the water in the pool be?

   (A) 1 foot
   (B) 2 feet
   (C) 3 feet
   (D) 4 feet
   (E) 5 feet

Workout #2

3. A cylinder has a diameter that is the same as its height and a volume of 54π cm³. What is the radius of the cylinder, in cm?

   Volume of cylinder = $\pi r^2 h$

   (A) $\frac{3}{2}$
   (B) 3
   (C) $3\sqrt[3]{2}$
   (D) 6
   (E) $6\sqrt[3]{2}$

4. A small cube has a base perimeter of 8 cm. Several of these small cubes are stacked to create a larger cube with a volume of 216 cm³. How many of the small cubes were stacked to create the larger cube?

   (A) 3
   (B) 6
   (C) 27
   (D) 54
   (E) 108

Here are some questions that test your ability to apply the concepts of angles and shapes:

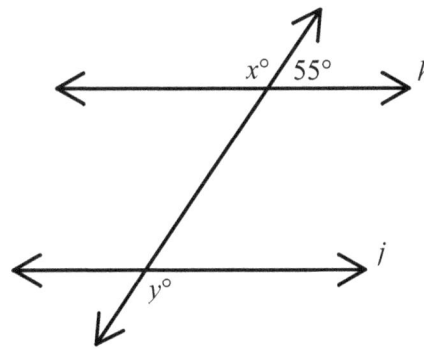

5. In the figure shown, lines h and j are parallel. What is the value of $x + y$?

   (A) 70
   (B) 110
   (C) 125
   (D) 250
   (E) 290

6. Which of the following could be the side lengths of a triangle?

   (A) 3 cm, 3 cm, 7 cm
   (B) 4 cm, 5 cm, 10 cm
   (C) 5 cm, 4 cm, 1 cm
   (D) 6 cm, 4 cm, 10 cm
   (E) 7 cm, 7 cm, 13 cm

7. What is the measure of each interior angle in a regular hexagon?

   (A) 90°
   (B) 108°
   (C) 120°
   (D) 540°
   (E) 720°

Finally, we have questions that test your ability to apply the Pythagorean theorem. What makes these questions difficult is not the math itself, but rather that you have to recognize that we must use the Pythagorean theorem in order to solve.

8. Bonnie lives 4 miles due south of the grocery store. Neil lives 5 miles due west of the grocery store. How many miles does Bonnie live from Neil?

   (A) 3 miles
   (B) 4.5 miles
   (C) $\sqrt{37}$ miles
   (D) $\sqrt{41}$ miles
   (E) 9 miles

9. An equilateral triangle has a perimeter of 15 cm. What is the area of the triangle?

   (A) $\frac{25\sqrt{3}}{4}$
   (B) $\frac{25}{2}$
   (C) $\frac{25\sqrt{3}}{2}$
   (D) $25\sqrt{3}$
   (E) $50\sqrt{3}$

Workout #2

10. A right isosceles triangle has an area of 18 in². What is the perimeter of this triangle?
    (A) 12 in
    (B) $12+3\sqrt{2}$ in
    (C) $12+6\sqrt{2}$ in
    (D) $12+18\sqrt{2}$ in
    (E) 36 in

Workout #2 Answers

Synonyms Practice

As you might have noticed as you went through the synonyms sections, the definition given is not always the one that was listed in the words to learn section. This is because there is often more than one synonym for a word and on test day, you may get a synonym other than the one listed.

When you check your work, if there are words that you do not know the meaning of, make flashcards for them and then study these flashcards after you complete each workout.

1. D — The word list states that *rue* means "regret," so choice D is correct. Perhaps you have heard someone say, "I rue the day I met that person," which means "I wish I had never met that person."

2. B — The word list for workout #1 states that *dogged* means "persistent." Choice B is correct. Be sure to study the words that you don't know from previous lessons — they will keep reappearing — so that you will know these words when test day comes.

3. E — The word list states that *quandary* means "predicament." A *predicament* is a problem that is tough to figure out a solution for, as is a *dilemma*. Choice E is correct.

4. C — The word list states that *laborious* means "arduous" or "difficult." Choice C is correct. We can use roots to remember this one — to labor is to work, so something that is laborious requires a lot of work or is difficult.

5. A — The word list states that *impertinent* means "insulting," so choice A is the correct answer. If you couldn't remember the meaning of the word, perhaps you could at least remember that it had a very negative meaning and eliminate *immense* (choice C), which means "very big," and *unerring* (choice E), which means "without error," since those do not have negative meanings. From there, you could guess since you only need to eliminate one answer choice before you come out ahead with guessing.

6. E — The word list states that *qualm* means "apprehension." This is not an answer choice, however. We do know that *qualm* has a negative meaning, so we could eliminate choices C and D because *junction* (joining) and *extension* (making longer) do not have negative meanings. *Apprehension* means "anxiety about something," so we have to decide if *skepticism*, *bedlam* (chaos), or *misgiving* fits with having anxiety about something. To have a misgiving is to have a doubt that something is a good idea, so choice E is correct.

7. B — The word lists states that *chagrin* means "disappointment." Answer choice B is correct.

8. D — The word list states that *havoc* means "devastation." *Devastation* is a very negative event. A *catastrophe* is also a very negative event, so choice D is correct.

9. C — The word list states that *somber* means "gloomy," so choice C is correct.

10. A — The word list states that *defile* means "to pollute." To pollute is to add contaminants. *Insult*, *rue* (regret), *buttress* (support), and *rend* (divide) do not mean "to pollute" or "to add contaminants." To *taint*, however, is to pollute or add contaminants, so choice A is the correct answer.

Analogies Practice

1. C — The relationship in this question is *opposites*: to *affront* is to offend someone, which is the opposite of *allaying* (soothing) him or her. *Ratify* and *approve* are synonyms, so choice A is not correct. *Defile* (pollute) is not related to *surrender*, *stifle* (discourage) is not related to *rue* (regret), and *rend* (divide) is not related to *embellish* (beautify), so choices B, D, and E can be eliminated. *Bolster* (support) is the opposite of *depreciate* (lose value), so choice C is the best answer.

2. E — The relationship in this question is *opposites*: a *bane* (curse) is the opposite of a *blessing*. *Havoc* and *chaos* are synonyms, so choice A is not correct. *Confusion* is not related to *ire* (anger), *revision* (change) is not related to *qualm* (apprehension), and *proclamation* (declaration) is not related to *contempt* (disrespect), so choices B, C, and D can be eliminated. *Tranquility* (calm) is the opposite of *bedlam* (chaos), so choice E is the correct answer.

3. A — The relationship in this question is *degree*: *cynical* is similar in meaning to *skeptical*, only more extreme. *Cursed* is similar to *hapless*, only more extreme, so choice A is the correct answer. *Impartial* (not taking sides) is unrelated to *invincible*, so choice B is not correct. *Excited* and *exuberant* are similar in meaning, only *excited* is less extreme than *exuberant* (the words are in the wrong order), so choice C can be eliminated. *Able* and *proficient* are similar in meaning, but *able* is not more extreme than *proficient*, so choice D can be ruled out. Finally, *laborious* (difficult) is not related to *benevolent* (kind), so choice E is not correct.

4. B — The relationship in this question is *degree*: to be *callous* is to be insensitive, while to be *contemptible* is to be openly disrespectful, which is more extreme. The relationship between being *timely* (well-timed) and being *diligent* (persevering) is a weak one, so we can rule out choice A. To be *unhappy* is similar to being *miserable*, only *miserable* is more extreme. Therefore, choice B is the correct answer. Choice C can be ruled out because *respected* is the opposite of *disreputable*. Choice D is not correct because *morbid* (gruesome) is not related to *impertinent* (insulting). Finally, being *dramatic* is unrelated to being *humane*, so choice E can be eliminated.

5. C — The relationship in this question is *opposites*: *benevolent* (kind) is the opposite of *atrocious* (dreadful). *Somber* and *gloomy* as well as *embarrassed* and *chagrined* are similar in meaning, so choices A and B can be ruled out. *Humdrum* (boring) is the opposite of *fascinating*, so choice C is the correct answer. *Prudent* (wise) is not the opposite of *unerring* (perfect), so choice D is

not correct. *Appalling* (horrific) is not the opposite of *despondent* (hopeless), so choice E can be eliminated.

Reading Practice

1. A — In the first paragraph, Emmeline Pankhurst is angry. She is pointing out that many would consider a man justified in revolting to get representative institutions but that women are treated differently and need to also adopt revolutionary methods. We can easily rule out choices C, D, and E because she is clearly not *forgiving*, *indifferent* (doesn't care), or *pleasant*. Now we have to decide if she is *indignant* (angry) or *resigned* (having given up). Since she is arguing that women should adopt revolutionary methods, she has not given up, and we can eliminate choice B. She is *indignant*, so choice A is correct.

2. C — The question asks why men are mentioned in the first paragraph. We can use the strategy of ruling out from most wrong to least wrong. Answer choice A is not correct because she is not calling upon men to join the fight in the first paragraph (or really in the entire passage). We can also eliminate E because she is mentioning men to contrast their treatment to that of women and not to describe how important representative rights are for all humans. Choice B is tempting because she is pointing out how men and women are no different in deserving human rights. However, in the first paragraph, the purpose isn't really to point out how men and women deserve equal treatment, but rather to point out that they are treated differently. Choice B is not the best answer and can be eliminated. Now we are down to choices C and D. Again, we look at the purpose of the paragraph. It is not to argue that men are justified when they use revolutionary methods; it is to argue that women and men are treated differently when they do employ revolutionary methods. Answer choice C best captures this meaning and is a better choice than choice D. Answer choice C is correct.

3. B — The passage describes men as people who "quite calmly acquiesce." The word *acquiesce* needs to go along with doing something calmly. Since to *fight vehemently* (strongly), *actively encourage*, or *stop suddenly* do not go along with doing something calmly, we can eliminate choices A, C, and E. We are down to choices B and D. Since *going along with* best fits with *calmly*, answer choice B is the correct answer. *Acquiesce* means "to give in and go along with," but even if you didn't know that, we can still get to the right answer using context clues and the process of elimination.

4. E — In lines 12-14, the passage states, "It is quite evident that you do not all realize we are human beings or it would not be necessary to argue with you that women may, suffering from intolerable injustice, be driven to adopt revolutionary methods." This is most directly restated by choice E, and that is the correct answer. While some of the other answer choices may be logical conclusions, only choice E has evidence that we can underline in the passage, so it is the best answer.

5. B — For main idea questions, it is often helpful to look at the last sentence of the passage. In the last sentence, she states, "I want to put a few political arguments before you — not

arguments for suffrage, because I said when I opened, I didn't mean to do that — but arguments for the adoption of militant methods in order to win political rights." This tells us that the purpose of her speech was not to generally explain why women should be able to vote, but rather to encourage the use of militant methods to achieve the right to vote. We can eliminate choices A, C, and E because they do not fit with this very specific purpose. We are down to choices B and D. Choice D is more extreme and specifically says that women should engage in armed combat — which is not something the passage advocates. Choice B better summarizes the idea that women should use militant methods (a particular approach) to gain political rights. Choice B is the best answer.

Math Practice

1. A — This is a shaded region problem. These problems require us to find the area of a larger figure and then subtract off the area of the unshaded region. In this case, the area of the larger figure is the smaller square located on the upper right side of the larger square. The area of a circle is found using the formula area = πr^2, where r is the length of the radius. If the area of the circle is 64π, then the radius must be 8 units since 8^2 is 64. The radius is also the side length of the smaller square. Since the area of a square is found by multiplying the side length by itself, the area of the square is 8×8, or 64 units^2. Now we have to subtract the area of the part of the circle within the square that is not shaded. The area of the circle that is within the smaller square is $\frac{1}{4}$ of the area of the total circle, so we can multiply $\frac{1}{4} \times 64\pi$ and find that the area of the $\frac{1}{4}$ circle within the smaller square is 16π units^2. Therefore, the area of the shaded region is the area of the smaller square (64 units^2) minus the area of the quarter circle which is not shaded (16π units^2) or $64 - 16\pi$, and answer choice A is correct.

2. E — The volume of the water in the pool before it is drained is 3,600 cubic feet (volume of a rectangular prism is found using volume = length × width × depth). The question tells us that the volume of the remaining water in the pool can be found using $v(m) = 3,600 - 600m$, where m is the number of minutes that the pool has been draining. Since the pool has been draining for 1 minute, we can substitute in 1 for m and find that the volume is $v(1) = 3,600 - 600(1) = 3,000$. Now we can substitute in 3,000 for the volume and solve for the new depth: $3,000 = 30 \times 20 \times$ depth. This simplifies to $3,000 = 600 \times$ depth. Now we divide both sides by 600 and the result is that $5 =$ depth, so choice E is correct.

3. B — The key to this question is that the question gives us the diameter, but the formula for volume of a cylinder uses the radius. The problem tells us that the diameter of the cylinder is

equal to the height. This means that the radius is equal to $\frac{1}{2}$ of the height. Let's represent the height as h and the radius as $\frac{1}{2}h$. Now we can substitute these into the volume formula:

$$\text{volume} = \pi r^2 h = \pi(\frac{1}{2}h)^2 \times h$$

This simplifies to volume = $\frac{1}{4}h^3\pi$ (remembering to square the $\frac{1}{2}$ as well). Now we can substitute in 54π for the volume and the result is $54\pi = \frac{1}{4}h^3\pi$. To isolate the variable h, we can start with dividing both sides by π. Our equation is now $54 = \frac{1}{4}h^3$. Multiplying both sides by 4 tells us that $216 = h^3$. Since the cube root of 216 is 6, the height is 6. Now we have to make sure that we answer the correct question. The question asks for the radius, which is half of the diameter. The diameter is equal to the height, so the radius of the cylinder is half of the height, or 3 cm. Answer choice B is correct.

4. C — The small cube has a base perimeter of 8 cm. Since the base is a square, we divide 8 by 4, and find that the side length of the small cube is 2 cm. Now we have to find the side length of the larger cube. We are given that the volume of the larger cube is 216 cm³. Since the volume of cube can be found by cubing the side length, we can take the cube root of 216 and find that the side length of the larger cube is 6 cm. In order to build the larger cube from the smaller cube, we would need to stack the smaller cubes 3 across, 3 deep, and 3 high to create a cube that is 6 cm by 6 cm by 6 cm. If we multiply 3 cubes across, 3 cubes deep, and 3 cubes high, then we find that 27 cubes are required to build the larger cube. Answer choice C is correct.

5. D — In the figure, we can see that $x°$ and 55° lie along a straight line. This means that they must add to 180°. If we subtract 55° from 180°, we find that $x° = 125°$. We can also see that the angles represented by $x°$ and $y°$ are alternate exterior angles, meaning that $x°$ must be equal to $y°$ and $y° = 125°$. Therefore, $x + y = 125 + 125 = 250$. Answer choice D is correct.

6. E — In a triangle, there are two important rules for side lengths:

The sum of the lengths of two sides must be greater than the length of the third side

The difference between the length of two sides must be less than the length of the third side

We can eliminate choice A because 3 cm + 3 cm is not greater than 7 cm. We can rule out choice B because 4 cm + 5 cm is not greater than 10 cm. Choice C is not correct because the difference between 5 cm and 4 cm is equal to 1 cm and not less than 1 cm. Choice D is also not correct because 6 cm + 4 cm is equal to 10 cm and not greater than 10 cm. Finally, choice

Workout #2

E is the correct answer because the 7 cm + 7cm is greater than 13 cm and 7 cm − 7 cm is less than 13 cm.

7. C — There is a formula you could use but it can be difficult to remember, so we will use reasoning instead. We can begin by dividing the hexagon into six pieces, as shown:

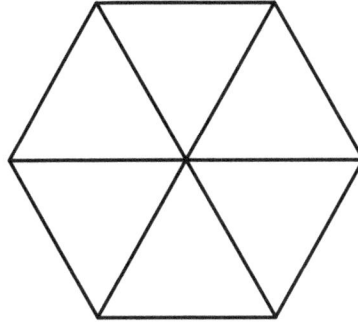

If we look at the center of the figure, where all the triangles come together, we can see that the 6 triangles form a full circle. Since a circle is 360°, we can divide 360° by 6 and find that the central angle of each triangle must be 60°, as shown:

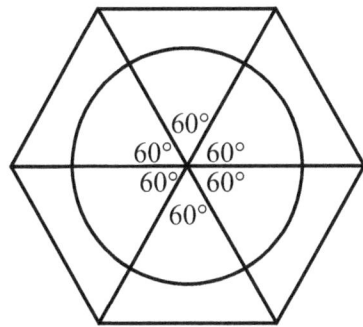

Since the triangles formed are isosceles (two sides are the same since they are both the distance from the center to the vertex in a regular hexagon), the two remaining angles must also be the same. These angles must add to 120°, since the third angle is 60° and the angles in a triangle add to 180°. If we divide 120° by 2, we find that these remaining angles of each triangle must also be 60° each, as shown:

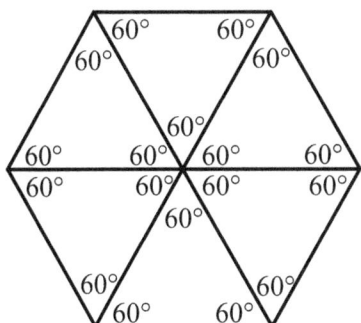

41

If we notice that each interior angle of the hexagon is made up of two angles from adjacent triangles, we can add 60° and 60° and find that the total interior angle measure is 120°. Answer choice C is correct.

8. D — The key to this question is to draw out what is described in words:

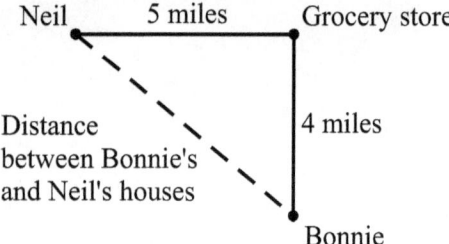

If we do this, we can see that a right triangle is formed and the hypotenuse of that right triangle is the distance between Bonnie's and Neil's houses. We can use the Pythagorean theorem: $a^2 + b^2 = c^2$, where a and b are leg lengths and c is the hypotenuse length (side opposite the right angle). If we substitute in the distances given, the result is $4^2 + 5^2 = c^2$. This simplifies to $16 + 25 = c^2$, or $41 = c^2$. Taking the square root of both sides results in $c = \sqrt{41}$. Since the length of the hypotenuse is also the distance between Bonnie's and Neil's houses, answer choice D is correct.

9. A — This is a question with a lot of steps. The formula for the area of a triangle is $\frac{1}{2}$ (base × height). In this case, however, we are not given the height since it is not a right triangle. We must solve for the height. Since it is an equilateral triangle, we can cut the triangle in half to create two right triangles:

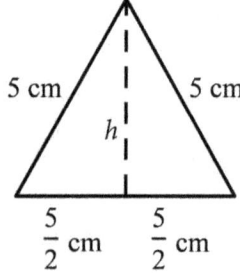

Note that we cut the base length in half as well. Now we have a right triangle where the length of one leg is also the height of the larger triangle, and we can use Pythagorean theorem to solve. In this case, however, we are given one leg, the hypotenuse, and we are solving for the other leg.

The math to solve for the other leg looks like this:

$$h^2 + \left(\frac{5}{2}\right)^2 = 5^2$$

$$h^2 + \frac{25}{4} = 25$$

$$h^2 + \frac{25}{4} = \frac{100}{4}$$

(Note: We turned 25 into $\frac{100}{4}$ to have a common denominator)

$$h^2 = \frac{100}{4} - \frac{25}{4}$$

$$h^2 = \frac{75}{4}$$

$$h = \sqrt{\frac{75}{4}}$$

Now we have to simplify the radical. We can do this by breaking apart the radical to take the square root of the numerator and denominator. The denominator is then a perfect square, so we don't need to do anything other than take the square root of 4. The numerator, however, can be simplified by breaking 75 into 25 × 3, since 25 is also a perfect square.

Here is what the math looks like:

$$\sqrt{\frac{75}{4}} = \frac{\sqrt{75}}{\sqrt{4}} = \frac{\sqrt{25}\sqrt{3}}{\sqrt{4}} = \frac{5\sqrt{3}}{2}$$

Now that we have the base (5) and height $\left(\frac{5\sqrt{3}}{2}\right)$ of the triangle, we can apply the formula for the area of a triangle to get the answer:

$$\text{Area} = \frac{1}{2}(\text{base} \times \text{height}) = \frac{1}{2}\left(5 \times \frac{5\sqrt{3}}{2}\right) = \frac{25\sqrt{3}}{4}$$

Choice A is correct.

10. C — In this case, we are given the area of the triangle and need to solve for the side lengths to find the perimeter. If the triangle is an isosceles right triangle, the base and height are the same (the word *isosceles* indicates that). We can call the length of each leg w and then substitute into the area formula:

$$\text{Area} = \frac{1}{2}(\text{base} \times \text{height})$$

$$18 = \frac{1}{2}(w \times w)$$

$$36 = w^2$$

$$6 = w$$

Now we know that the leg lengths of the right triangle are both 6 in. We can use the Pythagorean theorem to solve for the hypotenuse:

$$a^2 + b^2 = c^2$$

$$6^2 + 6^2 = c^2$$

$$36 + 36 = c^2$$

$$\sqrt{72} = c$$

If we look at our answer choices, we can see that we need to simplify the radical:

$$\sqrt{72} = \sqrt{36} \times \sqrt{2} = 6\sqrt{2}$$

Now we have all the side lengths, so we can add them together to find the perimeter:

$$6 + 6 + 6\sqrt{2} = 12 + 6\sqrt{2}$$

Answer choice C is correct.

Workout #3

Words to Learn

Below are the words used in Workout 3. Refer back to this list as needed as you move through the lesson.

Words related to gathering

Bevy:	group
Consolidate:	unite
Glean:	infer or gather
Compile:	gather
Medley:	mixture
Tabulate:	categorize

Words that mean to bring about an ending

Curtail:	cut back
Dispel:	get rid of
Eradicate:	exterminate
Evasion:	avoidance
Quell:	extinguish
Revoke:	take back
Revert:	regress

Words related to being polite

Demure:	reserved
Genteel:	elegant
Discretion:	good judgment

Words related to happiness

Enrapture:	enchant
Enthrall:	captivate
Revel:	merriment or merrymaking
Superlative:	outstanding
Incandescent:	glowing

Synonyms Practice

1. BEVY:
   - (A) mixture
   - (B) curse
   - (C) fixture
   - (D) group
   - (E) technique

2. REVEL:
   - (A) celebration
   - (B) drought
   - (C) predicament
   - (D) sponsor
   - (E) ardor

3. CONTEMPTIBLE:
   - (A) tough
   - (B) ridiculous
   - (C) disgusting
   - (D) spectacular
   - (E) benevolent

4. INCANDESCENT:
   - (A) disreputable
   - (B) glowing
   - (C) skeptical
   - (D) sorrowful
   - (E) impartial

5. ALLAY:
   - (A) gather
   - (B) defile
   - (C) revoke
   - (D) slump
   - (E) ease

6. GLEAN:
   - (A) gather
   - (B) captivate
   - (C) rustle
   - (D) enchant
   - (E) judge

7. TABULATE:
   - (A) regard
   - (B) speak
   - (C) correct
   - (D) catalogue
   - (E) curtail

8. DOGGED:
   - (A) humble
   - (B) reputable
   - (C) persistent
   - (D) elegant
   - (E) superlative

9. CONSOLIDATE:
   - (A) extinguish
   - (B) unite
   - (C) respond
   - (D) buttress
   - (E) predict

10. DISPEL:
    - (A) replicate
    - (B) evade
    - (C) track
    - (D) protect
    - (E) banish

Analogies Practice

1. Proficient is to superlative as

    (A) interested is to enthralled
    (B) laborious is to easy
    (C) genteel is to demure
    (D) despondent is to morbid
    (E) prudent is to impertinent

2. Quell is to rebellion as

    (A) rue is to mistake
    (B) depreciate is to evasion
    (C) suppress is to emotion
    (D) compile is to list
    (E) rectify is to accident

3. Bolster is to eradicate as

    (A) revoke is to curtail
    (B) tabulate is to rend
    (C) adorn is to embellish
    (D) bury is to defile
    (E) revert is to progress

4. Discretion is to affront as

    (A) chagrin is to embarrass
    (B) honesty is to deceive
    (C) qualm is to doubt
    (D) fluctuation is to ratify
    (E) reputation is to enrapture

5. Deft is to clumsy as

    (A) notable is to famous
    (B) atrocious is to appalling
    (C) exuberant is to demure
    (D) invincible is to robust
    (E) somber is to irate

Reading Practice

I was born in No-doyohn Cañon, Arizona, June, 1829.

In that country which lies around the headwaters of the Gila River I was reared. This range was our fatherland; among these mountains our wigwams were hidden; the scattered valleys contained our fields; the boundless prairies, stretching away on every side, were our pastures; the rocky caverns were our burying places.

I was fourth in a family of eight children—four boys and four girls. Of that family, only myself, my brother, Porico (White Horse), and my sister, Nah-da-ste, are yet alive. We are held as prisoners of war in this Military Reservation (Fort Sill).

As a babe, I rolled on the dirt floor of my father's tepee, hung in my tsoch (Apache name for cradle) at my mother's back, or suspended from the bough of a tree. I was warmed by the sun, rocked by the winds, and sheltered by the trees as other Indian babes.

When a child my mother taught me the legends of our people; taught me of the sun and sky, the moon and stars, the clouds and storms. She also taught me to kneel and pray to Usen for strength, health, wisdom, and protection. We never prayed against any person, but if we had aught against any individual we ourselves took vengeance. We were taught that Usen does not care for the petty quarrels of men.

My father had often told me of the brave deeds of our warriors, of the pleasures of the chase, and the glories of the warpath.

With my brothers and sisters, I played about my father's home. Sometimes we played at hide-and-seek among the rocks and pines; sometimes we loitered in the shade of the cottonwood trees or sought the shudock (a kind of wild cherry) while our parents worked in the field. Sometimes we played that we were warriors. We would practice stealing upon some object that represented an enemy, and in our childish imitation often perform the feats of war. Sometimes we would hide away from our mother to see if she could find us, and often when thus concealed go to sleep and perhaps remain hidden for many hours.

1. This passage would most likely be found in

    (A) an autobiography
    (B) an almanac
    (C) an encyclopedia
    (D) a history of western explorers
    (E) an editorial review

2. The primary focus of the passage is

    (A) why the narrator has been imprisoned
    (B) the settlement of the American west
    (C) the childhood experiences of the narrator
    (D) the injustice of Native Americans being imprisoned
    (E) the landscape of the Gila River valley

3. As used in line 14, the word "aught" most nearly means

   (A) slights
   (B) victories
   (C) surprises
   (D) fascination
   (E) grievances

4. The narrator's description of his childhood can best be described as

   (A) tumultuous
   (B) peaceful
   (C) agitated
   (D) nomadic
   (E) stifling

5. The second paragraph (lines 2-5) describes the land around the Gila River headwaters in order to show

   (A) how beautiful the country was where the narrator was raised
   (B) the challenges of farming around the Gila River headwaters
   (C) how connected the narrator's family was to that particular area
   (D) the diversity of the lands in which the narrator's family lived
   (E) the difficulties that the narrator's tribe experienced when it tried to move away

Math Practice

In this workout we will cover some math problems that are somewhat unique to the SSAT and difficult to answer. With practice, they become much easier to both recognize and solve. The writers of the SSAT classify these questions as "computational clue" and "classic problem solving."

Keep in mind the strategy of plugging in answer choices to see what works. This strategy doesn't apply to all these questions but, in general, if you think to yourself, "I need to set up an equation and solve," you can probably also try out answer choices and see what works.

Here are some examples for you to try:

1. What is the value of the least of 4 consecutive even integers if the greatest plus twice the least equals 0?

    (A) −2
    (B) 0
    (C) 2
    (D) 4
    (E) 10

2. A garage charges $2.50 for the first hour of parking and $0.60 for each additional half hour of parking. If Cameron paid $8.50 for parking in this garage, for how long did she park?

    (A) 5 hours
    (B) 5.5 hours
    (C) 6 hours
    (D) 10 hours
    (E) 11 hours

3. If the product of $2m$ and 4 less than m is equal to 42, what is one possible value of m?

    (A) −7
    (B) −3
    (C) −2
    (D) 3
    (E) 4

4. If the sum of 2 prime numbers is 12, what is their product?

    (A) 2
    (B) 5
    (C) 7
    (D) 22
    (E) 35

Workout #3

5. Marsha and Rodolfo both collect stamps. Twice the number of stamps that Marsha has plus 5 times the number of stamps that Rodolfo has is equal to 49. Three times the number of stamps that Marsha has decreased by 4 times the number of stamps that Rodolfo has is equal to 39. How many stamps did Marsha have?

   (A) 2
   (B) 3
   (C) 15
   (D) 17
   (E) 18

6. If the difference between 2 numbers is 8 and the product of those two numbers is 240, what is the greater of the two numbers?

   (A) 8
   (B) 12
   (C) 16
   (D) 20
   (E) 24

7. The sum of 5 consecutive numbers is 115. What is the sum of the greatest and the least number?

   (A) 21
   (B) 23
   (C) 25
   (D) 36
   (E) 46

8. The figure below shows an addition problem where W, X, Y, and Z represent distinct digits. Which of the following could be the sum of $W + X + Y + Z$?

   ```
       W  X  3
    +  Z  Y  X
    ─────────
    1  Y  4  2
   ```

   (A) 18
   (B) 22
   (C) 26
   (D) 31
   (E) 35

51

9. At a buffet restaurant, there is one price for adults and a different price for children. If 4 adults and 2 children cost $36, and 3 adults and 3 children cost $33, then what is the price for a child to eat at this restaurant?

   (A) $3
   (B) $4
   (C) $5
   (D) $6
   (E) $7

10. If $x < 5$, then which is a possible value for $4x + 7$?

    (A) 26
    (B) 27
    (C) 28
    (D) 29
    (E) 30

Workout #3 Answers

Synonyms Practice

As you might have noticed as you went through the synonyms sections, the definition given is not always the one that was listed in the words to learn section. This is because there is often more than one synonym for a word and on test day, you may get a synonym other than the one listed.

When you check your work, if there are words that you do not know the meaning of, make flashcards for them and then study these flashcards after you complete each workout.

1. D — The word list states that *bevy* means "group." Choice D is correct.

2. A — The word list states that *revel* means "merriment" or "merrymaking" — it can be both a noun and a verb. *Merriment* is to have a joyful gathering, or a celebration. Choice A is correct.

3. C — The word list from workout #2 states that *contemptible* means "despicable." Something despicable is something that is truly disgusting. Answer choice C is correct.

4. B — The word list states that *incandescent* means "glowing," so choice B is correct. To remember this meaning, notice that *incandescent* and *candle* both contain the *cand* root, and a candle glows.

5. E — The word list from workout #1 states that *allay* means "to soothe." To *soothe* is to reduce irritation or make something less difficult. To *ease* is also to make something less difficult. Choice E is correct.

6. A — The word list states that *glean* means "to gather." Answer choice A is correct.

7. D — The word list states that *tabulate* means "to categorize," or to list into categories. To *catalogue* is also to list, so choice D is the best answer. (Note that *categorize* and *catalogue* start the same way.)

8. C — The word list from workout #1 states that *dogged* means "persistent." Answer choice C is correct.

9. B — The word list states that *consolidate* means "to unite," so choice B is correct. To remember this word, the root *con* means "together" or "with," and *consolidate* means "to come together" or "unite."

10. E — The word list states that *dispel* means "to get rid of." *Banish* is another word that means "to get rid of," so choice E is correct. To remember the meaning of *dispel*, the root *dis* means "away" or "apart" and *pel* means "to push," so *dispel* literally means "to push away."

Analogies Practice

1. A — The relationship in this question is *degree*: *proficient* means "able to do something," while *superlative* means to be really good at something, making *superlative* is more extreme than *proficient*. Choice A is correct because *enthralled* has a similar meaning to *interested* but is more extreme. *Laborious* and *easy* are opposites, so choice B is not correct. *Demure* and *genteel* both describe someone who is polite, but *demure* is not more extreme than *genteel*, so choice C can be eliminated. *Despondent* means "totally hopeless," while *morbid* means "gruesome" and *morbid* is not more extreme than *despondent*, so choice D can be ruled out. Finally, *prudent* (wise) and *impertinent* (insulting) are not words that are similar only one is more extreme, so choice E is not correct.

2. C — The relationship here is *cause and effect*: to quell a rebellion is to stop it. The cause is to *quell*, and the effect is to stop the *rebellion*. To *rue* is to regret a mistake after it has happened (and not to stop it), so choice A can be ruled out. *Depreciate* (lose value) is not related to *evasion* (avoidance), so choice B can be ruled out. To *suppress* is to stop an *emotion*, so choice C is the correct answer. To *compile* is to gather a *list*, and not stop it, so choice D can be eliminated. Finally, to *rectify* (correct) would be to fix an *accident*, and not stop it, so choice E is not correct.

3. E — The relationship in this question is *opposites*: to *bolster* something is to support it, while to *eradicate* something is to eliminate it. *Revoke* (take back) and *curtail* (limit) are similar in meaning, so choice A can be ruled out. To *tabulate* (categorize) and to *rend* (divide) are not related, so choice B is also not correct. *Adorn* and *embellish* are similar in meaning, so choice C can be eliminated. Choice D is not correct because *bury* is not related to *defile* (pollute). Finally, *revert* is to go back and *progress* is to go forward, so choice E is the correct answer.

4. B — The relationship in this question is *means without*: showing *discretion* (sensitivity) means not *affronting* (offending) someone. *Chagrin* and *embarrassment* are similar in meaning, so choice A is not correct. To show *honesty* means not *deceiving* someone, so choice B is the correct answer. *Qualm* and *doubt* are similar in meaning, so choice C can be ruled out. *Fluctuation* (change) is unrelated to *ratify* (approve), and *reputation* is unrelated to *enrapture* (make someone extremely happy), so choices D and E are not correct.

5. C — The relationship in this question is *opposites*: *deft* is the opposite of *clumsy*. *Notable* and *famous* as well as *atrocious* and *appalling* are similar in meaning, so choices A and B are not correct. *Exuberant* means "showing extreme excitement," while *demure* is to show little emotion, so they are opposite in meaning, and choice C is correct. *Invincible* (undefeatable) and *robust* (strong) are similar in meaning, so choice D can be ruled out. Finally, *somber* means "gloomy" and *irate* means "angry," so they are not opposites, and choice E is not correct.

Reading Practice

1. A — This passage uses the first person voice for the narrator. This fits with an autobiography, so answer choice A is correct. An almanac (book of lists), encyclopedia, history of western explorers, or editorial review would not be written in the first person voice, so choices B, C, D, and E are not possible answers.

2. C — We can use the strategy of ruling out answer choices in order from most wrong to least wrong. The passage does not mention why the narrator has been imprisoned (only that he has been), so choice A can be ruled out. The passage also does not discuss the settlement of the American west, so choice B is not correct. The passage mentions that the narrator is imprisoned but does not generally discuss injustices, so choice D can also be eliminated. We are down to choices C or E. While the passage does discuss the Gila River Valley in the second paragraph, more of the passage discusses the childhood experiences of the narrator, so choice C is the best answer and choice E is not correct.

3. E — The passage states that when the narrator "had aught against any individual we ourselves took vengeance." This means that *aught* results in someone taking vengeance, or revenge. Someone would not take revenge if there were victories, surprises, or fascination, so choices B, C, and D are not correct. Vengeance might be taken if there are slights or grievances. *Grievances* is a stronger word, however, so people would be more likely to take vengeance if there were grievances, and choice E is the best answer choice while choice A is not correct.

4. B — The passage discusses the narrator living in a place with beautiful natural features, being warmed by the sun, rocked by the winds, and sheltered by the trees. Overall, this is a peaceful description, so choice B is the best answer.

5. C — This question asks why the description of the land around the Gila River headways was included. We can easily eliminate choices B and E because the passage does not mention that farming was difficult or that the narrator's tribe tried to move away. The second paragraph does describe beautiful lands as well as the diversity of the lands. However, the information was not included purely for the description of these features. The paragraph includes the information that the range was their fatherland, their wigwams were hidden in those mountains, the valleys were their fields, the prairies were their pastures, and the rocky caverns were their burial ground. The purpose of this description is to show the connection between the narrator's family and the land where they lived. Choice C best summarizes this and is the correct answer.

Math Practice

1. A — To answer this question we can set up expressions for each number. Let's say that x represents the smallest number because that is what we are looking for. Since the numbers are consecutive even numbers, the other numbers can be represented by $x + 2$, $x + 4$, and

$x + 6$. The question states that the value of the greatest of the 4 numbers ($x + 6$) plus twice the least ($2x$) is equal to 0. We can translate this into $x + 6 + 2x = 0$. If we combine like terms, the equation becomes $3x + 6 = 0$. Then we subtract 6 from both sides and the result is $3x = -6$. In order for this to be true, x must equal -2. Since we defined x as the least number, choice A is correct.

2. C — Cameron paid $2.50 for the first hour. That means that she paid $8.50 - $2.50 = $6.00 for the additional time. Since the garage charges $0.60 for each half hour, if we divide $6.00 by $0.60, we find that there were 10 additional half hours. This adds up to 5 additional hours. If we add in the first hour that she paid $2.50 for, this adds up to a total of 6 hours. Choice C is the correct answer.

3. B — We can translate the words of the question into an equation. Products means to multiply and "4 less than m" can be translated into $m - 4$. Therefore, $2m(m - 4) = 42$. At this point, we can multiply out the left side of the equation to get $2m^2 - 8m = 42$. This would require factoring to solve, however, and that is difficult for some students. It is easier to stop at the stage of $2m(m - 4) = 42$ and then plug in the answer choices for m and see which one makes the equation true. Let's try choice A first. If we substitute in -7 for m, the left side of the equation becomes $(2 \times -7)(-7 - 4)$. Since this simplifies to -14×-11, which is not equal to 42, choice A is not correct. Let's try choice B. If we substitute in -3 for m, the left side of the equation becomes $(2 \times -3)(-3 - 4)$. This simplifies to -6×-7, which is equal to 42, so choice B is the correct answer. Since we found an answer that works, we can stop there.

4. E — One approach is to list the positive integers that add to 12 (prime numbers are positive by definition):

    $1 + 11 = 12$

    $2 + 10 = 12$

    $3 + 9 = 12$

    $4 + 8 = 12$

    $5 + 7 = 12$

    $6 + 6 = 12$

    The only combination that includes two prime numbers is $5 + 7$, so our numbers are 5 and 7. Their product is 35, so choice E is correct. Note: the first combination of numbers (1 and 11) is not correct because 1 is neither prime nor composite.

5. D — One approach is to set up two equations. We can use M to represent the number of stamps that Marsha has and R to represent the number of stamps that Rodolfo has. We can turn "twice the number of stamps that Marsha has plus 5 times the number of stamps that

Rodolfo has is equal to 49," into $2M + 5R = 49$. We can also translate "3 times the number of stamps that Marsha has decreased by 4 times the number of stamps that Rodolfo has is equal to 39" into $3M - 4R = 39$.

Our equations are:

$2M + 5R = 49$

$3M - 4R = 39$

Using the elimination method to solve, we will first try to eliminate the R variables since we only need to solve for M. We can multiply the first equation by 4 and the second equation by 5:

$4(2M + 5R = 49)$

$5(3M - 4R = 39)$

This becomes:

$8M + 20R = 196$

$15M - 20R = 195$

If we add these together, $20R$ and $-20R$ cancel each other out, and we are left with $23M = 391$. If we divide both sides by 23, we find that $M = 17$. Marsha has 17 stamps, and choice D is correct.

6. D — We can define the larger number as x since we are looking for the greater number. Since the difference between the two numbers is 8, we can represent the second number as $x - 8$. The question tells us that the product of these numbers is 240, so $x(x - 8) = 240$. From here, we could multiply out and then have to factor to solve, but it might be easier to just substitute in answer choices to see what works. We are looking for the answer choice that makes the equation $x(x - 8) = 240$ true. Let's start with choice C since it is in the middle. We can substitute in 16 for x, then the left side of the equation becomes $16(16 - 8)$, which simplifies to 16×8, or 128. Since this is less than 240, we know that choice C doesn't work and we need a larger number. Let's try choice D. If we substitute in 20 for x, then the left side of the equation becomes $20(20 - 8)$. This simplifies to $20(12)$. Since this simplifies to 240, answer choice D is correct.

7. E — If the sum of 5 numbers is 115, we can divide 115 by 5 to find that the mean of the 5 numbers is 23. Since the numbers are consecutive, the mean is also the middle number. If the middle number is 23, then all 5 numbers are 21, 22, 23, 24, and 25. Since the least number is 21 and the greatest number is 25, the sum of the least and the greatest numbers is $21 + 25$, or 46. Answer choice E is correct.

8. C — We can start with the right column. We know that 3 + X equals something that ends in a units digit of 2. Since there is no positive digit that adds with 3 to get 2 and no two single digits can add to a number greater than 18, we know that 3 + X must equal 12. Therefore, X must equal 9. We also know that 1 must be carried over to the next column. Now we can use 9 for the value of X in the second-to-right column. If we substitute in 9 for X in the second-to-right column and remember to carry the 1 from the previous column, we can see that 1 + 9 + Y is equal to a number with a units digit of 4. Since 10 is greater than 4, the digits must add to 14. In order for this to be true, Y must be equal to 4 and we need to carry over 1 to the column on the left. So far, we know that X is equal to 9 and Y is equal to 4. If we look at the column on the left, and substitute in 4 for Y in the answer, we know that W + Z + 1 (carried over) is equal to 14. Therefore, W + Z is equal to 13. We can't know what W and Z are each equal to, but the question does not require that. We just need to be able to find the sum of W + X + Y + Z. Since X is equal to 9, Y is equal to 4, and W + X is equal to 13, we can add 9 + 4 +13 and find that W + X + Y + Z is equal to 26. Answer choice C is correct.

9. B — We can set up two equations to answer this question. Let's make A represent the cost of each adult and C represent the cost of each child. We multiply the cost of each adult/child by the number of adults/children to find the cost for each group. Given that 4 adults and 2 children cost $36, one of our equations is 4A + 2C = 36. The question also tells us that 3 adults and 3 children cost $33, so our second equation is 3A + 3C = 33.

Our equations are:

4A + 2C = 36

3A + 3C = 33

Now we can use the elimination method. We should eliminate the A variables since the question asks us to solve for the price of a child. We can multiply the first equation by 3 and the second equation by -4:

3(4A + 2C = 36)

−4(3A + 3C = 33)

If we distribute, our equations are now:

12A + 6C = 108

−12A − 12C = −132

Now we add the equations together. When we do this, 12A and −12A cancel each other out and we are left with −6C = −24. If we divide both sides by −6, the result is C = 4. Choice B is correct.

10. A — Let's start with figuring out what the value of $4x + 7$ is if x is equal to 5. If we substitute in 5 for x, the result is $4(5) + 7$, which is equal to 27. Since x is less than 5, however, the expression must be less than 27. Since A is the only answer choice with a number less than 27, choice A is correct.

Workout #4

Words to Learn

Below are the words used in Workout 4. Refer back to this list as needed as you move through the lesson.

Words used for name calling

Glutton:	one who overindulges
Hovel:	shack
Parochial:	narrow-minded
Naïve:	unsophisticated
Nonchalant:	unconcerned
Portly:	stout
Provincial:	unsophisticated
Putrid:	decaying
Tawdry:	cheap
Uncouth:	awkward

Words related to something not real

Cryptic:	mysterious
Dupe:	trick
Fallacy:	misconception
Feign:	pretend
Furtive:	stealthy
Hoax:	fraud
Bogus:	counterfeit

Words related to confusion

Mystical:	mysterious
Opaque:	murky
Disconcert:	perplex

Synonyms Practice

1. HOAX:
   - (A) fraud
   - (B) ritual
   - (C) skepticism
   - (D) focus
   - (E) ardor

2. COMPILE:
   - (A) embellish
   - (B) affront
   - (C) accumulate
   - (D) bolster
   - (E) disconcert

3. ALLURE:
   - (A) fallacy
   - (B) appeal
   - (C) chagrin
   - (D) glimpse
   - (E) stability

4. FEIGN:
   - (A) omit
   - (B) ratify
   - (C) doubt
   - (D) pretend
   - (E) dispel

5. DEFILE:
   - (A) glean
   - (B) enchant
   - (C) taint
   - (D) revoke
   - (E) count

6. BANE:
   - (A) revelation
   - (B) medley
   - (C) shack
   - (D) glutton
   - (E) curse

7. HAVOC:
   - (A) hovel
   - (B) calamity
   - (C) bevy
   - (D) collection
   - (E) portion

8. PAROCHIAL:
   - (A) curtailed
   - (B) cranky
   - (C) superlative
   - (D) gloomy
   - (E) provincial

9. FURTIVE:
   - (A) secretive
   - (B) uncouth
   - (C) disreputable
   - (D) crude
   - (E) irate

10. TAWDRY:
    - (A) unerring
    - (B) disconcerting
    - (C) cheap
    - (D) exuberant
    - (E) noteworthy

Analogies Practice

1. Smelly is to putrid as
    - (A) discouraged is to despondent
    - (B) appalling is to disgusting
    - (C) tranquil is to genteel
    - (D) somber is to callous
    - (E) insulting is to enthralled

2. Naïve is to worldly as
    - (A) flexible is to nimble
    - (B) harmful is to diligent
    - (C) transparent is to cryptic
    - (D) demure is to extreme
    - (E) laborious is to nonchalant

3. Gaunt is to portly as
    - (A) incandescent is to glowing
    - (B) authentic is to bogus
    - (C) honorable is to deft
    - (D) preserved is to opaque
    - (E) atrocious is to morbid

4. Consolidate is to rend as
    - (A) revert is to turn
    - (B) burst is to bundle
    - (C) enrapture is to please
    - (D) provide is to depreciate
    - (E) encourage is to quell

5. Prudent is to sage as
    - (A) mystical is to archaeologist
    - (B) impertinent is to child
    - (C) timely is to teacher
    - (D) proficient is to expert
    - (E) genteel is to owner

Reading Practice

The following speech was delivered by Senator Margaret Chase Smith on June 1, 1950.

Those of us who shout the loudest about Americanism in making character assassinations are all too frequently those who, by our own words and acts, ignore some of the basic principles of Americanism:

The right to criticize.

Line 5   The right to hold unpopular beliefs.

The right to protest.

The right of independent thought.

The exercise of these rights should not cost one single American citizen his reputation or his right to a livelihood nor should he be in danger of losing his reputation or livelihood merely
10   because he happens to know someone who holds unpopular beliefs. Who of us does not? Otherwise none of us could call our souls our own. Otherwise thought control would have set in. The American people are sick and tired of being afraid to speak their minds lest they be politically smeared as "Communists" or "Fascists" by their opponents. Freedom of speech is not what it used to be in America. It has been so abused by some that it is not exercised by others.
15   The American people are sick and tired of seeing innocent people smeared and guilty people whitewashed. But there have been enough proved cases, such as the Amerasia case, the Hiss case, the Coplon case, the Gold case, to cause nationwide distrust and strong suspicion that there may be something to the unproved, sensational accusations.

1. In this passage, Senator Margaret Chase Smith is primarily concerned with

    (A) naming individuals who had engaged in un-American activities.
    (B) arguing for greater enforcement of anticommunist laws.
    (C) describing the reasons why laws should be changed given recent cases of anti-American acts.
    (D) pointing out the ways in which freedom of speech had been diminished in the United States.
    (E) outlining basic American freedoms.

2. The author views unpopular beliefs as

    (A) something to be eradicated.
    (B) a basic part of being human.
    (C) necessary for maintaining an American identity.
    (D) a frustrating part of being an American.
    (E) not protected by freedom of speech.

3. The author portrays "those of us who shout the loudest about Americanism" as

   (A) hypocrites.
   (B) true patriots.
   (C) pure evildoers.
   (D) protectors of American rights.
   (E) independent thinkers.

4. Which of the following could replace the term "whitewashed" (line 16) without changing the author's meaning?

   (A) excoriated
   (B) cast aside
   (C) encouraged
   (D) promoted
   (E) exonerated

5. In this passage, Senator Margaret Chase Smith implies which of the following about "Communism" and "Fascism?"

   (A) They are evils that need to be eliminated.
   (B) They are terms that are used incorrectly in order to discredit opponents.
   (C) They represent un-American values.
   (D) They can be protected against by allowing freedom of speech.
   (E) They are labels that have been unfairly applied to her.

Workout #4

Math Practice

In this section, we will work on questions that involve exponential expressions, radicals, and scientific notation. These questions are difficult not because they are tricky but rather because they involve more advanced math concepts.

We will start with questions that require you to apply the rules of exponential expressions.

1. $\dfrac{3^{-2}a^{-3}b^{-1}c^5}{6b^{-2}c^2} =$

    (A) $\dfrac{3c^3}{2a^3b}$

    (B) $\dfrac{bc^3}{2a^3}$

    (C) $\dfrac{3bc^3}{2a^3}$

    (D) $\dfrac{c^7}{27a^3b}$

    (E) $\dfrac{bc^3}{54a^3}$

2. Which expression is equivalent to $\left(\dfrac{1}{x^{-8}}\right)^2$?

    (A) $\dfrac{1}{x^8}$

    (B) $\dfrac{1}{x^{16}}$

    (C) x^{10}

    (D) x^{16}

    (E) x^{24}

3. Which expression has the least value?

    (A) $\left(\dfrac{3}{4}\right)^{-2}$

    (B) $\left(\dfrac{4}{3}\right)^{-2}$

    (C) $\left(\dfrac{3}{4}\right)^{-1}$

    (D) $\dfrac{3}{4}$

    (E) $\dfrac{4}{3}$

4. Harold opened a bank account with $4,000. He deposits no more money into it. The expression $4{,}000(1.05)^t$ represents how much money is in the account after t years. By what percent does the balance in his bank account increase each year?

   (A) 0.05%
   (B) 0.5%
   (C) 1.05%
   (D) 5%
   (E) 105%

Now we will work on some problems with radical expressions. Hint: remember that we can factor numbers under a radical. Also, remember that we can turn radicals into fractional exponents.

5. Which expression is equivalent to $\sqrt[4]{x^5 y^9}$?

   (A) xy^5
   (B) $x^{20} y^{36}$
   (C) $xy^2 \sqrt[4]{xy}$
   (D) $xy^2 \sqrt{xy}$
   (E) $x^{\frac{4}{5}} y^{\frac{4}{9}}$

6. Which expression is equivalent to $\sqrt{\sqrt{\sqrt{m^{32}}}}$?

   (A) m^4
   (B) m^8
   (C) $m^{\frac{32}{3}}$
   (D) m^{16}
   (E) m^{29}

7. Which expression is equivalent to $\dfrac{4}{\sqrt{2}} + \dfrac{3}{\sqrt{3}}$?

   (A) $2\sqrt{2} + 3\sqrt{3}$
   (B) $2\sqrt{2} + \sqrt{3}$
   (C) $\dfrac{7\sqrt{6}}{6}$
   (D) $7\sqrt{6}$
   (E) 42

Finally, we have some scientific notation questions.

8. Which of the following is equivalent to $\dfrac{1}{5{,}000}$?

    (A) 2×10^{-5}
    (B) 2×10^{-4}
    (C) 2×10^{-3}
    (D) 5×10^{-4}
    (E) 5×10^{-3}

9. The population of country X is 1.6×10^4. The population of country Y is 4.8×10^8. How many times greater is the population of country Y than the population of country X?

    (A) 3×10^{-4}
    (B) 3×10^{-2}
    (C) 3×10^2
    (D) 3×10^4
    (E) 3.2×10^4

10. Which shows 0.03% written in scientific notation?

    (A) 3×10^4
    (B) 3×10^2
    (C) 3×10^{-2}
    (D) 3×10^{-3}
    (E) 3×10^{-4}

Workout #4 Answers

Synonyms Practice

1. A — The word list states that *hoax* means "fraud," so choice A is the right answer.

2. C — The word list from workout #3 states that *compile* means "to gather." *Accumulate* also means "to gather," so choice C is correct. Note that *compile* has the root *com* and *accumulate* has the related root *cum*. Both of these roots mean "together," so *complete* and *accumulate* both mean "to gather together."

3. B — The word list from workout #1 states that *allure* means "attraction." *Appeal* is another word for *attraction*, so choice B is the correct answer.

4. D — The word list states that *feign* means "to pretend." Answer choice D is correct.

5. C — The word list from workout #2 states that *defile* means "pollute." It also states that *taint* means "pollute." Since *taint* and *defile* both mean "pollute," they are synonyms, and choice C is correct.

6. E — The word list in workout #2 states that *bane* means "curse." Answer choice E is correct.

7. B — The word list from workout #2 states that *havoc* means "devastation." That is not an answer choice, however. *Calamity* also means "devastation," so choice B is correct.

8. E — The word list states that *provincial* means "unsophisticated." *Curtailed* (limited), *cranky* (grumpy), *superlative* (outstanding), and *gloomy* do not mean "unsophisticated." We are left with *provincial*, which describes a person who is unsophisticated, so choice E is correct.

9. A — The word list states that *furtive* means "stealthy." *Stealthy* describes performing an action while taking care for other people not to find out about it. This is also being *secretive*, so choice A is correct.

10. C — The word list states that *tawdry* means "cheap." Answer choice C is correct.

Analogies Practice

1. A — The relationship in this question is *degree*: something that is really *smelly* is *putrid*, and *putrid* is more extreme than *smelly*. If a person was really discouraged, they would be despondent. Since *despondent* is more extreme than *discouraged*, answer choice A is correct. *Appalling* is more extreme than *disgusting*, so choice B is not correct because the words are in the wrong order. *Genteel* is not more extreme than *tranquil*, so choice C can be ruled out. *Somber* (gloomy) and *callous* (insensitive) as well as *insulting* and *enthralled* (captivated) are not related, so choices D and E are not correct.

Workout #4

2. C — The relationship in this question is *opposites*: *naïve* (unsophisticated) is the opposite of *worldly* (having knowledge of the world). *Flexible* is a synonym for *nimble*, so choice A is not correct. *Harmful* is not related to *diligent* (persevering), so choice B can be ruled out. *Transparent* (clear) is the opposite of *cryptic* (mysterious), so choice C is the correct answer. *Demure* (reserved) and *extreme* as well as *laborious* (difficult) and *nonchalant* (unconcerned) are not related, so choices D and E can be eliminated.

3. B — The relationship in this question is *opposites*: *gaunt* (very thin) and *portly* (stout) are opposites. *Incandescent* and *glowing* are synonyms, so choice A is not correct. *Authentic* (real) is the opposite of *bogus* (fake), so choice B is the correct answer. *Honorable* and *deft* (nimble) as well as *preserved* and *opaque* (murky) are not related, so choices C and D can be ruled out. *Atrocious* and *morbid* are similar in meaning and not opposites, so choice E can be eliminated.

4. E — The relationship in this question is *opposites*: *consolidate* (unite) is the opposite of *rend* (divide). To *revert* is to turn back, which is not the opposite of *turn*, so choice A can be ruled out. *Burst* and *bundle* are not related, so choice B can be eliminated. *Enrapture* is an extreme version of *please* (and not opposite of it), so choice C is not correct. *Provide* is not related to *depreciate* (lost value), so choice D is also not the correct answer. *Encourage* is the opposite of *quell* (extinguish), so choice E is the correct answer.

5. D — The relationship in this question is *characteristic of*: *prudent* (wise) is a characteristic of a *sage* (wise person). *Mystical* (mysterious) is not necessarily a characteristic of an *archaeologist*, so choice A is not correct. *Impertinent* (insulting) is also not necessarily a characteristic of a *child*, and *timely* doesn't have to be a characteristic of a *teacher*, so choices B and C can be ruled out. By definition, an *expert* is *proficient* (experienced) in what he or she does, so choice D is the correct answer. An *owner* is not *genteel* by definition, so choice E is not correct.

Reading Practice

1. D — This question is asking for the main point that Senator Margaret Chase Smith is making in this speech. We can easily eliminate choices A, B, and C because she is not naming individuals, is against the strict enforcement of anticommunist laws, and does not advocate for a change in laws. We are down to choices D and E. While she does advocate for the freedom of speech, she is not outlining basic American freedoms in general, so choice E is not the best answer. She is giving examples of how people are labeled fascists or communists for speaking their minds, which diminishes freedom of speech, so choice D is the best answer.

2. B — In line 10, Senator Margaret Chase Smith mentions unpopular beliefs. She then goes on to ask, "Who of us does not?" in reference to holding unpopular beliefs. She is pointing out that every person at some point has a belief that others find unpopular, so it is a part of being human, and choice B is correct.

3. A — The beginning of the passage states, "Those of us who shout the loudest about Americanism in making character assassinations are all too frequently those who, by our own

words and acts, ignore some of the basic principles of Americanism." She is pointing out that people who shout about Americanism are not following their own values, which makes them hypocrites, so choice A is correct.

4. E — In lines 15-16, the passage states, "innocent people smeared and guilty people whitewashed." The passage is contrasting innocent and guilty people and smeared with whitewashed. Since smeared is to paint someone as bad or guilty, whitewashed would be to portray that person as good or innocent. To be exonerated means to be declared innocent of a crime, so choice E is the correct answer.

5. B — In lines 12-13, the passage states, "The American people are sick and tired of being afraid to speak their minds lest they be politically smeared as "Communists" or "Fascists" by their opponents." Since being politically smeared would be the same thing as being discredited and she implies that those terms are applied incorrectly, answer choice B is the correct answer.

Math Practice

1. E — We can start by breaking apart the expression so that we simplify like terms:

$$\frac{3^{-2}}{6} \times \frac{a^{-3}}{1} \times \frac{b^{-1}}{b^{-2}} \times \frac{c^5}{c^2}$$

Our next step is to rewrite the terms to eliminate the negative exponents. To do this, we move each term that has a negative exponent in the numerator to the denominator and each term that has a negative exponent in the denominator to the numerator and make the exponent positive:

$$\frac{1}{3^2 \times 6} \times \frac{1}{a^3} \times \frac{b^2}{b^1} \times \frac{c^5}{c^2}$$

Finally, we simplify each term and then multiply them back together:

$$\frac{1}{54} \times \frac{1}{a^3} \times \frac{b}{1} \times \frac{c^3}{1} = \frac{bc^3}{54a^3}$$

Answer choice E is correct.

2. D — Our first step is to eliminate the negative exponent. We do this by moving x^{-8} from the denominator to the numerator and making it x^8. Our expression is now $(x^8)^2$. To simplify, we multiply the exponents together and the result is x^{16}. Answer choice D is correct.

3. B — Our first step is to eliminate the negative exponents in choices A, B, and C. We can start with first reversing the numerators and denominators in each choice and making the exponent positive. Then we can distribute the exponent to the numerator and denominator in each answer choice. Finally, we can simplify:

(A) $\left(\dfrac{3}{4}\right)^{-2} = \left(\dfrac{4}{3}\right)^{2} = \dfrac{4^2}{3^2} = \dfrac{16}{9}$

(B) $\left(\dfrac{4}{3}\right)^{-2} = \left(\dfrac{3}{4}\right)^{2} = \dfrac{3^2}{4^2} = \dfrac{9}{16}$

(C) $\left(\dfrac{3}{4}\right)^{-1} = \left(\dfrac{4}{3}\right)^{1} = \dfrac{4}{3}$

We are looking for the least answer and some of our answer choices are greater than 1 and some of them are less than 1. We can rule out choices A, C, and E because they are all greater than 1 and therefore can't have the least value. Now we have to compare $\dfrac{9}{16}$ (choice B) and $\dfrac{3}{4}$ (choice D). In order to do so, we can give the two fractions a common denominator. Since 4 is a factor of 16, we will multiply $\dfrac{3}{4}$ by $\dfrac{4}{4}$ and the result is $\dfrac{12}{16}$. Therefore $\dfrac{3}{4}$ is equal to $\dfrac{12}{16}$ and $\dfrac{3}{4}$ is greater than $\dfrac{9}{16}$. Since $\dfrac{9}{16}$ is less than $\dfrac{12}{16}$, choice B is the correct answer.

4. D — This question applies the formula $A = P(1 + r)^t$, where A is the amount, P is the principle (starting amount), r is the rate of increase or decrease, and t is the time that has passed. The equation given for how much money Harold has in the bank shows that he started with $4,000 and that $(1 + r)$ is equal to 1.05. Therefore, r (or the rate of increase) must be equal to 0.05. The question asks for the rate as a percent, however, so we multiply 0.05 by 100% and find that the rate of increase is 5%. Choice D is correct.

5. C — We can start by turning the fourth root radical into a fraction exponent. The expression becomes:

$$\left(x^5 y^9\right)^{\frac{1}{4}}$$

If we distribute the exponent, the expression is now:

$$x^{\frac{5}{4}} y^{\frac{9}{4}}$$

Now we will break apart the fractional exponent so that we can simplify:

$$x^{\frac{4}{4}} x^{\frac{1}{4}} y^{\frac{8}{4}} y^{\frac{1}{4}}$$

We can use the commutative property to rearrange the terms:

$$x^{\frac{4}{4}} y^{\frac{8}{4}} x^{\frac{1}{4}} y^{\frac{1}{4}}$$

This simplifies to:

$$xy^2 \sqrt[4]{xy}$$

Answer choice C is correct.

6. A — To answer this question, we can start at the inside and use fractional exponents to simplify. We can turn the inner radical into an exponent of $\frac{1}{2}$ so that our expression becomes:

$$\sqrt{\sqrt{\sqrt{m^{32 \times \frac{1}{2}}}}} = \sqrt{\sqrt{\sqrt{m^{16}}}}$$

Now we can turn the next radical into a fractional exponent:

$$\sqrt{\sqrt{m^{16 \times \frac{1}{2}}}} = \sqrt{\sqrt{m^8}}$$

Finally, we turn the last radical into a fractional exponent and the expression is now:

$$m^{8 \times \frac{1}{2}} = m^4$$

Answer choice A is correct.

7. B — Our first step is to create a common denominator. In this case, $\sqrt{2}$ and $\sqrt{3}$ are both factors of $\sqrt{6}$, so our common denominator is $\sqrt{6}$. To do this, we have to multiply the first fraction by $\frac{\sqrt{3}}{\sqrt{3}}$ and the second fraction by $\frac{\sqrt{2}}{\sqrt{2}}$. Then we add the two expressions together:

$$\left(\frac{4}{\sqrt{2}} \times \frac{\sqrt{3}}{\sqrt{3}}\right) + \left(\frac{3}{\sqrt{3}} \times \frac{\sqrt{2}}{\sqrt{2}}\right) = \frac{4\sqrt{3}}{\sqrt{6}} + \frac{3\sqrt{2}}{\sqrt{6}} = \frac{4\sqrt{3} + 3\sqrt{2}}{\sqrt{6}}$$

Now we have an expression with a radical in the denominator so we need to rationalize the expression. We can do this by multiplying both the numerator and the denominator by $\sqrt{6}$:

$$\frac{4\sqrt{3} + 3\sqrt{2}}{\sqrt{6}} \cdot \frac{\sqrt{6}}{\sqrt{6}} = \frac{4\sqrt{3} \cdot \sqrt{6} + 3\sqrt{2} \cdot \sqrt{6}}{6} = \frac{4\sqrt{18} + 3\sqrt{12}}{6}$$

Now we have to simplify the radicals in the numerator by factoring:

$$\frac{4\sqrt{18}+3\sqrt{12}}{6} = \frac{4\cdot\sqrt{9}\cdot\sqrt{2}+3\cdot\sqrt{4}\cdot\sqrt{3}}{6} = \frac{4\cdot 3\cdot\sqrt{2}+3\cdot 2\cdot\sqrt{3}}{6} = \frac{12\sqrt{2}+6\sqrt{3}}{6}$$

Finally, we can simplify by dividing both terms in the numerator by 6, which results in $2\sqrt{2}+\sqrt{3}$. Answer choice B is correct.

8. B — One approach is to create an equivalent fraction to $\frac{1}{5,000}$ that has 10, 100, 1,000, 10,000, etc., as a denominator since those are the place values. We can multiply $\frac{1}{5,000} \times \frac{2}{2}$ and find that $\frac{1}{5,000}$ is equivalent to $\frac{2}{10,000}$. Another way to say $\frac{2}{10,000}$ is two-ten-thousandths. The 2 should go in the ten-thousandths place, so we would write the decimal as 0.0002. Now we need to convert this into scientific notation. We need to move the decimal place 4 places to the right in order to do that, so our number becomes 2×10^{-4}. Answer choice B is correct.

9. D — This question is asking what we have to multiply 1.6×10^4 by in order to get 4.8×10^8. We need to multiply 1.6 by 3 to get 4.8, so we know the first number must be 3. Then we would need to multiply 10^4 by 10^4 in order to get 10^8. Therefore, all together we need to multiply 1.6×10^4 by 3×10^4 in order to get 4.8×10^8. Answer choice D is correct.

10. E — Our first step is to convert from a percent into a decimal. We do this by moving the decimal two places to the left so that 0.03% becomes 0.0003. Now we have to turn this decimal into scientific notation. In order to do that, we move the decimal 4 places to the right and the number becomes 3×10^{-4}. Answer choice E is correct.

Workout #5

Words to Learn

Below are the words used in Workout 5. Refer back to this list as needed as you move through the lesson.

Words related to activity

Inert:	unmoving
Invigorating:	energizing
Dormant:	inactive
Listless:	spiritless
Slothful:	lazy
Wan:	feeble

Words related to fighting

Brandish:	wield
Incite:	encourage
Incriminate:	accuse
Parry:	deflect
Radical:	extreme
Rebuff:	reject
Rift:	disagreement
Skirmish:	conflict
Tumult:	riot

Words related to height

Apex:	peak
Dominant:	most powerful
Pinnacle:	peak
Ultimate:	highest

Words related to humor

Droll:	witty
Satire:	parody
Banter:	joke

Synonyms Practice

1. NONCHALANT:
   - (A) challenging
   - (B) mellow
   - (C) benevolent
   - (D) responsible
   - (E) demure

2. ALLAY:
   - (A) rue
   - (B) insult
   - (C) encourage
   - (D) glean
   - (E) ease

3. DEFT:
   - (A) agile
   - (B) cryptic
   - (C) enthralled
   - (D) putrid
   - (E) superlative

4. ERADICATE:
   - (A) gather
   - (B) astonish
   - (C) destroy
   - (D) trample
   - (E) restrict

5. INERT:
   - (A) furtive
   - (B) dormant
   - (C) atrocious
   - (D) invigorating
   - (E) callous

6. DOGGED:
   - (A) genteel
   - (B) wondrous
   - (C) listless
   - (D) drastic
   - (E) determined

7. APEX:
   - (A) drift
   - (B) glutton
   - (C) trough
   - (D) captivity
   - (E) pinnacle

8. SATIRE:
   - (A) hoax
   - (B) medley
   - (C) ceremony
   - (D) parody
   - (E) result

9. DISCRETION:
   - (A) prudence
   - (B) awkwardness
   - (C) mystique
   - (D) accusation
   - (E) bevy

10. DUPE:
    - (A) rebuff
    - (B) deflect
    - (C) deceive
    - (D) curtail
    - (E) rectify

Analogies Practice

1. Humdrum is to invigorating as
   - (A) bogus is to furtive
   - (B) portly is to morbid
   - (C) wan is to exuberant
   - (D) cynical is to hapless
   - (E) tawdry is to incandescent

2. Incite is to bedlam as
   - (A) enchant is to training
   - (B) defile is to evasion
   - (C) parry is to fallacy
   - (D) flatter is to humor
   - (E) ignite is to blaze

3. Opaque is to clarity as
   - (A) slothful is to laziness
   - (B) uncouth is to sophistication
   - (C) handy is to skills
   - (D) parochial is to ideals
   - (E) somber is to tragedy

4. Skirmish is to tumult as
   - (A) suspicion is to incrimination
   - (B) drought is to tsunami
   - (C) rift is to disagreement
   - (D) quandary is to guilt
   - (E) conversation is to banter

5. House is to hovel as
   - (A) chagrin is to distaste
   - (B) process is to restraint
   - (C) suitcase is to sack
   - (D) cabinet is to desk
   - (E) havoc is to chaos

Reading Practice

> On and on, always on and on
> Away from you, parted by a life-parting.
> Going from one another ten thousand "li,"
> Each in a different corner of the World.
> Line 5 The way between is difficult and long,
> Face to face how shall we meet again?
> The Tartar horse prefers the North wind,
> The bird from Yüeh nests on the Southern branch.
> Since we parted the time is already long,
> 10 Daily my clothes hang looser round my waist.
> Floating clouds obscure the white sun,
> The wandering one has quite forgotten home.
> Thinking of you has made me suddenly old,
> The months and years swiftly draw to their close.
> 15 I'll put you out of my mind and forget for ever
> And try with all my might to eat and thrive.

1. This poem is primarily concerned with

    (A) describing the process of aging.
    (B) illustrating how hard it is to leave where a person has grown up.
    (C) describing the experience of missing another person.
    (D) mourning the death of a close friend.
    (E) explaining the disadvantages of traveling away from home.

2. It can be inferred from the poem that a "life-parting" occurs when

    (A) one person dies and the other person remains living.
    (B) two people are parted by the circumstances of their lives.
    (C) a person leaves a place without expecting to return.
    (D) two people have a major disagreement.
    (E) people grow apart even though they live in the same place

3. The author uses the examples of the "Tartar horse" and "the bird from Yueh" to represent

    (A) how hard it is to part from a friend.
    (B) that people are often very similar to animals in the wild.
    (C) the natural progression of life.
    (D) life and the afterlife.
    (E) people who are drawn to different places.

4. The author writes, "Daily my clothes hang looser round my waist," in order to illustrate how

    (A) hard it is to find food while traveling.
    (B) long it has been since the author's friend has died.
    (C) far the author has traveled since he left home.
    (D) long it has been since the author has seen his friend.
    (E) sudden it seemed when the author's friend left home.

5. The final two lines, "I'll put you out of my mind and forget for ever / And try with all my might to eat and thrive," indicate that the author

    (A) will never forget his friend.
    (B) is saying goodbye to his friend so that he can prosper.
    (C) wishes to forget that he ever knew his friend.
    (D) is returning to see his friend again.
    (E) would like to see his friend one last time.

Workout #5

Math Practice

In this workout we will practice problems that involve the coordinate grid. These include questions involving transformations, slope, and problems that require you to apply the Pythagorean theorem to answer the question.

Some coordinate questions are relatively simple and just require you to understand how the basic coordinate grid works. We are focusing on the difficult problems here, however, so we will skip to the harder ones.

1. In the *xy*-coordinate plane, the graph of a line with the equation $4x - 2y = 6$ intersects the *y*-axis at point *B*. What are the coordinates of point *B*?

    (A) (0, –3)
    (B) (–3, 0)
    (C) (0, 3)
    (D) (0, 1.5)
    (E) (1.5, 0)

2. In the *xy*-coordinate plane, a circle has a radius of 3 units and its center is located at the point (6, 7). Which point is NOT on the circle?

    (A) (6, 4)
    (B) (3, 7)
    (C) (3, 4)
    (D) (9, 7)
    (E) (6, 10)

3. A line segment has one endpoint at the coordinates (9, 5) and a midpoint of (1, 3). What is the other endpoint of this line segment?

    (A) (17, 7)
    (B) (5, 4)
    (C) (4, 3)
    (D) (–4, –3)
    (E) (–7, 1)

Now we will work on some transformation problems.

4. In the *xy*-coordinate plane, the point *B* (5, 4) is reflected across the *x*-axis and then translated up 6 units to create point *B'*. What are the coordinates of point *B'*?

    (A) (–5, –10)
    (B) (–5, –4)
    (C) (5, 2)
    (D) (5, 4)
    (E) (5, 10)

5. The triangle XYZ is rotated 90° clockwise about the origin and then translated up 2 units to create the triangle X'Y'Z'?

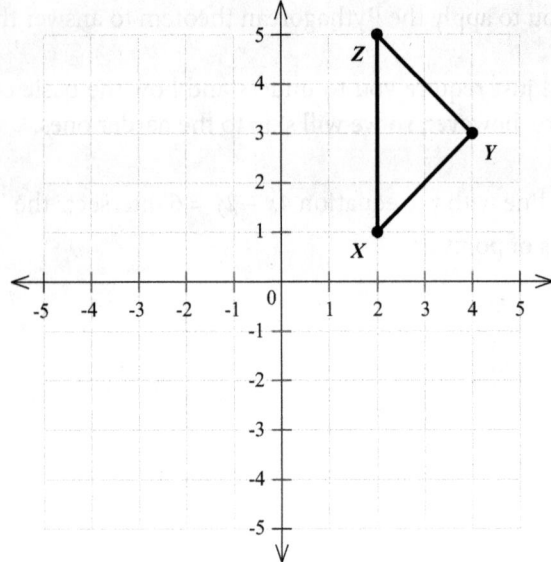

What are the coordinates of point Y'?

(A) (–3, 6)
(B) (–3, 4)
(C) (–4, 3)
(D) (–4, 5)
(E) (3, –2)

The following are some problems that use slope. While they don't use the word *slope*, they do require you to apply the principles of slope.

6. Line *m* is perpendicular to a line with the equation $4x + 2y = 6$. If two points on line *m* are $(3, -3)$ and $(4, k)$, what is the value of *k*?

(A) –5
(B) $\frac{-7}{2}$
(C) $\frac{-5}{2}$
(D) $\frac{2}{5}$
(E) 5

Workout #5

7. If the line *b* is parallel to the graph of $3x + 2y = 5$ on the coordinate grid, which could be the equation of line *b*?

   (A) $y = \dfrac{-2}{3}x + 4$

   (B) $y = -4x + 8$

   (C) $y = \dfrac{2x + 7}{3}$

   (D) $y = \dfrac{-3x + 7}{2}$

   (E) $y = \dfrac{3x + 6}{2}$

8. Which set of coordinates could describe point *P* if triangle *LMP* is a right triangle?

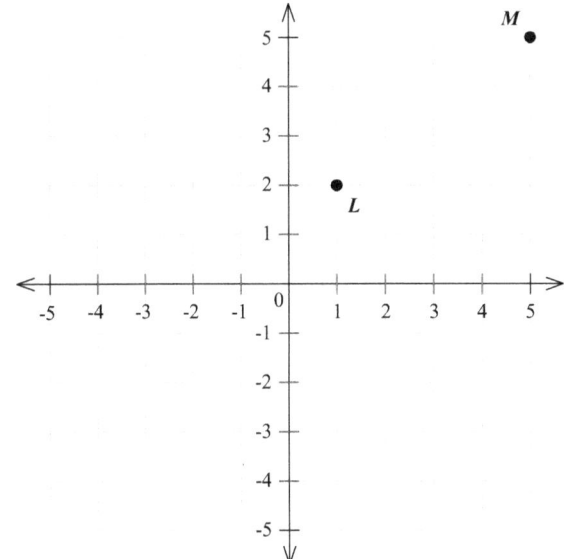

   (A) (2, 1)
   (B) (3, 1)
   (C) (3, 2)
   (D) (4, 1)
   (E) (5, 1)

81

Finally, we have some problems that are on the coordinate grid but can be solved by applying the Pythagorean theorem. Hint: Keep in mind that to find the distance between two points we can create a right triangle and use the Pythagorean theorem to solve for the hypotenuse, or distance between the two points.

9. In the *xy*-coordinate plane, points $P\,(5, 2)$, $Q\,(5, 7)$, and $R\,(7, 5)$ form a triangle. What is the length of side $\overline{PR}$?

   (A) $2\sqrt{2}$
   (B) $\sqrt{13}$
   (C) 5
   (D) $\sqrt{20}$
   (E) 6

10. In the *xy*-coordinate plane, the points $(1, 3)$ and $(7, p)$ are 10 units apart. Which is a possible value for p?

    (A) −5
    (B) −3
    (C) 1
    (D) 3
    (E) 5

Workout #5 Answers

Synonyms Practice

1. B — The word list from lesson #4 states that *nonchalant* means "unconcerned." Another word for a person who does not have concerns is *mellow*. Choice B is correct.

2. E — The word list from workout #1 states that *allay* means "to soothe." To soothe is to reduce irritation or make something easier, or ease a situation. Answer choice E is correct.

3. A — The word list from workout #1 states that *deft* means "nimble." *Agile* has the same meaning as *nimble*, so choice A is correct.

4. C — The word list from workout #3 states that *eradicate* means "to exterminate." *Exterminate* means "to get rid of something completely," or "to destroy it," so choice C is the best answer. You may have been tempted by choices D or E, but to *trample* or *restrict* would be to limit something, but not to get rid of it completely, so choice C is the best answer.

5. B — The word list states that *inert* means "unmoving." *Dormant* also means "unmoving," so choice B is the correct answer.

6. E — The word list from workout #1 states that *dogged* means "persistent." To be persistent is to follow through on a goal until it is completed. *Determined* also describes this behavior, so choice E is the correct answer.

7. E — The word list states that *apex* means "peak." The word list also states that *pinnacle* means "peak." Since *apex* and *pinnacle* both mean "peak," they are synonyms, and choice E is correct.

8. D — The word list tells us that *satire* means "parody," so choice D is the correct answer. A *satire* (or parody) is a work of art that mocks or makes fun of something or someone.

9. A — The word list from workout #3 states that *discretion* means "good judgment." The word list from workout #1 states that *prudent* means "wise." *Prudence* is the noun form of *prudent* and means "to show wisdom or good judgment." *Discretion* and *prudence* are synonyms, so choice A is correct.

10. C — The word list from workout #4 states that *dupe* means "to trick." To trick a person is to convince him or her of something that is not true, or *deceive* him or her. Choice C is correct.

Analogies Practice

1. C — The relationship in this question is *opposites*: *humdrum* (boring) is the opposite of *invigorating* (energizing). *Bogus* (fake) is not the opposite of *furtive* (secretive) and *portly* (stout) is not the opposite of *morbid* (gruesome), so choices A and B are not correct. *Wan* (feeble or lacking energy) is the opposite of *exuberant* (excited), so choice C is the correct answer. *Cynical* (pessimistic) and *hapless* (unlucky) as well as *tawdry* (cheap) and *incandescent* (glowing) are not opposites, so choices D and E can be eliminated.

2. E — The relationship in this question is *cause and effect*: to *incite* is to cause *bedlam* (or chaos). *Enchant* and *training* are unrelated, as are *defile* (pollute) and *evasion* (avoidance), so choices A and B are not correct. To *parry* (deflect) does not lead to *fallacy* (lie) and *flatter* does not lead to *humor*, so choices C and D can be ruled out. Finally, to *ignite* is to cause a *blaze* to start, so choice E is the best answer.

3. B — The relationship in this question is *means without*: *opaque* means without *clarity*. *Slothful* means with *laziness* (not without), so choice A can be ruled out. *Uncouth* does mean without *sophistication*, so choice B is the correct answer. *Handy* means with *skills*, so we can eliminate choice C. *Parochial* (unsophisticated) is unrelated to having *ideals*, and *somber* is the result of a *tragedy* (and not without tragedy), so choices D and E are not correct.

4. A — The relationship here is *degree*: a *skirmish* is a small fight, and a *tumult* is a large riot, so *tumult* is more extreme than *skirmish*. *Suspicion* is to suspect a person of doing something wrong, while *incrimination* is to openly blame them. Therefore, *incrimination* is more extreme than *suspicion*, and choice A is the correct answer. A *drought* and a *tsunami* are opposites, and *tsunami* is not a more extreme *drought*, so we can rule out choice B. A *rift* is more extreme than a *disagreement* (the words are in the wrong order), so choice C is not correct. *Quandary* (dilemma) and *guilt* are unrelated, and *banter* is a lighter form of *conversation* (the words are in the wrong order), so we can rule out choices D and E.

5. C — The relationship here is *type of*: a shabby type of *house* is a *hovel*. *Chagrin* (embarrassment) and *distaste* as well as *process* and *restraint* are unrelated, so choices A and B are not correct. A shabby type of *suitcase* is a *sack*, so choice C is the correct answer. A shabby type of *cabinet* is not a *desk*, and *havoc* and *chaos* are synonyms, so we can rule out choices D and E.

Reading Practice

1. C — The poem begins with talking about how far apart two people are and questioning whether they will meet again. Then the poem discusses how long the two people have been apart from each other. Finally, it describes how thinking of the other person has made the speaker feel old and how he needs to put the other person out of his mind so that he might thrive. The poem is primarily about missing another person and choice C is correct.

2. C — The poem states, "Away from you, parted by a life-parting. / Going from one another ten thousand 'li,' / Each in a different corner of the World." The speaker then asks, "Face to face how shall we meet again?" Therefore, a *life-parting* involves going a great distance from each other and maybe never meeting face to face again. We can rule out choices D and E because there is no indication of a disagreement or that the two people live in the same place. Choices A, B, and C are very similar. Choice A states that one person has died, and this is not mentioned in the poem, so choice A is not correct. Choice B is tempting because the speaker and his friend are parted by the circumstances of their lives (one leaves), but choice C is the better answer because this poem is not just about being parted by circumstances but rather about the specific circumstances of one person leaving a place. Choice C is correct.

3. E — The poem states, "The Tartar horse prefers the North wind, / The bird from Yueh nests on the Southern Branch." This represents how two people can simply prefer different parts of the world, so choice E is the correct answer.

4. D — The poem states, "Since we parted the time is already long, / Daily my clothes hang looser round my waist." The clothes are being used to illustrate how long the time is since the friends have parted, so choice D is the correct answer.

5. B — The poem states, "I'll put you out of my mind and forget for ever / And try with all my might to eat and thrive." The speaker is drawing a connection between forgetting his friend and *thriving*, which is another word for *prospering*. Choice B best restates this and is the correct answer.

Math Practice

1. A — When a line crosses the y-axis, the x-coordinate of that point is 0. Therefore, we can substitute in 0 for x in the equation $4x - 2y = 6$ and it becomes $4(0) - 2y = 6$. This simplifies to $0 - 2y = 6$ or $-2y = 6$. In order for this to be true, y has to be equal to -3. We have already established that the x-coordinate is 0 when the line crosses the y-axis, so the coordinate point is $(0, -3)$ and choice A is correct.

2. C — We can start by writing the equation of a circle. The general form for the equation of a circle is $(x - h)^2 + (y - k)^2 = r^2$, where the center of the circle is (h, k) and r is the length of the radius. If we substitute in, the equation of this circle is $(x - 6)^2 + (y - 7)^2 = 3^2$. Now we have to look for the point that does NOT make the equation $(x - 6)^2 + (y - 7)^2 = 9$ true. Let's start with choice A, $(6, 4)$: $(6 - 6)^2 + (4 - 7)^2 = 9$. This simplifies to $0^2 + (-3)^2 = 9$. Since this simplifies to $9 = 9$, the point $(6, 4)$ is on the line and we can eliminate choice A. Now let's try choice B, $(3, 7)$: $(3 - 6)^2 + (7 - 7)^2 = 9$. This simplifies to $(-3)^2 + 0^2 = 9$ or $9 = 9$. Since $(3, 7)$ made the equation of the circle true, it is on the circle and we can eliminate choice B. We can try choice C, $(3, 4)$, next: $(3 - 6)^2 + (4 - 7)^2 = 9$. This simplifies to $(-3)^2 + (-3)^2 = 9$ or $18 = 9$. Since this is NOT true, the point $(3, 4)$ is not on the line and choice C is correct. We can stop there since

we found the right answer but if you were to substitute in the coordinates given in the other answer choices, you would find that those points are on the circle as well.

3. E — We can apply the formula for finding a midpoint:

$$\left(\frac{x_1+x_2}{2}, \frac{y_1+y_2}{2}\right)$$

In this case, we are given the midpoint and one endpoint and we need to find the other endpoint. Let's start with solving for the x-coordinate:

$$\frac{9+x_2}{2} = 1$$

Now we multiply both sides by 2 and find $9 + x_2 = 2$ and $x_2 = -7$. Now we can solve for the y-coordinate:

$$\frac{5+y_2}{2} = 3$$

If we multiply both sides by 3, the result is $5 + y_2 = 6$, or $y_2 = 1$. The coordinates of the midpoint are (–7, 1) and choice E is correct.

4. C — We can start by doing a sketch of point B and reflecting point B across the x-axis:

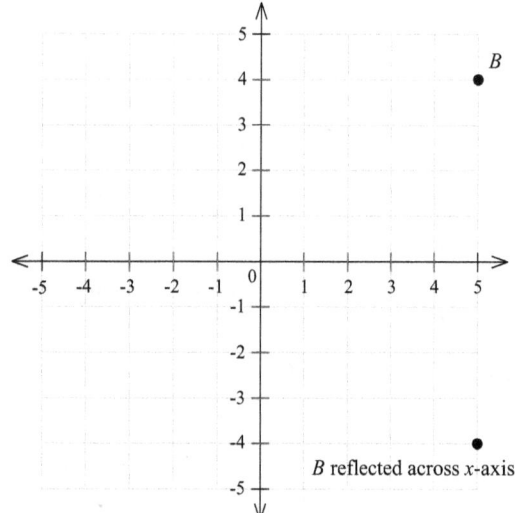

Now we have to complete the second step of moving the point up 6 units:

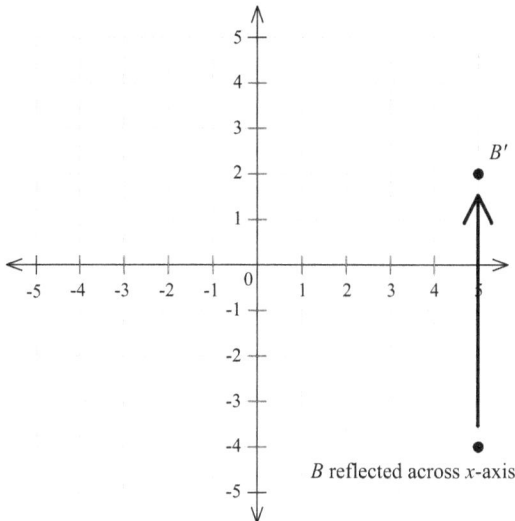

Answer choice C is correct.

5. E — We can start by rotating triangle XYZ 90° clockwise around the origin. One way to do this is to picture an arm that runs from the origin to each point. For example, an arm that connects the origin to point Y would go over 4 units and up 3 units. Now we can rotate that arm clockwise 90° and it goes down 4 units and 3 units to the right. We'll refer to this point at the end of the rotated arm as Y″, and its coordinates are (3, −4). Here is a picture showing the result of the rotation:

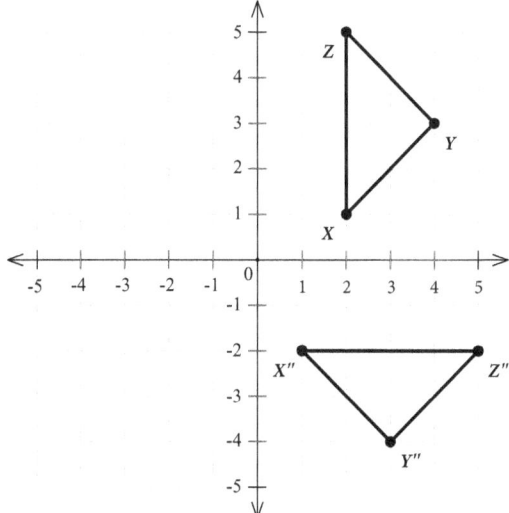

We're not done yet, as the triangle is also moved up 2 units. Since the question only asks about point Y′, we can move Y″ up 2 units to find that the point Y′ is at (3, −2). Answer choice E is correct.

6. C — We need to start with solving for the slope of the line given (the word perpendicular almost always means we need to use the fact that the slopes of perpendicular lines are negative reciprocals of each other). We can transform the equation $4x + 2y = 6$ into $y = mx + b$ form, where m is the slope. First we can subtract $4x$ from both sides and our equation becomes $2y = -4x + 6$. Now we divide both sides by 2 and the equation is $y = -2x + 3$. In this equation, $m = -2$ so the slope is -2. Therefore, the slope of the perpendicular line is $\frac{1}{2}$. Now we can use the slope formula for when we are given two points:

$$m = \frac{y_1 - y_2}{x_1 - x_2}$$

If we substitute in $\frac{1}{2}$ for m and the coordinates of $(3, -3)$ and $(4, k)$, the equation becomes:

$$\frac{1}{2} = \frac{-3 - k}{3 - 4}$$

This simplifies to:

$$\frac{1}{2} = \frac{-3 - k}{-1}$$

Now we can cross-multiply and the equation becomes $1(-1) = 2(-3 - k)$ or $-1 = -6 - 2k$. If we add 6 to both sides, the equation is now $5 = -2k$. Finally, we divide both sides by -2 and find that $k = -\frac{5}{2}$. Choice C is correct.

7. D — The word *parallel* tells us that the two lines must have the same slope. We can start by transforming the equation $3x + 2y = 5$ into $y = mx + b$ form. Our first step is to subtract $3x$ from both sides and now the equation is $2y = -3x + 5$. The next step is to divide both sides by 2 and the result is:

$$y = -\frac{3}{2}x + \frac{5}{2}$$

Since parallel lines have the same slope, we are looking for the answer choice with a slope of $-\frac{3}{2}$. We can transform the equation given in choice D into:

$$y = -\frac{3}{2}x + \frac{7}{2}$$

Since this equation has a slope of $-\dfrac{3}{2}$, answer choice D is correct.

8. B — In order for triangle *LMP* to be a right triangle, the two legs of the triangle would need to be perpendicular to one another, or have slopes that are negative reciprocals.

Let's try out answer choices. If we start with choice A, let's plot point *P* as (2, 1):

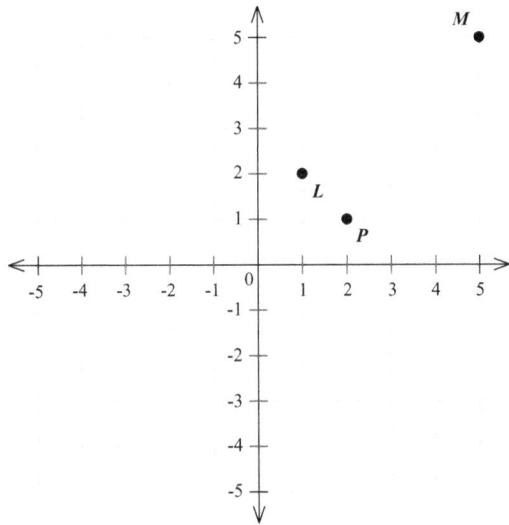

Remembering that slope is rise over run, we can use the picture to determine the slope between the different points:

Slope between *L* and *P* = −1

Slope between *P* and *M* = $\dfrac{4}{3}$

Slope between *L* and *M* = $\dfrac{3}{4}$

None of these slopes are negative reciprocals of one another, so choice A is not correct (the slope between *P* and *M* and the slope between *L* and *M* are reciprocals but not negative reciprocals).

Now let's try choice B, where the coordinates of point *P* are (3, 1):

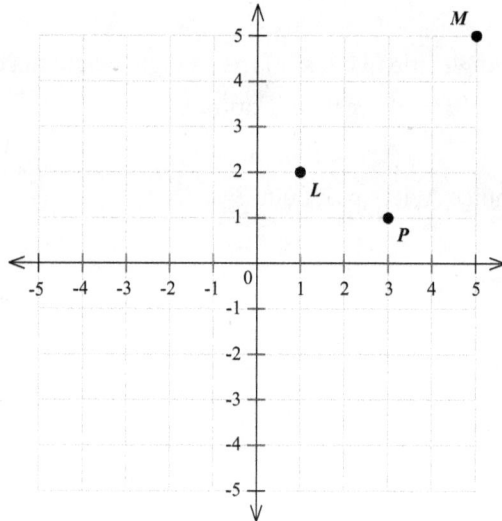

Using the graph to find the slope between the points,

Slope between *L* and *P* = $-\dfrac{1}{2}$

Slope between *P* and *M* = $\dfrac{4}{2} = 2$

Slope between *L* and *M* = $\dfrac{3}{4}$

Since $-\dfrac{1}{2}$ and 2 are negative reciprocals of one another, sides *LP* and *PM* are perpendicular to one another and a right angle is formed, which makes triangle *LPM* a right triangle. Choice B is correct. We can stop there since we found an answer that works. If you were to keep going, however, you would find that no other triangles include a pair of perpendicular sides, so no other placements given for point *P* would form a right triangle.

9. B — We can start by sketching out the points given and then sketching in a right triangle that has side $\overline{PR}$ as the hypotenuse (for clarity, the right angle is labeled as point *A* although that is not given in the question):

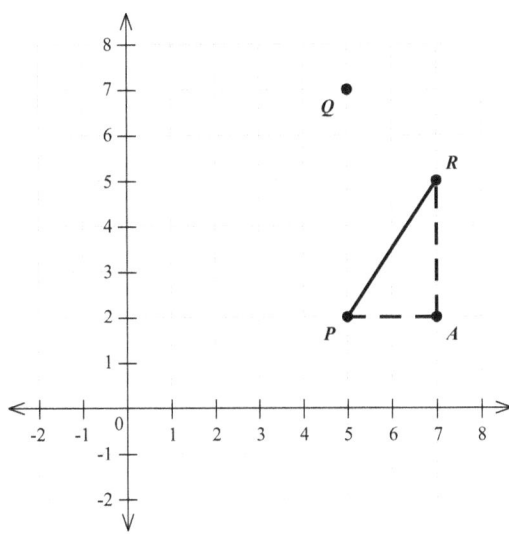

Now we have a right triangle where the legs are $\overline{AP}$ and $\overline{AR}$. Since these legs run parallel to the axes, it is easy to see that the length of $\overline{AP}$ is 2 and the length of $\overline{AR}$ is 3. Now substitute into the Pythagorean theorem ($a^2 + b^2 = c^2$): $2^2 + 3^2 = \overline{PR}^2$. If we simplify, this gives us $4 + 9 = \overline{PR}^2$ or $13 = \overline{PR}^2$. If we take the square root of both sides, the length of $\overline{PR}$ is equal to the square root of 13 and choice B is correct.

10. A — To answer this question, we can use a variation of the distance formula that is derived from the Pythagorean theorem: $(x_1 - x_2)^2 + (y_1 - y_2)^2 = d^2$, where d is the distance between the points (x_1, y_1) and (x_2, y_2). If we substitute in the points given and the distance, the equation becomes $(1 - 7)^2 + (3 - p)^2 = 10^2$. This simplifies to $(-6)^2 + (3 - p)^2 = 100$ or $36 + (3 - p)^2 = 100$. If we subtract 36 from both sides, the equation becomes $(3 - p)^2 = 64$. Now we have to remember that if we take the square root of a number, there is both a positive and a negative square root. In this case, squaring both 8 and –8 would result in 64, so $3 - p = 8$ and $3 - p = -8$ would both make the equation true.

Let's solve each equation:

$3 - p = 8$ $3 - p = -8$

$-p = 5$ $-p = -11$

$p = -5$ $p = 11$

This tells us that p could be equal to –5 or 11 in order to make the equation true. The question asks for one possible value for p, so choice A is correct.

Workout #6

Words to Learn

Below are the words used in Workout 6. Refer back to this list as needed as you move through the lesson.

Words related to fighting

Accost:	attack
Assail:	attack
Contend:	compete
Pugnacious:	quarrelsome
Incendiary:	inflammatory
Renegade:	dissenter
Tirade:	diatribe (speech against something)
Transgress:	violate

Words related to being a good person

Affable:	friendly
Judicious:	responsible
Congenial:	friendly
Scruple:	moral
Adage:	proverb (wise saying)
Mien:	demeanor
Mettle:	courage

Words that describe length and size

Abridge:	shorten
Amplitude:	magnitude
Brevity:	shortness
Terse:	concise

Synonyms Practice

1. CONTEND:
   - (A) consolidate
   - (B) compare
   - (C) conquer
   - (D) compete
   - (E) confide

2. GLEAN:
   - (A) hesitate
   - (B) parry
   - (C) bustle
   - (D) slash
   - (E) compile

3. PROVINCIAL:
   - (A) hapless
   - (B) reserved
   - (C) parochial
   - (D) spiritual
   - (E) impertinent

4. ADAGE:
   - (A) proverb
   - (B) mien
   - (C) treatise
   - (D) hoax
   - (E) force

5. LABORIOUS:
   - (A) flourishing
   - (B) arduous
   - (C) worrisome
   - (D) droll
   - (E) mundane

6. APEX:
   - (A) pinnacle
   - (B) trigger
   - (C) hovel
   - (D) gear
   - (E) bane

7. REVEL:
   - (A) sacrifice
   - (B) qualm
   - (C) fluke
   - (D) merriment
   - (E) fraud

8. PORTLY:
   - (A) listless
   - (B) transparent
   - (C) overweight
   - (D) betrayed
   - (E) appalling

9. ASSAIL:
   - (A) revive
   - (B) accost
   - (C) lessen
   - (D) banter
   - (E) transmit

10. TERSE:
    - (A) mystical
    - (B) judicious
    - (C) dismissed
    - (D) nonchalant
    - (E) brief

Analogies Practice

1. Reputable is to scruples as

    (A) timely is to irrelevance
    (B) flexible is to preparation
    (C) corrupt is to evasion
    (D) brave is to mettle
    (E) opaque is to fallacy

2. Dominant is to wan as

    (A) difficult is to tawdry
    (B) cryptic is to puzzling
    (C) preferable is to inert
    (D) slothful is to dormant
    (E) soothing is to incendiary

3. Amplitude is to size as

    (A) inch is to length
    (B) volume is to sound
    (C) postage is to stamp
    (D) tumult is to conflict
    (E) skirmish is to depression

4. Affable is to pugnacious as

    (A) unerring is to impartial
    (B) furtive is to invigorating
    (C) authentic is to bogus
    (D) specific is to detailed
    (E) congenial is to wise

5. Skepticism is to renegade as

    (A) daring is to pioneer
    (B) brevity is to tirade
    (C) naivety is to radical
    (D) diligence is to correspondent
    (E) transgression is to tourist

Reading Practice

An HYMN to the EVENING.

SOON as the sun forsook the eastern main
The pealing thunder shook the heav'nly plain;
Majestic grandeur! From the zephyr's wing,
Exhales the incense of the blooming spring.
Soft purl the streams, the birds renew their notes,
And through the air their mingled music floats.
   Through all the heav'ns what beauteous dies are spread!
But the west glories in the deepest red:
So may our breasts with ev'ry virtue glow,
The living temples of our God below!
   Fill'd with the praise of him who gives the light,
And draws the sable curtains of the night,
Let placid slumbers sooth each weary mind,
At morn to wake more heav'nly, more refin'd;
So shall the labours of the day begin
More pure, more guarded from the snares of sin.
   Night's leaden sceptre seals my drowsy eyes,
Then cease, my song, till fair Aurora rise.

1. Lines 1-10 (Soon as…below!), are mainly concerned with comparing

   (A) a beautiful sunset to the experience of faith.
   (B) bird songs to the colors of the night sky.
   (C) sunrise to sunset.
   (D) the times before and after a storm.
   (E) a storm to the blossoms of spring.

2. As used in line 13, the word "placid" is closest in meaning to

   (A) perturbed.
   (B) ignored.
   (C) stunned.
   (D) restless.
   (E) tranquil.

3. Lines 14-16 (At morn... sin) describe the morning as

    (A) vastly different than the experience of watching the sunset.
    (B) a time to start anew in living a pure life.
    (C) the same every day.
    (D) a time to cease your labors.
    (E) protected by sable curtains.

4. In line 6, "mingled music" is an example of which literary device?

    (A) metaphor
    (B) simile
    (C) hyperbole
    (D) alliteration
    (E) allegory

5. The poem describes night as a time

    (A) that is dangerous.
    (B) when God is no longer present.
    (C) to renew one's spirit.
    (D) when creatures roam the earth.
    (E) to allow one's mind to wander.

Workout #6

Math Practice

In this workout we will practice sequences and patterns, percents, and unit analysis questions. While many of these questions are not terribly difficult, these will focus just on the trickier aspects of each problem type.

The first question type we will work on is sequences and patterns. For these questions, it is particularly important to keep straight whether the question is looking for a particular term or the sum of the sequence up to a particular term.

1. Omar is collecting bottle caps. On day 1, he collects 2 bottle caps, on day 2 he collects 4 bottle caps, on day 3, he collects 6 bottle caps, and so on. If this pattern continues, how many bottle caps will he have collected after 20 days?

    (A) 40
    (B) 80
    (C) 210
    (D) 360
    (E) 420

2. Use the following information to answer the question.

    $3^1 = 3$
    $3^2 = 9$
    $3^3 = 27$
    $3^4 = 81$
    $3^5 = 243$
    $3^6 = 729$

    Based on this information, what is the units digit of 3^{20}?

    (A) 1
    (B) 3
    (C) 5
    (D) 7
    (E) 9

3. Steve is saving up to buy a new computer that costs $741. He saves $1.00 the first week, $2.00 the second week, $3.00 the third week. If this pattern continues, how many weeks will it take for him to save up enough money to buy the computer?

    (A) 6
    (B) 15
    (C) 20
    (D) 38
    (E) 39

97

4. Use the following information to answer the question.

   1 + 3 + 5 = 9
   3 + 5 + 7 = 15
   5 + 7 + 9 = 21
   7 + 9 + 11 = 27
   9 + 11 + 13 = 33
   11 + 13 + 15 = 39

   Which number could be the sum of 3 consecutive odd numbers?

   (A) 66
   (B) 99
   (C) 100
   (D) 102
   (E) 103

Now we will practice some tricky questions involving percentages. The key to these questions is to remember that when we take multiple percent increases or decreases, we can't just take the percent increase or decrease off of the original number each time.

5. The length of a rectangle was increased by 10% and the width was decreased by 10%. The area of the resulting rectangle was what percent of the area of the original rectangle?

   (A) 90%
   (B) 99%
   (C) 100%
   (D) 101%
   (E) 110%

6. At a particular store, all prices are reduced by 25% on Mondays. On Tuesdays, the prices return to normal. The prices at this store on Tuesdays are what fraction of the prices at the store on Mondays?

   (A) $\dfrac{1}{4}$

   (B) $\dfrac{1}{3}$

   (C) $\dfrac{1}{2}$

   (D) $\dfrac{5}{4}$

   (E) $\dfrac{4}{3}$

Workout #6

7. What is 15% of 48% of 640?

    (A) 46.08
    (B) 48.24
    (C) 50.6
    (D) 52.04
    (E) 55.01

8. 3 minutes and 36 seconds is what percent of 3 hours?

    (A) 0.02%
    (B) 0.2%
    (C) 2%
    (D) 6%
    (E) 10%

That last question leads us into the final question type for this workout: unit analysis. These problems aren't that tricky, they just have many steps and take practice. Keep in mind that you should always check to see if you can simplify before doing long calculations.

9. The fastest horse ever recorded could run 24.4 meters in one second. What was this speed in miles per hour? (1.61 kilometer = 1 mile)

    (A) 5.5
    (B) 20.6
    (C) 54.9
    (D) 70.2
    (E) 90.5

10. A penny weighs 3.11 grams. A bag weighing 8 grams contains 600 pennies. What is the total weight of the bag and the pennies it contains in kilograms?

    (A) 0.1874
    (B) 1.874
    (C) 2.94
    (D) 187.4
    (E) 1,874

Workout #6 Answers

Synonyms Practice

1. D — The word list states that *contend* means "compete," so choice D is correct. Note that choice C is not correct because *contend* means "compete" but not necessarily "win" or "conquer".

2. E — The word list from workout #3 states that *glean* and *compile* can both mean "gather." Therefore, *glean* and *compile* are synonyms, and choice E is the correct answer.

3. C — The word list from workout #4 states that *parochial* means "narrow-minded" and *provincial* means "unsophisticated." Since *unsophisticated* can describe a person who has a very narrow point of view, *parochial* is a synonym for *provincial*, and choice C is correct.

4. A — The word list tells us that *adage* means "a proverb or wise saying." Answer choice A is correct.

5. B — The word list from workout #2 states that *laborious* means "arduous," so choice B is the correct answer.

6. A — The word list from workout #5 states that *apex* and *pinnacle* both mean "peak." Therefore, they are synonyms, and choice A is correct.

7. D — The word list from workout #3 states that *revel* means "merriment," so choice D is the correct answer.

8. C — The word list from workout #4 states that *portly* means "stout." Since *stout* is another word for *overweight*, choice C is the correct answer.

9. B — The word list states that *accost* and *assail* both mean "attack." Therefore, they are synonyms, and choice B is correct.

10. E — The word list tells us that *terse* means "concise." Since *concise* is another word for *brief*, answer choice E is correct.

Analogies Practice

1. D — The relationship in this question is *characteristic of*: a characteristic of a *reputable* person is that he or she has *scruples* (morals). Being *timely* (well-timed) is unrelated to *irrelevance* (not being relevant), so choice A is not correct. Being *flexible* does not have a strong relationship to *preparation*, so we can eliminate choice B. While a person who is *corrupt* might practice *evasion*, the relationship is not strong, so choice C can be ruled out. A characteristic

Workout #6

of a *brave* person is that he or she has *mettle* (courage), so choice D is the correct answer. If something is *opaque*, it is hard to see through but not necessarily false, so *opaque* is not related to *fallacy*, and choice E is not correct.

2. E — The relationship in this question is *opposites*: *dominant* is the opposite of *wan* (feeble). *Difficult* is unrelated to *tawdry* (cheap), so choice A is not correct. *Cryptic* and *puzzling* are similar in meaning (and not opposites), so choice B can be ruled out. *Preferable* is not related to *inert* (unmoving), so we can rule out choice C. *Slothful* (lazy) and *dormant* (inactive) are similar in meaning, so choice D can be eliminated. Finally, *soothing* is the opposite of *incendiary* (inflammatory), so choice E is the correct answer.

3. B — The relationship in this question is *one thing describes the other*: *amplitude* describes *size*. An *inch* is a unit of *length*, not a bigger concept that describes *length*, so choice A is not the best answer. *Volume* does describe *sound*, so choice B is the correct answer. *Postage* doesn't describe *stamp* (a *stamp* is a type of *postage*), so choice C can be ruled out. The relationship in choice D is *degree* (*tumult* is a big *conflict*), so choice D is not the best answer. Finally, *skirmish* (conflict) and *depression* are not related, so choice E can be eliminated.

4. C — The relationship in this question is *opposites*: *affable* (friendly) is the opposite of *pugnacious* (quarrelsome). *Unerring* (perfect) is not related to *impartial* (without bias), so choice A can be ruled out. *Furtive* (secretive) is also not related to *invigorating* (energizing), so choice B is not correct. *Authentic* is the opposite of *bogus* (counterfeit or fake), so choice C is the correct answer. *Specific* and *detailed* are similar in meaning, so choice D can be eliminated. *Congenial* (friendly) is not related to *wise*, so choice E is not correct.

5. A — The relationship in this question is *characteristic of*: *skepticism* is a characteristic of a *renegade*. *Daring* is a characteristic of *pioneer*, so choice A is the correct answer. *Brevity* (shortness) is not a characteristic of a *tirade* (long rant), so choice B can be ruled out. *Naivety* (lack of sophistication) is not necessarily a characteristic of a *radical*, so choice C is not correct. *Diligence* (responsibility) is not necessarily a characteristic of a *correspondent*, and *transgression* (violation of rules) is not necessarily a characteristic of a *tourist*, so choices D and E can be eliminated.

Reading Practice

1. A — In lines 1-10, the speaker of the poem describes the sun rising up from the east and then setting in the west where "beauteous dies are spread" and "the west glories in the deepest red." This describes a beautiful sunset. In lines 9-10, the speaker states, "So may our breasts with ev'ry virtue glow, / The living temple of our God below!" This is comparing the experience of glowing with virtue to that of the sunset. Answer choice A best restates this and is the correct answer.

2. E — The poem describes "placid slumbers" that "sooth each weary mind." Placid slumbers are soothing, so we are looking for something that goes with *soothing*. We can eliminate *perturbed*

(irritated), *ignored*, *stunned* (surprised), and *restless* (agitated) because these words do not go with *soothing*. However, something *tranquil* (calm) is soothing, so choice E is the correct answer.

3. B — The poem states, "At morn to wake more heav'nly, more refin'd; / So shall the labours of day begin / More pure, more guarded from the snares of sin." The speaker is describing the morning where a person begins working, feeling more pure and protected from sin, or evil. Answer choice B best summarizes this experience and is the correct answer.

4. D — The words "mingled music" repeat the same initial consonant sound and are therefore an example of alliteration. Answer choice D is correct.

5. C — The poem begins by describing the sunset, or the beginning of night. Then the poem describes how sleep soothes the weary mind. Finally, the poem describes waking in the morning more pure and ready to go about the day's labors. Therefore, night is described as a time when a person is renewed, and choice C is correct.

Math Practice

1. E — We can use the formula for the sum of a sequence:

$$S_n = n\left(\frac{a_1 + a_n}{2}\right)$$

In this formula, S_n is the sum of a sequence with n terms, where a_1 is the first term and a_n is the last term. (This equation is derived from the formula for finding mean: sum ÷ number of numbers = mean. If we rearrange this, we get sum = mean × number of numbers. To find the mean of a sequence, we add the first and last terms and divide by 2.) On the first day, he collected 2 caps and since we can find the number of caps collected by multiplying the day number by 2, on day 20 he collected 40 caps. We can substitute in the information given:

$$S_n = 20\left(\frac{2 + 40}{2}\right) = 20(21) = 420$$

Answer choice E is correct.

2. A — Since the question asks about the units digit, we want to look for a pattern with the units digits. The units digits of the numbers given are 3, 9, 7, 1, 3, 9. Therefore, the pattern of units digits is 3, 9, 7, 1, and then it repeats. There are 4 elements in the pattern. If we divide the exponent by 4, what matters is the remainder. If the remainder is 1, then the units digit is the first element in the pattern (3); if the remainder is 2, then the units digit is the second element in the pattern (9); if the remainder is 3, then the units digit is the third element in the pattern

(7); and if there is no remainder, then the units digit is the last element in the pattern (1). If we divide 20 by 4, there is no remainder, so the units digit is 1 and choice A is correct.

3. D — This is essentially a sum of the sequence question. We want to know how many weeks it will take for the sum of the sequence to be 741. We can use the formula:

$$S_n = n\left(\frac{a_1 + a_n}{2}\right)$$

In this formula, S_n is the sum of a sequence with n terms, where a_1 is the first term and a_n is the last term. In this case:

$$741 = n\left(\frac{1 + a_n}{2}\right)$$

At this point, we can plug in answer choices to see what works. We will start with choice C, plugging in 20 for both n and a_n since the amount saved is equal to the ordinal number of the week (1st, 2nd, 3rd, etc). Now our equation is:

$$741 = 20\left(\frac{1 + 20}{2}\right)$$

This simplifies to 741 = 210 and that is not a true statement, so choice C is not correct. We also know that n and a_n must be larger than 20 since 210 is less than 741. Let's try choice D and substitute in 38 for n and a_n:

$$741 = 38\left(\frac{1 + 38}{2}\right)$$

Since this does simplify to 741 = 741, answer choice D is correct.

4. B — Since the question gives us a list of the sums of different sets of three consecutive odd numbers, we know there must be a pattern that we can use. If we look at all of the sums, they are all odd numbers. Since answer choices A, C, and D are all even numbers, we can eliminate them. However, both choice B (99) and choice E (103) are odd numbers, so we need to find another pattern. All of the sums are also multiples of 3. The number 99 is a multiple of 3 since both digits are divisible by 3. However, if we add together the digits of 103, the sum is 4 and since 4 is not divisible by 3, the number 103 is not divisible by 3. Answer choice B is the only one that is both odd and divisible by 3, so it is the correct answer choice. If we want to check it, the mean of three consecutive numbers is also the middle number. If we divide 99 by 3 we get 33, so the middle number is 33 and the numbers are 31, 33, 35.

5. B — We can use the strategy of plugging in our own numbers. We can make each side of the rectangle 10 since this is an easy number to work with. Therefore, the area of the original rectangle is 100 square units. Now, if we increase the length by 10%, the new length is 11 and if we decrease the width by 10%, the new width is 9. The area of a rectangle that is 11 × 9 units is 99 units squared. Since 99 is 99% of 100, the new area is 99% of the original area and choice B is correct.

6. E — Let's plug in our own prices. We can say that the normal price of something is $100. If it is reduced by 25% on Mondays, the price on Monday is $75. Therefore, the price on Tuesday is $\frac{100}{75}$ of what is was on Monday. If we divide both the numerator and denominator by 25, this fraction reduces to $\frac{4}{3}$. Answer choice E is correct.

7. A — The key to this question is to remember that the word "of" can be translated as multiplication. We also need to change 15% into 0.15 and 48% into 0.48 in order to set up an expression. Therefore, 15% of 48% of 640 can be turned into 0.15 × 0.48 × 640. If we first multiply 0.15 × 0.48, the result is 0.072. If we multiply 0.072 × 640, the result is 46.08 and answer choice A is correct.

8. C — In order to determine what percent 3 minutes and 36 seconds is of 3 hours, we can start by putting all of the numbers into the same units. In this case, we can put them all into seconds. To find the number of seconds in 3 minutes, we multiply 3 by 60 since there are 60 seconds in 1 minute. This results in 180 seconds and if we add back in the 36 seconds, 3 minutes and 36 seconds is equal to 216 seconds. Now we have to change 3 hours into seconds. We first multiply 3 by 60 to change the time into minutes. We find that 3 hours is equal to 180 minutes. Then we have to multiply 180 by 60 to change minutes into seconds and find that 3 hours is equal to 10,800 seconds. Now we have to find what percent 216 seconds is of 10,800 seconds:

$$\frac{\text{part}}{\text{whole}} = \frac{\text{percent}}{100}$$

$$\frac{216}{10,800} = \frac{\text{percent}}{100}$$

At this stage, we can use estimating since the answer choices are relatively far apart. We can round off 216 to 200 and 10,800 to 10,000. Our problem is now $\frac{200}{10,000} = \frac{\text{percent}}{100\%}$. If we then cross-multiply, we find that 10,000 × percent = 200 × 100%, or 10,000 × percent = 20,000%. When we divide both sides by 10,000, we find that the answer is 2%. Answer choice C is correct.

9. C — We can start by using dimensional analysis to create an expression. Essentially, what we are doing is writing conversions as proportions, lining them up so that the units we don't want cancel and only the units we want remain. For example, if we are trying to convert $\frac{24.4 \text{ m}}{1 \text{ sec}}$ into km / sec, we write the conversion unit as $\frac{1 \text{ km}}{1,000 \text{ m}}$ (and not as $\frac{1,000 \text{ m}}{1 \text{ km}}$) so that the "m" in the numerator and denominator cancel and we are left with the speed in km / sec.

   Here is what the expression looks like if we first convert meters into miles and then seconds into hours:

   $$\frac{24.4 \text{ m}}{1 \text{ sec}} \times \frac{1 \text{ km}}{1,000 \text{ m}} \times \frac{1 \text{ mile}}{1.6 \text{ km}} \times \frac{60 \text{ sec}}{1 \text{ min}} \times \frac{60 \text{ min}}{1 \text{ hr}}$$

   We know this is correct because all of the units canceled except for miles per hour.

   Now we can rewrite this expression without units:

   $$\frac{24.4 \times 60 \times 60}{1,000 \times 1.6}$$

   At this point, we should round since the answer choices are relatively far apart. We can also divide both the numerator and denominator by 100 and the expression becomes:

   $$\frac{25 \times 6 \times 6}{10 \times 1.6} = \frac{150 \times 6}{16} = \frac{900}{16}$$

   We can make this easier by rounding 16 to 15 (15 divides evenly into 900), and 900 divided by 15 is 60. This is closest to answer choice C (54.9), so choice C is the correct answer.

10. B — If we look at the answer choices, they are relatively far apart, so we know that we can estimate. We can round the mass of each penny (3.11 grams) down to 3 grams. Then we multiply this by 600 since there are 600 pennies and find that the weight of the pennies is about 1,800 grams. If we add the weight of the bag, it is 1,808 grams. Now we have to turn this into kilograms since that is what the question asks for. Since there are 1,000 grams in 1 kilogram, we divide grams by 1,000 to find kilograms. Since 1,808 divided by 1,000 is 1.808, the weight of the pennies and the bag is about 1.808 kg. Since we rounded off, we just want to find the answer that is closest to 1.808. Since choice B (1.874) is the closest to 1.808, answer choice B is correct.

Workout #7

Words to Learn

Below are the words used in Workout 7. Refer back to this list as needed as you move through the lesson.

Words related to wanting something

Acquisition:	possession
Bequeath:	grant
Covet:	desire
Procure:	obtain
Pillage:	plunder
Forbearance:	self-control

Words related to approval

Condone:	approve
Consecrate:	sanctify
Sanction:	approve

Words related to disapproval

Indict:	accuse
Refute:	disprove
Unfounded:	unjustified

More words about making things worse

Adulterated:	cheapened
Alienate:	estrange
Discredit:	tarnish
Deplete:	reduce
Relinquish:	give up
Detriment:	disadvantage
Fetter:	restrain
Impediment:	obstacle

Synonyms Practice

1. QUELL:
   - (A) appeal
   - (B) compile
   - (C) testify
   - (D) hover
   - (E) extinguish

2. FETTER:
   - (A) writhe
   - (B) disconcert
   - (C) splinter
   - (D) curtail
   - (E) precede

3. CRYPTIC:
   - (A) veiled
   - (B) hostile
   - (C) jubilant
   - (D) radical
   - (E) dreadful

4. WAN:
   - (A) wretched
   - (B) listless
   - (C) rigid
   - (D) bogus
   - (E) noticeable

5. DOMINANT:
   - (A) inert
   - (B) nonchalant
   - (C) humane
   - (D) dramatic
   - (E) commanding

6. ACQUISITION:
   - (A) possession
   - (B) disappointment
   - (C) hoax
   - (D) glutton
   - (E) attraction

7. INCITE:
   - (A) accuse
   - (B) consolidate
   - (C) flee
   - (D) encourage
   - (E) speculate

8. AFFABLE:
   - (A) congenial
   - (B) murky
   - (C) depreciated
   - (D) awkward
   - (E) singular

9. METTLE:
   - (A) demeanor
   - (B) tumult
   - (C) courage
   - (D) novelty
   - (E) impediment

10. DROLL:
    - (A) legible
    - (B) witty
    - (C) courteous
    - (D) opaque
    - (E) blistering

Analogies Practice

1. Adulterated is to tawdry as

    (A) indicted is to unfounded
    (B) disrupted is to slothful
    (C) condoned is to sanctioned
    (D) feigned is to restrained
    (E) duped is to incendiary

2. Judicious is to discretion as

    (A) witty is to reverence
    (B) diligent is to brevity
    (C) continuous is to chagrin
    (D) terse is to ardor
    (E) demure is to forbearance

3. Covet is to alluring as

    (A) present is to pugnacious
    (B) assail is to practical
    (C) tabulate is to corrupt
    (D) rue is to regretful
    (E) disperse is to ignorant

4. Bolster is to discredit as

    (A) rectify is to defile
    (B) transgress is to rend
    (C) enthrall is to revert
    (D) inspect is to abridge
    (E) adorn is to embellish

5. Rebuff is to alienate as

    (A) know is to bequeath
    (B) steal is to pillage
    (C) undertake is to hurdle
    (D) allay is to clatter
    (E) begrudge is to procure

Reading Practice

The Rainy Day

The day is cold, and dark, and dreary;
It rains, and the wind is never weary;
The vine still clings to the mouldering wall,
But at every gust the dead leaves fall,
And the day is dark and dreary.

My life is cold, and dark, and dreary;
It rains, and the wind is never weary;
My thoughts still cling to the mouldering past,
But the hopes of youth fall thick in the blast,
And the days are dark and dreary.

Be still, sad heart! and cease repining;
Behind the clouds is the sun still shining;
Thy fate is the common fate of all,
Into each life some rain must fall,
Some days must be dark and dreary.

H.W. Longfellow.

1. The main point that the poem makes about life is

   (A) youth can never be recaptured.
   (B) it eventually turns bleak for everyone.
   (C) there are good days and there are bad days.
   (D) death cannot be avoided.
   (E) it is best to stay inside on rainy days.

2. In this poem, the vine clinging to the wall represents

   (A) rainy weather.
   (B) the dismal nature of life.
   (C) optimism for a better future.
   (D) the author's thoughts of the past.
   (E) the fragile nature of life.

3. The author most likely repeats the phrase, "It rains and the wind is never weary" in order to

    (A) emphasize the connection between the patterns of nature and those of humans.
    (B) show how desolate life really is.
    (C) personify the wind.
    (D) show how fleeting youth can be.
    (E) introduce a new theme.

4. The phrase, "Behind the clouds is the sun still shining," is included in order to

    (A) emphasize how difficult it is to cheer up when it is dark and dreary.
    (B) offer hope to the reader.
    (C) show that youth does not really disappear.
    (D) illustrate how quickly the weather can change.
    (E) contrast the effects of rainy and sunny weather.

5. Which line most appeals to the visual sense?

    (A) "It rains, and the wind is never weary"
    (B) "My thoughts still cling to the mouldering past"
    (C) "Be still, sad heart! and cease repining;"
    (D) "Thy fate is the common fate of all"
    (E) "The vine still clings to the mouldering wall"

Workout #7

Math Practice

In this workout, we will cover problems that test divisibility, linear equations, and inequalities.

First, let's look at problems with divisibility. Keep in mind that *divisible* means a number can be divided by another number and the answer is an integer.

1. If m can be divided by 8 with no remainder, then $3(m + 4)$ can be divided by which number with no remainder?

    (A) 12
    (B) 14
    (C) 15
    (D) 18
    (E) 20

2. A camp director divides campers into groups. If the average number of campers in a group is exactly 15, which could be the total number of campers?

    (A) 685
    (B) 905
    (C) 930
    (D) 940
    (E) 955

3. When the number 54,162 is divided by p, the result is an integer. Which of the following could NOT be the value of p?

    (A) 2
    (B) 3
    (C) 4
    (D) 6
    (E) 9

4. If r is divisible by 7 and s is divisible by 3, which of the following MUST be divisible by 21?

    (A) $s(r + 3)$
    (B) $s(r + 7)$
    (C) $3(r + s)$
    (D) $7(r + s)$
    (E) $\dfrac{rs}{7}$

111

Now we will work on questions involving linear equations. Linear equations are those with graphs that are a straight line. On the SSAT, the difficult linear equation questions often have many steps, variables on both sides of the equal sign, and require applying the rules operations for negative numbers.

Here are some examples for you to try:

5. If $12x - 3(3x - 4) + 10 = -4x - 3$, then what is the value of x?

    (A) -7

    (B) $-\dfrac{25}{7}$

    (C) $-\dfrac{1}{7}$

    (D) $\dfrac{7}{25}$

    (E) $\dfrac{25}{7}$

6. Which expression shows the result of solving for x in the equation $3x + Ax - 5 = 7$?

    (A) $\dfrac{7}{A}$

    (B) $\dfrac{12 - A}{3}$

    (C) $\dfrac{2}{3 + A}$

    (D) $\dfrac{3 + A}{12}$

    (E) $\dfrac{12}{3 + A}$

7. How many solutions does the equation $-2(x - 9) = -2x + 18$ have?

    (A) 0
    (B) 2
    (C) 3
    (D) 4
    (E) infinitely many

Workout #7

Now we will work on solving inequalities. The rules are very similar to solving linear equations; we just have to remember to flip the inequality sign if we divide or multiply by a negative number.

8. Which represents all possible solutions of $24x - 6(5x - 4) > -12x + 6$?

    (A) $x > -3$
    (B) $x < -3$
    (C) $x < 3$
    (D) $x > 3$
    (E) $x > 5$

9. Which number line represents all possible solutions to the inequality $-4(x + 3) - 7 \leq -9$?

    (A) number line with closed circle at -2, shaded left
    (B) number line with closed circle at -2, shaded right
    (C) number line with closed circles at -7 and 5, shaded between
    (D) number line with closed circle at 2, shaded right
    (E) number line with closed circle at 1, shaded left

10. Which inequality represents the possible solutions of $6 > -2x + 4$ or $3x + 1 > 10$?

    (A) $-3 < x < -1$
    (B) $-3 < x < 1$
    (C) $x > -1$ or $x < 3$
    (D) $-1 < x$
    (E) $-1 > x$ or $x > 3$

Workout #7 Answers

Synonyms Practice

1. E — The word list from workout #3 states that *quell* means "to extinguish." Choice E is correct.

2. D — The word list states that *fetter* means "restrain." The word list from workout #3 states that *curtail* means "cut back." Since *cut back* is another way to describe *restraining* something, choice D is the correct answer.

3. A — The word list from workout #4 states that *cryptic* means "mysterious." If something is *veiled*, it is covered or hard to see, or mysterious. Answer choice A is correct.

4. B — The word list from workout #5 states that *wan* means "feeble." It also states that *listless* means "spiritless." Since *feeble* and *spiritless* are synonyms, *wan* is also a synonym for *listless*, and choice B is correct.

5. E — Workout #5 states that *dominant* means "most powerful." *Inert* (unmoving), *nonchalant* (unconcerned), *humane* (compassionate), and *dramatic* have nothing to do with having power, so choices A, B, C, and D can be ruled out. However, a person who is *commanding* has power over others, so choice E is the correct answer.

6. A — The word list states that *acquisition* means "possession," so choice A is correct. The word *acquisition* is related to *acquire*, which means "to get something." A *possession* is something that you have acquired.

7. D — The word list from workout #5 states that *incite* means "encourage." Choice D is correct.

8. A — The word list from workout #6 states that *affable* and *congenial* mean "friendly." Therefore, they are synonyms, and choice A is correct.

9. C — The word list from workout #6 states that *mettle* means "courage," so choice C is correct.

10. B — The word list from workout #5 states that *droll* means "witty," so choice B is correct.

Analogies Practice

1. C — The relationship in this question is *cause and effect*: if something is *adulterated* (contaminated) it becomes *tawdry* (cheap). If someone is *indicted* (formally charged with crime) they do not become *unfounded* (without evidence), so choice A is not correct. *Disrupted* and *slothful* (lazy) are not related, so choice B can be ruled out. If something is *condoned* (approved), it becomes *sanctioned* (approved of), so choice C is correct. *Feigned* (pretended) is not related to *restrained*, and *duped* (fooled) is not related to *incendiary* (inflammatory), so choices D and E are not correct.

2. E — The relationship in this question is *one word means showing the other*: being *judicious* means showing *discretion*. To be *witty* (humorous) is not related to showing *reverence* (respect), to be *diligent* (responsible) has nothing to do with *brevity* (shortness), *continuous* (ongoing) is not related to *chagrin* (disappointment), and *terse* (concise) is not related to *ardor* (passion), so choices A, B, C, and D are not correct. To be *demure* (reserved) is to show *forbearance* (restraint), so choice E is the correct answer.

3. D — The relationship in this question is *cause and effect*: if you *covet* (desire) something, it is because it is *alluring* (attractive). You don't *present* something if it is *pugnacious* (quarrelsome), *assail* (attack) something if it is *practical*, or *tabulate* (categorize) something if it is *corrupt* (dishonest), so choices A, B, and C can be ruled out. You would *rue* (regret) something if it is *regretful*, so choice D is the best answer. Choice E is not correct because you don't *disperse* (spread out) something if it is *ignorant* (lacking knowledge).

4. A — The relationship in this question is *opposites*: *bolster* (support) is the opposite of *discredit* (tarnish). To *rectify* (correct) something is the opposite of to *defile* (pollute) it, so choice A is correct. *Transgress* (violate) is not related to *rend* (divide), *enthrall* (fascinate) is not related to *revert* (go back), and *inspect* (examine) is not related to *abridge* (shorten), so choices B, C, and D are not correct. *Adorn* (decorate) and *embellish* are synonyms, so choice E can be ruled out.

5. B — The relationship in this question is *degree*: to *rebuff* (reject) is less extreme than to *alienate* (estrange or sever ties with a person). To *know* is unrelated to *bequeath* (grant), so choice A is not correct. To *steal* is less extreme than to *pillage* (plunder or ransack), so choice B is correct. To *undertake* (attempt) is not more extreme than to *hurdle* (jump over), so choice C can be ruled out. To *allay* (soothe) is not more extreme than to *clatter* (make a loud noise), and *begrudge* (resent) is not related to *procure* (obtain or get), so choices D and E are not correct.

Reading Practice

1. **C** — The poem begins by discussing a cold and dreary day. Then it discusses how cold and dreary the speaker's life is. Finally, the poem describes that there is still sun shining from behind the clouds and reminds the reader that some days must be dark and dreary. The poem is about life being full of both rainy, dreary days, as well as days with the sun still shining. Answer choice C best restates this and is the correct answer.

2. **D** — In line 3, the poem states, "the vine still clings to the mouldering wall," and this imagery is repeated later in line 8 with, "my thoughts still cling to the mouldering past." Therefore, the speaker is equating the vine on the mouldering wall with his thoughts of the mouldering past, and choice D is the correct answer.

3. **A** — This question is asking us why the phrase "It rains and the wind is never weary" is repeated. We can eliminate choices B and D because the poem is not showing how desolate life is (although it sometimes can be) or how fleeting (quickly) youth goes away. We can eliminate choice E because the lines do not introduce a new theme. The lines do personify the wind, but they are not included just to personify the wind, so choice C is not the best answer. The poem personifies the wind to show the connection between nature (the wind) and human nature, so choice A is the best answer.

4. **B** — Most of the poem is dark and dreary, but in line 11, the speaker states, "be still, sad heart! and cease repining." These lines say that not all is sadness, and then the speaker mentions that "behind the clouds is the sun still shining" as evidence that not all is sadness. This offers hope to the reader, so choice B is correct.

5. **E** — Answer choices B, C, and D are easy to eliminate because they do not give a visual image. Now we have to decide whether "It rains, and the wind is weary" or "The vine still clings to the mouldering wall" creates a stronger visual. The first choice is more tactile — rain is wet and the wind is something we feel. However, the vine clinging to the mouldering wall is something that we perceive through the sense of sight, so choice E is the best answer.

Math Practice

1. A — We can use the strategy of substituting in a number to answer this question. Let's start by substituting in 8 for *m* since that is the smallest number that would make *m* divisible by 8. If we substitute in 8 for *m*, then 3(*m* + 4) becomes 3(8 + 4), which is equal to 36. Now we look at the answer choices. Since 36 can be divided by 12 with no remainder, we will keep choice A. The number 36 cannot be divided by 14 or 15 with no remainder, so choices B and C are not correct. However, 36 can be divided by 18 with no remainder, so we need to keep choice D. The number 36 can't be divided by 20 with no remainder, so choice E is not correct. Since choice A and choice D both work, we need to choose another number for *m*. Let's try 16 since that is the next largest number that is divisible by 8. If *m* is equal to 16, then 3(16 + 4) is equal to 60. Since 60 is divisible by 12, we can still keep choice A. However, 60 cannot be divided by 18 with no remainder, so choice D can be ruled out. We are left with choice A and that is the correct answer.

2. C — To answer this question, we can use the rules of divisibility. If the average is exactly 15 students, then the total number of students must be divisible by 15. If a number is divisible by another number, it is also divisible by its factors. Since the factors of 15 (other than itself and 1) are 3 and 5, if a number is divisible by 15 then it is also divisible by 3 and 5. All of the answer choices end in a 0 or 5, so they are all divisible by 5 and we can't use that to rule out answer choices. To see if an answer choice is divisible by 3, we can add together the digits and see if the sum is divisible by 3:

    (A) 685 = 6 + 8 + 5 = 19 — not divisible by 3

    (B) 905 = 9 + 0 + 5 = 14 — not divisible by 3

    (C) 930 = 9 + 3 + 0 = 12 — is divisible by 3

    (D) 940 = 9 + 4 + 0 = 13 — not divisible by 3

    (E) 955 = 9 + 5 + 5 =1 9 — not divisible by 3

    Since only answer choice C is divisible by both 3 and 5, it is the only answer choice that is divisible by 15 and it is the correct answer.

3. C — This question is asking us to identify which number 54,162 is NOT divisible by. It is an even number, so it can be divided by 2 with no remainder and choice A can be ruled out. If we add up the digits of the number, we get $5 + 4 + 1 + 6 + 2 = 18$. Since this sum is divisible by 3, the number is divisible by 3 and we can rule out choice B. We can also rule out choice D because the number is divisible by 2 and 3 and therefore is also divisible by 6. Choice E can also be eliminated because the sum (18) is divisible by 9, so the whole number is divisible by 9. We have ruled out every choice but C. We know C is the correct answer because the last two digits of the number (62) are not divisible by 4, so the entire number is not divisible by 4.

4. B — We can use the strategy of substituting in numbers to see what works. Let's make r equal to 7 since that is the smallest number divisible by 7 and s equal to 3 since that is the smallest number divisible by 3. Now we can substitute in to answer choices and see what is divisible by 21:

    (A) $s(r + 3) = 3(7 + 3) = 30$ — not divisible by 21

    (B) $s(r + 7) = 3(7 + 7) = 42$ — IS divisible by 21

    (C) $3(r + s) = 3(3 + 7) = 30$ — not divisible by 21

    (D) $7(r + s) = 7(3 + 7) = 70$ — not divisible by 21

    (E) $\dfrac{rs}{7} = \dfrac{3 \times 7}{7} = 3$ — not divisible by 21

    Since only answer choice B gave us a number divisible by 21 when we substituted in possible values for r and s, choice B is correct.

5. B — Our fist step in solving this equation is to eliminated the parentheses. We can do this by distributing the –3 to the terms in the parentheses and $12x - 3(3x - 4) + 10 = -4x - 3$ becomes $12x - 9x + 12 + 10 = -4x - 3$. If we combine like terms on the left, the equation is now $3x + 22 = -4x - 3$. We can add $4x$ to both sides and subtract 22 from both sides so that we have terms with variables on one side and integers on the other. The equation becomes $7x = -25$. If we divide both sides by 7, we find that x is equal to $-\dfrac{25}{7}$ and choice B is correct.

6. E — The tricky part of this problem is that x is in more than one term. We can begin by adding 5 to each side so that we have the terms with variables on one side and the integers on the other. Our equation is now $3x + Ax = 12$. Our next step is the factor x in the left side of the equation: $x(3 + A) = 12$. Finally, to isolate x we divide both sides by $3 + A$ and the result is $x = \dfrac{12}{3+A}$, so answer choice E is correct.

7. E — Before we begin to solve, we should always look at the answer choices. If we do this, we see that choice E is "infinitely many solutions." If this is the correct answer, then the two sides of the equation would be equal to one another. Let's distribute the –2 on the left side of the equation and see what the result is. If we do this, the result is $-2x + 18 = -2x + 18$. Since the two sides of the equation are the same, they represent the same line and there are infinitely many solutions. Choice E is correct.

8. A — We can begin by distributing the –6 on the left side of the inequality and the inequality becomes $24x - 30x + 24 > -12x + 6$. Now we combine like terms on the left side and the inequality is now $-6x + 24 > -12x + 6$. To have the terms with variables on one side of the inequality and the integers on the other, we have to add $12x$ to both sides and subtract 24 from both sides. The result is $6x > -18$. Finally, we divide both sides by 6 and the final inequality is $x > -3$ and choice A is correct. Note that we did NOT flip the inequality sign in this problem because while there were negative numbers, we did not multiply or divide by a negative number at any point.

9. B — We can begin by distributing the –4: $-4x - 12 - 7 \leq -9$. Now we can combine like terms and the result is $-4x - 19 \leq -9$. If we add 19 to both sides, the result is $-4x \leq 10$. Finally, we divide both sides by –4. Since we are dividing by a negative number, we have to flip the inequality sign at this point and the inequality is now $x \geq -\dfrac{10}{4}$ or $x \geq -2.5$. Answer choice B represents this on the number line and is the correct answer.

10. D — To answer this question, we need to solve each inequality individually. Let's start with $6 > -2x + 4$. If we subtract 4 from each side, the inequality becomes $2 > -2x$. Now we divide both sides by –2 (remembering to flip the inequality sign) and our final inequality is $-1 < x$. We have the second inequality to solve now. We can start by subtracting 1 from both sides and the inequality becomes $3x > 9$. Then we divide both sides by 3 and the result is $x > 3$. Our two solutions are $-1 < x$ and $x > 3$. Since an "or" statement was used, we want all numbers that fit either inequality. Since numbers that are greater than 3 are also greater than –1, we can simply say that the solution is all numbers that are greater than –1. Choice D is correct.

Workout #8

Words to Learn

Below are the words used in Workout 8. Refer back to this list as needed as you move through the lesson.

Things you don't like

Aversion:	disliking
Odious:	offensive
Revulsion:	disliking

Don't be so mean!

Condescending:	patronizing
Contemptuous:	disrespectful
Disdain:	disrespect
Reproof:	criticism
Extortion:	blackmail
Ominous:	threatening
Overbearing:	domineering
Affectation:	pretension

Not quite true

Dubious:	doubtful
Erroneous:	wrong
Fabricate:	invent
Concoct:	make up
Devious:	crafty
Ruse:	trick
Incredulous:	skeptical
Awry:	wrong

Synonyms Practice

Workout #8

1. OVERBEARING:
   - (A) domineering
   - (B) honest
   - (C) anonymous
   - (D) naïve
   - (E) splashy

2. BRANDISH:
   - (A) tabulate
   - (B) enthrall
   - (C) identify
   - (D) wield
   - (E) dread

3. UNCOUTH:
   - (A) dramatic
   - (B) inelegant
   - (C) ideal
   - (D) splendid
   - (E) unerring

4. MORBID:
   - (A) brutal
   - (B) convincing
   - (C) ghoulish
   - (D) treacherous
   - (E) deft

5. ADAGE:
   - (A) trance
   - (B) brevity
   - (C) magnitude
   - (D) grant
   - (E) proverb

6. CONDONE:
   - (A) transport
   - (B) approve
   - (C) huddle
   - (D) credit
   - (E) depreciate

7. RUSE:
   - (A) hoax
   - (B) anxiety
   - (C) illustration
   - (D) understanding
   - (E) scruple

8. CONSECRATE:
   - (A) procure
   - (B) refute
   - (C) sanctify
   - (D) alienate
   - (E) disconcert

9. ADULTERATE:
   - (A) revert
   - (B) abridge
   - (C) contradict
   - (D) taint
   - (E) latch

10. AVERSION:
    - (A) precaution
    - (B) revulsion
    - (C) nuisance
    - (D) resolution
    - (E) qualm

Analogies Practice

1. Erroneous is to fallacy as

    (A) congenial is to acquisition
    (B) radical is to impediment
    (C) ominous is to threat
    (D) putrid is to proficiency
    (E) ultimate is to extortion

2. Dubious is to skeptical as

    (A) affable is to incredulous
    (B) concise is to noteworthy
    (C) fluttering is to relinquished
    (D) devious is to furtive
    (E) pugnacious is to mystical

3. Fabricate is to excuse as

    (A) transgress is to amplitude
    (B) banter is to mien
    (C) compose is to symphony
    (D) incriminate is to skirmish
    (E) revoke is to revel

4. Diatribe is to renegade as

    (A) soliloquy is to actor
    (B) pinnacle is to apex
    (C) detriment is to holiday
    (D) food is to glutton
    (E) bravery is to mettle

5. Condescending is to contemptuous as

    (A) invigorating is to slothful
    (B) depleted is to eradicated
    (C) opaque is to provincial
    (D) hapless is to humdrum
    (E) odious is to judicious

Reading Practice

The following is an excerpt from "The Rime of the Ancient Mariner" by Samuel Taylor Coleridge.

It is an ancient Mariner,
And he stoppeth one of three.
"By thy long grey beard and glittering eye,
Now wherefore stopp'st thou me?

Line 5
The bridegroom's doors are opened wide,
And I am next of kin;
The guests are met, the feast is set:
May'st hear the merry din."

He holds him with his skinny hand,
10
"There was a ship," quoth he.
"Hold off! unhand me, grey-beard loon!"
Eftsoons his hand dropt he.

He holds him with his glittering eye—
The Wedding-Guest stood still,
15
And listens like a three years' child:
The Mariner hath his will.

The Wedding-Guest sat on a stone:
He cannot choose but hear;
And thus spake on that ancient man,
20
The bright-eyed Mariner.

"The ship was cheered, the harbor cleared,
Merrily did we drop
Below the kirk, below the hill,
Below the lighthouse top.

25
The sun came up upon the left,
Out of the sea came he!
And he shone bright, and on the right
Went down into the sea.

Higher and higher every day,
30
Till over the mast at noon—"
The Wedding-Guest here beat his breast,
For he heard the loud bassoon.

1. This passage is primarily about
   - (A) a wedding between two people unsuitable to be married.
   - (B) a sailor who attends a wedding and tells a story.
   - (C) a shipwreck that happened a long time ago.
   - (D) a joyous wedding day.
   - (E) a sailor preparing to go on a journey.

2. The line "By thy long grey beard and glittering eye" is an example of which literary convention?
   - (A) alliteration
   - (B) assonance
   - (C) hyperbole
   - (D) exposition
   - (E) synechdoche

3. Which best describes the mood of the poem?
   - (A) gleeful
   - (B) gory
   - (C) indifferent
   - (D) ominous
   - (E) pessimistic

4. The bridegroom commands the mariner to drop his hand because
   - (A) the bridegroom is offended by the appearance of the mariner.
   - (B) the bridegroom is not interested in the story that the mariner has to tell.
   - (C) the bridegroom does not want others to know that they are kin.
   - (D) it is bad luck for the bridegroom to see a mariner before his wedding.
   - (E) the mariner has threatened the bridegroom.

5. According to the poem, which came out of the sea?
   - (A) the bride
   - (B) the bridegroom
   - (C) the mariner
   - (D) a ship
   - (E) the sun

Math Practice

In this workout, we will focus on questions that involve factoring and quadratic equations. These questions involve equations and expressions that include variables with exponents that are 2 or greater.

First we will look at quadratic equations and solving them. These questions can be solved by factoring, but keep in mind that this is a multiple-choice test and sometimes the easiest path to answering the question is to plug in answer choices and see what works. Another concept to keep in mind is that when we take the square root of a positive number, there are two answers: one positive and one negative.

1. What are the possible solutions to $2x^2 + 8x - 42 = 0$?

    (A) 7, 3
    (B) −7, −3
    (C) −7, 3
    (D) 7, −3
    (E) 2, −8

2. Which are the solutions for the equation $(x - 3)^2 - 18 = 0$?

    (A) -21
    (B) $-21, 15$
    (C) $-3+3\sqrt{2},\ -3-3\sqrt{2}$
    (D) $3\sqrt{2},\ -3\sqrt{2}$
    (E) $3+3\sqrt{2},\ 3-3\sqrt{2}$

3. A rocket is launched into the air and the rocket's height h (in cm) above the ground is a function of time (in seconds) and can be modeled by the function:

    $h(t) = -16t^2 + 32t + 128$

    How many seconds after the rocket is launched will it hit the ground?

    (A) 1
    (B) 2
    (C) 3
    (D) 4
    (E) 8

Now we will work on some questions that use factoring. Again, first think about whether you can try out answer choices to see what works.

4. Which expression is equivalent to $-3x^2 + 5x + 2$?

   (A) $(3x + 1)(x - 2)$
   (B) $-(3x + 1)(x - 2)$
   (C) $(3x - 1)(x + 2)$
   (D) $(-3x + 1)(x - 2)$
   (E) $(3x - 1)(x - 2)$

5. Which expression is equivalent to $16x^2 - 25y^2$

   (A) $(4x - 5y)(4x + 5y)$
   (B) $(4x + 5y)^2$
   (C) $(4x - 5y)^2$
   (D) $(4x - 5)(4x + 5)$
   (E) $y(4x + 5)(4x - 5)$

6. Which is equivalent to $x^3 + 3x^2 - 9x - 27$?

   (A) $(x - 3)(x - 3)(x + 3)$
   (B) $(x + 3)(x^2 - 9)$
   (C) $(x - 3)^3$
   (D) $-(x + 3)^3$
   (E) $(x - 3)^2(x + 3)$

Now we will work on greatest common factor and least common multiple questions.

7. What is the least common multiple of $9m^2n^7p$, $6m^3n^5p^4$, and $12m^5n^2$?

   (A) $3m^2n^2$
   (B) $3m^2n^2p$
   (C) $12m^2n^2$
   (D) $36m^2n^2p$
   (E) $36m^5n^7p^4$

8. Which is equivalent to the least common multiple of $2(x^2 + x - 2)$ and $3(x^2 + 3x + 2)$?

   (A) $x + 2$
   (B) $6x + 6$
   (C) $6(x + 2)$
   (D) $6(x + 2)(x^2 - 1)$
   (E) $6(x + 2)(x - 1)^2$

Workout #8

9. What is the greatest common factor of $6x^4y^5z$, $9x^3y^6z^2$, and $12x^2z^4$?

    (A) $3x^2z$
    (B) $3x^2y^5z$
    (C) $6x^2z$
    (D) $6x^2y^5z$
    (E) $36x^4y^6z^4$

10. What is the greatest common factor of $5(6x^2 - x - 2)$ and $5(12x^2 - 11x + 2)$?

    (A) 5
    (B) $3x - 2$
    (C) $15x - 10$
    (D) $30x - 10$
    (E) $30x + 15$

Workout #8 Answers

Synonyms Practice

1. A — The word list states that *overbearing* means "domineering," so choice A is correct.

2. D — The word list from workout #5 states that *brandish* means "wield," so choice D is correct. To *brandish* (or wield) is to wave something in a menacing manner — it is frequently used to describe what people do with weapons.

3. B — The word list from workout #4 states that *uncouth* means "awkward." Since *awkward* and *inelegant* (lacking elegance) are synonyms, answer choice B is correct.

4. C — The word list from workout #2 states that *morbid* means "gruesome." Since *gruesome* and *ghoulish* are synonyms, answer choice C is correct.

5. E — The word list from workout #6 states that *adage* is a proverb or wise saying. Answer choice E is correct.

6. B — The word list from workout #7 states that *condone* means "approve." Answer choice B is correct.

7. A — The word list states that *ruse* means "trick." The word list from workout #4 states that *hoax* means "fraud." To *defraud* people is to trick them into doing something that is bad for themselves, so *fraud* and *trick* can have the same meaning, and *ruse* and *hoax* can also have the same meaning. Choice A is correct.

8. C — The word list from workout #7 states that *consecrate* means "sanctify." Answer choice C is correct. Both words mean "to make something holy" or "to recognize that something is holy."

9. D — The word list from workout #7 states that *adulterated* means "cheapened." Therefore, the verb form of that word (adulterate) means "to cheapen," or make less valuable. Since *taint* means "make something less pure or less valuable," answer choice D is correct.

10. B — The word list states that *aversion* means "disliking." *Revulsion* also means "disliking," so *aversion* and *revulsion* are synonyms, and choice B is correct. Note: the prefix *a-* means "away" and the root *ver* means "to turn." Therefore, *aversion* means to "turn away."

Analogies Practice

1. C — The relationship in this question is *characteristic of*: *erroneous* (wrong) is a characteristic of a *fallacy* (something that is false). *Congenial* (friendly) is not a characteristic of an *acquisition* (possession), and *radical* (extreme) is not a characteristic of an *impediment*

(obstacle), so choices A and B can be eliminated. *Ominous* (threatening) is a characteristic of a *threat*, so choice C is correct. *Putrid* (decaying) is not a characteristic of *proficiency* (ability), and *ultimate* (highest) is not a characteristic of *extortion* (blackmail), so choices D and E are not correct.

2. D — The relationship in this question is *synonyms*: *dubious* is a synonym of *skeptical* (they both mean "doubting"). *Affable* (friendly) is not related to *incredulous* (skeptical), *concise* (brief) is not related to *noteworthy* (famous), and *fluttering* is not related to *relinquished* (given up), so choices A, B, and C can be ruled out. *Devious* (dishonest) is a synonym for *furtive*, so choice D is the correct answer. Finally, *pugnacious* (quarrelsome) is not related to *mystical* (mysterious), so choice E is not correct.

3. C — The relationship in this question is *one thing is to make up another*: *fabricate* is to make up an *excuse*. *Transgress* (violate) is not to make up an *amplitude* (size), and *banter* (chat) is not to make up a *mien* (demeanor), so choices A and B are not correct. To *compose* is to make up a *symphony*, so choice C is correct. *Incriminate* (blame) could be related to a *skirmish*, but it is not to make up a *skirmish*, so choice D can be ruled out. Finally, to *revoke* (take back) is not related to *revel* (merriment), so choice E can be eliminated.

4. A — The relationship here is *one thing is given by the other*: a *diatribe* is a speech given by a *renegade*. A *soliloquy* is a speech given by an *actor*, so choice A is the correct answer. *Pinnacle* and *apex* are synonyms, and one is not given by the other, so choice B is not correct. *Detriment* (disadvantage) is not related to *holiday*, so choice C can be ruled out. *Food* is over-consumed by a *glutton*, not something given by a *glutton*, so choice D can be eliminated. *Bravery* and *mettle* are *synonyms*, so choice E is not correct. (Note: even if you weren't sure of the words in the question, you could have eliminated both choices B and E because they have the same relationship and there can only be one correct answer.)

5. B — The relationship in this question is *degree*: a more extreme version of *condescending* (looking down on another person) is *contemptuous* (obviously disrespectful). *Invigorating* (energizing) is the opposite of *slothful*, not a less extreme version of it, so choice A can be eliminated. *Depleted* (reduced) is a less extreme version of *eradicated* (eliminated), so choice B is the correct answer. *Opaque* (murky) is not related to *provincial* (unsophisticated), *hapless* (unlucky) is not related to *humdrum* (boring), and *odious* (offensive) is the opposite of *judicious* (responsible), so choices C, D, and E are not correct.

Reading Practice

1. B — We can use the process of elimination to answer this question. The poem does not imply that the people being married are unsuitable, so we can rule out choice A. The poem does describe a sailor (mariner) who attends a wedding and tells a story, so we will leave choice B. There is no mention of a shipwreck or that the sailor is about to go on a journey, so choices C and E can be eliminated. The poem does describe the "merry din" of the wedding, so we will

leave choice D for now. Now we have to decide whether the poem is primarily (or mainly) about the sailor telling a story or about the joyous wedding. Since most of the poem is about the sailor, choice B is the best answer and is correct.

2. B — In the line given, there is a repetition of a vowel sound: by, thy, and eye all have the same vowel sound. This is an example of assonance, so choice B is correct.

3. D — We can use the process of elimination for this question. The poem is not *gleeful* (very happy), *gory* (bloody), or *indifferent* (uncaring), so we can rule out answer choices A, B, and C. We are down to *ominous* (seems like something bad will happen) and *pessimistic* (the worst will most likely happen). Since *ominous* is less extreme, choice D is the better answer and is correct. The mariner has begun to tell a story where a ship has disappeared from civilization, so there is an ominous tone to the poem.

4. B — We can use the process of elimination to answer this question. There is no evidence that the bridegroom doesn't want other people to know that he is related to the mariner, that it is bad luck for the bridegroom to see the mariner, or that the mariner has threatened the groom, so we can eliminate choices C, D, and E. We have to decide whether the bridegroom is offended by the appearance of the mariner or is not interested in the mariner's story. In line 9, right before the bridegroom tells the mariner to unhand him, the mariner starts to tell the bridegroom a story about a ship. Therefore, it is a more logical conclusion that the bridegroom does not want to hear the story, so choice B is the best answer and is correct.

5. E — In lines 25-26, the poem states, "The sun came up upon the left, / Out of the sea came he!" Therefore, it was the sun that came out of the sea, and choice E is correct.

Math Practice

1. C — We can solve this problem by factoring. First, we can factor out a 2 from all of the terms on the left side of the equation: $2(x^2 + 4x - 21) = 0$. If we divide both sides by 2, the result is $x^2 + 4x - 21 = 0$. Now we have to list the factor pairs of -21:

    1, -21

    -1, 21

    -3, 7

    3, -7

Workout #8

We are looking for the factor pair of –21 (the last term) that adds to +4 (the coefficient of the middle term). Since –3 and 7 add to +4, the factored form of $x^2 + 4x - 21 = 0$ is $(x - 3)(x + 7) = 0$. Now we can set each set of parentheses equal to 0 since when either of these factors equals 0, the entire left side of the equation also equals 0. Therefore, $x - 3 = 0$ and $x + 7 = 0$ will yield our solutions. In order for these equations to be true, x could equal 3 or –7. Answer choice C is correct.

2. E — Our first step is to add 18 to both sides. Now our equation is $(x - 3)^2 = 18$. The next step is to take the square root of both sides. The trick here is that we have to remember that taking the square root results in both a positive and negative answer. We now have 2 equations: $x - 3 = \sqrt{18}$ and $x - 3 = -\sqrt{18}$. We can add 3 in both equations and they become $x = 3 + \sqrt{18}$ and $x = 3 - \sqrt{18}$. These are not answer choices, however, because we need to simplify $\sqrt{18}$. We can factor $\sqrt{18}$ into $\sqrt{9} \times \sqrt{2}$, which simplifies to $3\sqrt{2}$. If we substitute this simplified form back into the equations, our solutions are $3 + 3\sqrt{2}$ and $3 - 3\sqrt{2}$. Answer choice E is correct.

3. D — In order to answer this question, we need to set the function given equal to 0 (the height will be 0 when the rocket hits the ground) and then solve for t (or time). To solve the equation $-16t^2 + 32t + 128 = 0$, we can begin by factoring –16 out of each term on the left. The equation becomes $-16(t^2 - 2t - 8) = 0$. Dividing both sides by –16 results in $t^2 - 2t - 8 = 0$. This can be factored into $(t - 4)(t + 2) = 0$. If $t = 4$ or if $t = -2$ then the equation would be true. However, in this case, we can't have a negative solution since t represents time. Therefore, the only solution that works is $t = 4$ and answer choice D is correct.

4. B — We can use the process of elimination to answer this question. At a glance, we can see that choices A, C, and E don't have a negative sign in front of the expressions nor are either of the first terms in either set of parentheses negative, so they can be eliminated since it would not be possible to get $-3x^2$ as the first term if these answer choices were multiplied out. We are left with choices B and D, so let's multiply them out and see which one matches the expression given in the question. We will start with choice B. If we use FOIL (first outer inner last), the expression becomes $-(3x^2 - 6x + x - 2)$. If we combine like terms, it becomes $-(3x^2 - 5x - 2)$. Distributing the negative sign yields $-3x^2 + 5x + 2$. Since this matches the expression in the question, answer choice B is correct and we don't need to test out choice D since there can only be one correct answer choice.

5. A — The key to this question is recognizing that $16x^2 - 25y^2$ is a difference of the squares expression (the expression is one perfect square minus another perfect square). If an expression is the difference of the squares, then it factors into the square root of the first term plus the square root of the second term times the square root of the first term minus the square root of the second term. Since the square root of $16x^2$ is $4x$ and the square root of $25y^2$ is $5y$, the expression $16x^2 - 25y^2$ factors into $(4x + 5y)(4x - 5y)$. Answer choice A is correct.

6. B — We can use the process of elimination to answer this question. It is easy to eliminate choice D because there is no negative sign in front of the first term of the expression given

in the question. Also, if we were to write out choice E, it would become $(x - 3)(x - 3)(x + 3)$. Since this is the same as choice A, we can rule out both choices A and E since there cannot be two right answers. We are left with choices B and C. We can use FOIL to put choice B in the same form as the expression in the question: $(x + 3)(x^2 - 9) = x^3 - 9x + 3x^2 - 27$. If we rewrite this expression in descending order, it becomes $x^3 + 3x^2 - 9x - 27$. Since this matches the expression in the question, answer choice B is correct.

7. E — We can start with identifying the integer portion of the least common multiple. The integer portions of the terms given are 9, 6, and 12. Since the least common multiple of 9, 6, and 12 is 36, the answer must start with 36 (hint: if you didn't know the least common multiple of 9, 6, and 12, look at the answer choices and your only options are 3, 12, and 36). Answer choice D or E must be correct. Now we look at the variable portions. The least common multiple must contain all the variables in the terms given and each variable should have the highest exponent that it is given in the terms. Therefore, the least common multiple should contain m^5, n^7, and p^4. If we put this all together, the least common multiple is $36m^5n^7p^4$ and choice E is correct.

8. D — In order to answer this question, we need to factor each of the expressions given. The first expression factors to $2(x + 2)(x - 1)$ and the second expression factors to $3(x + 1)(x + 2)$. Since the least common multiple is the product of all unique prime factors, we multiply $3 \times 2 \times (x + 2)(x - 1)(x + 1)$ and the result is $6(x + 2)(x - 1)(x + 1)$. This is not an answer choice, however. We can rule out choices A, B, and C, however, since they all have x in the first degree and that would not be true if we multiplied out the factors. We are down to D and E. If we look at these choices, we can see that we need to combine $(x + 1)(x - 1)$ in our least common multiple. Since $(x + 1)(x - 1)$ is a difference of the squares expression, it multiplies to $x^2 - 1$ and our least common multiple is $6(x + 2)(x^2 - 1)$ and answer choice D is correct.

9. A — We can begin by identifying the integer portion of the greatest common factor. Since the integer portion of the expressions given are 6, 9, and 12, and the greatest common factor of these numbers is 3, the integer portion of our greatest common factor should be 3. Answer choice A or B must be correct. Now we look at the variable portions. The greatest common factor only has variables that are in all the terms given and the exponent is the lowest exponent given for that variable. Therefore, the greatest common factor should include x^2 and z (there is no y in the greatest common factor because the last term does not contain y). If we put this together, our greatest common factor is $3x^2z$ and choice A is correct.

10. C — In order to answer this question, we need to factor the expressions given. We can factor the first expression to $5(3x - 2)(2x + 1)$ and the second expression to $5(3x - 2)(4x - 1)$. The factors that these expressions have in common are 5 and $(3x - 2)$. If we put this together, the greatest common factor is $5(3x - 2)$, but that is not an answer choice. We have to multiply out $5(3x - 2)$ and the result is $15x - 10$. Answer choice C is correct.

Workout #9

Words to Learn

Below are the words used in Workout 9. Refer back to this list as needed as you move through the lesson.

Clear... or not so clear

Ambiguous:	unclear
Contort:	twist
Precarious:	insecure
Tentative:	uncertain
Erratic:	unpredictable
Translucent:	clear

Words for when you want to be dramatic

Celestial:	heavenly
Eminent:	distinguished
Emphatic:	definite
Fervent:	enthusiastic
Fervor:	enthusiasm
Immaculate:	spotless
Nullify:	invalidate
Obliterate:	destroy
Rampant:	widespread
Resplendent:	gleaming
Scourge:	plague
Vehement:	insistent
Zenith:	peak
Rabid:	extreme

Synonyms Practice

1. ZENITH:
   - (A) dependent
   - (B) tirade
   - (C) motto
   - (D) apex
   - (E) wisdom

2. COVET:
   - (A) wither
   - (B) sanction
   - (C) accuse
   - (D) practice
   - (E) desire

3. INCRIMINATE:
   - (A) condone
   - (B) relinquish
   - (C) indict
   - (D) postpone
   - (E) gamble

4. BOLSTER:
   - (A) buckle
   - (B) buttress
   - (C) badger
   - (D) brandish
   - (E) beckon

5. DUBIOUS:
   - (A) eminent
   - (B) restricted
   - (C) ominous
   - (D) doubtful
   - (E) ashamed

6. TAWDRY:
   - (A) cheap
   - (B) bulging
   - (C) strange
   - (D) unfounded
   - (E) cryptic

7. FABRICATE:
   - (A) concoct
   - (B) gather
   - (C) revoke
   - (D) appoint
   - (E) tabulate

8. ERRATIC:
   - (A) affable
   - (B) unpredictable
   - (C) bashful
   - (D) modest
   - (E) successful

9. REND:
   - (A) deplete
   - (B) wonder
   - (C) release
   - (D) apologize
   - (E) fracture

10. SCOURGE:
    - (A) impediment
    - (B) peak
    - (C) plague
    - (D) blunder
    - (E) adapt

Analogies Practice

1. Extortion is to crime as

    (A) hovel is to house
    (B) affectation is to aversion
    (C) forbearance is to detriment
    (D) acquisition is to fervor
    (E) renegade is to satire

2. Diligent is to dogged as

    (A) unjustified is to condescending
    (B) bogus is to dormant
    (C) compiled is to gleaned
    (D) odious is to disdainful
    (E) tentative is to definite

3. Fervent is to rabid as

    (A) tranquil is to emphatic
    (B) devious is to pugnacious
    (C) slothful is to eminent
    (D) clean is to immaculate
    (E) legible is to drab

4. Precarious is to invincible as

    (A) spiritual is to resistant
    (B) critical is to despondent
    (C) benevolent is to atrocious
    (D) impertinent is to droll
    (E) hysterical is to perturbed

5. Translucent is to opaque as

    (A) urgent is to ambiguous
    (B) incredulous is to naïve
    (C) proficient is to flimsy
    (D) concise is to terse
    (E) judicious is to apologetic

Reading Practice

> Philosophy is at once the most sublime and the most trivial of human pursuits. It works in the minutest crannies and it opens out the widest vistas. It 'bakes no bread,' as has been said, but it can inspire our souls with courage; and repugnant as its manners, its doubting and challenging, its quibbling and dialectics, often are to common people, no one of us can get along without the far-
> Line 5 flashing beams of light it sends over the world's perspectives. These illuminations at least, and the contrast-effects of darkness and mystery that accompany them, give to what it says an interest that is much more than professional.
>
> The history of philosophy is to a great extent that of a certain clash of human temperaments. Undignified as such a treatment may seem to some of my colleagues, I shall have to take account
> 10 of this clash and explain a good many of the divergencies of philosophers by it. Of whatever temperament a professional philosopher is, he tries when philosophizing to sink the fact of his temperament. Temperament is no conventionally recognized reason, so he urges impersonal reasons only for his conclusions. Yet his temperament really gives him a stronger bias than any of his more strictly objective premises. It loads the evidence for him one way or the other,
> 15 making for a more sentimental or a more hard-hearted view of the universe, just as this fact or that principle would. He trusts his temperament. Wanting a universe that suits it, he believes in any representation of the universe that does suit it. He feels men of opposite temper to be out of key with the world's character, and in his heart considers them incompetent and 'not in it,' in the philosophic business, even tho they may far excel him in dialectical ability.

1. According to the passage, a philosopher is most likely to adopt theories that fit with

    (A) what is best understood by common people.
    (B) what his or her peers believe to be true.
    (C) his or her own rational arguments.
    (D) the evidence that points to a conclusion.
    (E) his or her own view of the world based on temperament.

2. The author implies that most philosophers view temperament as

    (A) a source of conflict among common people.
    (B) not a source of bias.
    (C) a basis for rational arguments.
    (D) based on strictly objective observations.
    (E) quickly changing.

3. As used in line 2, the idiom "'bakes no bread" points out that philosophy

   (A) is useless.
   (B) is limited by the people who create it.
   (C) does not create a physical product.
   (D) is the greatest human contribution.
   (E) differentiates great thinkers from others.

4. According to the passage, common people

   (A) find the fighting among philosophers odious.
   (B) do not understand theories that philosophers develop.
   (C) have never heard of most philosophers.
   (D) are guided only by their biases.
   (E) cannot form arguments as effectively as philosophers can.

5. Which best expresses the main idea of this passage?

   (A) Philosophers should be influenced more by their temperaments.
   (B) Philosophy is really the study of various temperaments.
   (C) The job of a philosopher is to shine light on different perspectives.
   (D) Philosophers are guided mainly by temperament, even if they deny it.
   (E) Without philosophy, there would be less courage in the world.

Math Practice

The math in this workout builds on the last section. We will work on problems that test the rules of rational and polynomial expressions.

We will start with rational expressions. These questions require you to manipulate expressions to create equivalent expressions.

1. Which expression is equivalent to $\dfrac{x+3}{3} - \left(\dfrac{2}{3} - 2x\right)$?

    (A) $\dfrac{3x+1}{3}$

    (B) $\dfrac{1-x}{3}$

    (C) $\dfrac{1}{3}$

    (D) $\dfrac{7x+1}{3}$

    (E) $\dfrac{5-x}{3}$

2. If $g = 3h$ and $4h = 5j$, then what is the value of $\dfrac{g}{j}$?

    (A) $\dfrac{4}{15}$

    (B) $\dfrac{5}{12}$

    (C) $\dfrac{3}{5}$

    (D) $\dfrac{5}{3}$

    (E) $\dfrac{15}{4}$

Workout #9

3. Which expression is equivalent to $\left(\dfrac{4}{x+2}\right)\left(\dfrac{2x^2+2x-4}{x-2}\right)$?

   (A) $\dfrac{8x-8}{x-2}$

   (B) $\dfrac{4x-1}{x-2}$

   (C) $\dfrac{8x+8}{x+2}$

   (D) $\dfrac{4x-2}{x^2-4}$

   (E) $\dfrac{2x^2-16}{x^2-4}$

4. If $\dfrac{x}{x+2}=0.6$ then what is the value of $\dfrac{x+1}{x+2}$?

   (A) 0.4
   (B) 0.6
   (C) 0.8
   (D) 1.0
   (E) 1.2

5. Which expression is equivalent to $\dfrac{3}{x^2-16}+\dfrac{2}{x+4}$?

   (A) $\dfrac{5}{x^2-16}$

   (B) $\dfrac{2x-5}{x^2-16}$

   (C) $\dfrac{11+2x}{x^2-16}$

   (D) $\dfrac{5}{x^3+4x^2-16x-64}$

   (E) $\dfrac{2x-5}{x^3+4x^2-16x-64}$

Now we will work on polynomial expressions. These problems require a lot of attention to detail. Be sure to track both the number of the exponents as well as positive and negative signs.

6. Which expression is equivalent to $(2x^2 + 3x - 4) - (3x^2 - 2x + 1) - (4x - 3)$?

    (A) $-x^2 + x - 2$
    (B) $-x^2 + x + 2$
    (C) $x^2 + x - 5$
    (D) $x^2 - x - 2$
    (E) $x^2 - 7x - 11$

7. Which expression is equivalent to $-3b(c - 4d)$?

    (A) $-3bc - 12bd$
    (B) $-3bc - 4d$
    (C) $4d - 3bc$
    (D) $12bd - 3bc$
    (E) $12bd + 3bc$

8. When $3(x - y)^2$ is written in expanded form, what is the coefficient of the term that contains xy?

    (A) -6
    (B) -3
    (C) -1
    (D) 3
    (E) 6

9. Which expression is equivalent to $(x - 3)(x^2 - 4x + 7)$?

    (A) $x^2 - 3x + 4$
    (B) $x^3 - 7x^2 - 19x - 21$
    (C) $x^3 - 4x^2 + 12x - 21$
    (D) $x^3 - 3x^2 - 5x - 21$
    (E) $x^3 - 7x^2 + 19x - 21$

10. What is $(4x^3 - 2x + 6) - (2x^3 + 3x^2 - 3)$ in simplified form?

    (A) $2x^3 + x^2 + 9$
    (B) $2x^3 - 5x^2 + 9$
    (C) $2x^3 - 3x^2 - 2x + 9$
    (D) $2x^3 + 3x^2 - 2x + 3$
    (E) $2x^3 - 5x^2 - 2x + 3$

Workout #9 Answers

Synonyms Practice

1. D — The word list states that *zenith* means "peak." The word list from workout #5 states that *apex* also means "peak." Therefore, *zenith* and *apex* are synonyms, and choice D is correct.

2. E — The word list from workout #7 states that *covet* means "desire." Answer choice E is correct.

3. C — The word list from workout #5 states that *incriminate* means "accuse." The word list from workout #7 states that *indict* also means "accuse." Therefore, *incriminate* and *indict* have the same meaning, and choice C is correct.

4. B — The word list from workout #1 states that both *bolster* and *buttress* mean "support." Therefore, *bolster* and *buttress* are synonyms, and choice B is correct.

5. D — The word list from workout #8 states that *dubious* means "doubtful," so answer choice D is correct. (Note: *dubious* and *doubtful* are similar at the beginning — even though the spelling is not exactly the same, that is a good sign that the words are related in meaning.)

6. A — The word list from workout #4 states that *tawdry* means "cheap." Answer choice A is correct.

7. A — The word list from workout #8 states that *fabricate* means "invent." Since *concoct* means "to make up" (or invent), answer choice A is correct.

8. B — The word list states that *erratic* means "unpredictable." Answer choice B is correct.

9. E — The word list from workout #2 states that *rend* means "to divide." *Fracture* means "to break," or "divide," so choice E is correct.

10. C — The word list states that *scourge* means "plague," so choice C is correct.

Analogies Practice

1. A — The relationship in this question is *type of*: *extortion* (blackmail) is a type of *crime*. A *hovel* is a type of *house* (a hovel is a house that is falling apart), so choice A is correct. *Affectation* (pretension) is not a type of *aversion* (disliking), even though you might have an aversion to affectation, so choice B can be ruled out. *Forbearance* (self-control) is not related to *detriment* (disadvantage), *acquisition* (possession) is not related to *fervor* (enthusiasm), and *renegade* (dissenter) is not a type of *satire* (parody), so choices C, D, and E are not correct.

2. E — The relationship in this question is *degree*: *diligent* (persevering) is less extreme than *dogged*, which has the connotation of not giving up until a goal is achieved. *Unjustified* is not related to *condescending* (patronizing), and *bogus* (fake) is not related to *dormant* (inactive), so choices A and B are not correct. While *compiled* and *gleaned* are similar in meaning, *gleaned* is not more extreme than *compiled*, so choice C can be ruled out. If we look at answer choice D, *odious* (offensive) is more extreme than *disdainful* (disapproving), so the words are in the wrong order, and choice D is not correct. *Tentative* (uncertain) is less extreme than *definite*, so choice E is the correct answer. To think of it another way, if you have *tentative* plans, that is less extreme than having *definite* plans.

3. D — The relationship in this question is *degree*: if a person is more *fervent* (enthusiastic) then he would be *rabid* (extreme). *Tranquil* (calm) is unrelated to *emphatic* (definite), *devious* (deceitful) is not related to *pugnacious* (quarrelsome), and *slothful* (lazy) is not related to *eminent* (distinguished), so choices A, B, and C can be ruled out. A more extreme form of *clean* is *immaculate*, so choice D is the correct answer. *Legible* (clear) is not related to *drab* (boring), so choice E can be eliminated.

4. C — The relationship in this question is *opposites*: *precarious* (insecure) is the opposite of *invincible* (undefeatable). *Spiritual* is not related to *resistant*, and *critical* (important) is not related to *despondent* (hopeless), so choices A and B can be ruled out. *Benevolent* (kind) is the opposite of *atrocious* (dreadful), so choice C is correct. *Impertinent* (insulting) is not the opposite of *droll* (witty), so choice D can be eliminated. Finally, *hysterical* is a more extreme version of *perturbed* (disturbed), and they are not opposites, so choice E can be ruled out.

5. B — The relationship here is *opposites*: *translucent* (clear) is the opposite of *opaque* (murky). *Urgent* (needing immediate attention) is not the opposite of *ambiguous* (unclear), so choice A can be eliminated. *Incredulous* (skeptical) is the opposite of *naïve* (unsophisticated or lacking worldly knowledge), so choice B is the correct answer. *Proficient* (capable) and *flimsy* are not related, so we can eliminate choice C. *Concise* and *terse* are similar in meaning (and not opposites), so choice D is not correct. *Judicious* (responsible) and *apologetic* are not related, so choice E is not correct.

Reading Practice

1. E — In lines 13-17, the passage states, "Yet his temperament really gives him a stronger bias than any of his more strictly objective premises. It loads the evidence for him one way or the other… He trusts his temperament. Wanting a universe that suits it, he believes in any representation of the universe that does suit it." This part of the passage is saying that a philosopher adopts the worldview that suits his temperament. Choice E best restates this and is the correct answer.

2. B — In lines 12-13, the passage states, "temperament is no conventionally recognized reason, so he urges impersonal reason only for his conclusions." This implies that most philosophers

believe that their views are based purely on reason, even though the author states otherwise. The question doesn't ask what the author believes, however, only what he thinks most philosophers believe. Since most philosophers believe their view is based on objective reasons and not temperament, they do not view temperament as a source of bias, and choice B is the best answer.

3. C — The passage contrasts baking bread with inspiring souls with courage. The point here is that while philosophy does not create an actual product, i.e. bread, it has other benefits that are intangible. Therefore, the author comments that philosophy bakes no bread to show that no product is produced, and choice C is the best answer.

4. A — The passage discusses common people in the first paragraph when it states, "and repugnant as its manners, its doubting and challenging, its quibbling and dialectics, often are to common people." These lines are stating the common people find all of the challenging and quibbling (fighting over) to be *repugnant*, which is another word for *odious*. Therefore, answer choice A best restates the passage and is the correct answer.

5. D — We can use the process of elimination to answer this question. A good portion of the passage is about temperament, so we can eliminate choices C and E as they do not discuss temperament. The author says that philosophers are guided by their temperaments, but does not suggest that they should be guided more by their temperaments, so choice A can be ruled out. The passage also does not state that philosophy is the study of temperaments because the passage says that most of philosophy ignores the influence of temperaments. The passage does say that most philosophers are influenced by their temperament even while saying that, "temperament is no conventionally recognized reason, so he urges impersonal reasons only for his conclusion" (lines 12-13). Therefore, most philosophers deny that their thoughts are a product of their temperaments and both parts of choice D are supported with evidence from the passage. Choice D is correct.

Math Practice

1. D — In order to combine terms, we need a common denominator. The first two terms have a denominator of 3 so we need $-2x$ to have a denominator of 3 as well. In order to achieve this, we can multiply $-2x$ by $\frac{3}{3}$ so that the last term becomes $\frac{-6x}{3}$. The expression is now:

$$\frac{x+3}{3} - \left(\frac{2}{3} - \frac{6x}{3}\right)$$

If we eliminate the parentheses, remembering to distribute the negative sign, the expression becomes:

$$\frac{x+3-2+6x}{3}$$

Finally, we combine like terms and now the expression is:

$$\frac{7x+1}{3}$$

Answer choice D is correct.

2. E — One way to answer this question is to multiply the first equation by 4 and the second equation by 3 so that both equations have $12h$. If we do this, the first equation becomes $4g = 12h$ and the second equation becomes $12h = 15j$. Now we know that $4g = 15j$ since $4g$ and $15j$ are both equal to $12h$. Now we just need to rearrange $4g = 15j$ so that we have $\frac{g}{j}$. We can do this by dividing both sides by 4 and both sides by j. This results in $\frac{g}{j} = \frac{15}{4}$. Answer choice E is correct.

3. A — This problem has multiplication so we do not need a common denominator. However, we do need to fully factor in order to be able to simplify. If we multiply out the terms, the expression becomes:

$$\frac{4(2x^2+2x-4)}{(x+2)(x-2)}$$

We can further factor the numerator by factoring a 2 from the terms in the parentheses: $4 \times 2(x^2 + x - 2)$, which simplifies to $8(x^2 + x - 2)$. We can factor $x^2 + x - 2$ into $(x + 2)(x - 1)$ and our full expression is:

$$\frac{8(x+2)(x-1)}{(x+2)(x-2)}$$

We can divide both the numerator and denominator by $x + 2$ and distribute the 8:

$$\frac{8(x-1)}{x-2} = \frac{8x-8}{x-2}$$

Answer choice A is correct.

4. C — One approach is to solve for x. We can do this by multiplying both sides of the equation by x + 2. This results in x = 0.6(x + 2). If we distribute the 0.6, the equation becomes x = 0.6x + 1.2. Subtracting 0.6x from both sides results in 0.4x = 1.2. Finally, we divide by 0.4 and find that x is equal to 3. Now we can just substitute in and find that x + 1 is equal to 4 and x + 2 is equal to 5. Therefore, the value of $\frac{x+1}{x+2}$ is $\frac{4}{5}$. If we write this as a decimal, it is 0.8 since $\frac{4}{5}$ is equal to $\frac{8}{10}$ or 8 tenths. Answer choice C is correct.

5. B — In order to perform addition, we need to find a common denominator. We could multiply the denominators by each other but that would make the math really ugly. If we notice that $x^2 - 16$ is a difference of the squares problem, then we can factor the denominator in the first term to (x + 4)(x − 4). Our expression is now:

$$\frac{3}{(x+4)(x-4)} + \frac{2}{x+4}$$

We can then multiply both the numerator and denominator in the second term by x − 4 and the expression becomes:

$$\frac{3}{(x+4)(x-4)} + \frac{2(x-4)}{(x+4)(x-4)}$$

We can now add the numerators: 3 + 2(x − 4). In order to combine like terms, however, we need to distribute the 2 and the expression is now 3 + 2x − 8, which becomes 2x − 5. If we include the common denominator, our final answer is:

$$\frac{2x-5}{(x+4)(x-4)} = \frac{2x-5}{x^2-16}$$

Answer choice B is correct.

6. A — Our first step is to eliminate the parentheses. In order to do this, we need to distribute the negative signs to the last two sets of parentheses. This results in:

$2x^2 + 3x - 4 - 3x^2 + 2x - 1 - 4x + 3$

We can then use the commutative property to move around terms. We just have to remember that each term should take the + or − sign in front of it when it moves. The expression is now:

$2x^2 − 3x^2 + 3x + 2x − 4x − 4 − 1 + 3$

If we combine like terms, the final expression is $−x^2 + x − 2$. Answer choice A is correct.

7. D — We can begin by distributing $−3b$ to each term in the parentheses. This results in $−3bc + 12bd$. However, this is not one of the answer choices. We can use the commutative property to move the terms around, remembering that each term takes the + or − sign in front of it when it moves. The expression becomes $12bd − 3bc$. Answer choice D is correct.

8. A — The first step is to rewrite the expression as $3(x − y)(x − y)$. Now we use FOIL (first outer inner last) to multiply $(x − y)(x − y)$, which results in $3(x^2 - 2xy - y^2)$. The next step is to distribute the 3: $3x^2 - 6xy - 3y^2$. The coefficient of a term is the integer or fraction portion in front of the variables, so the coefficient of the term with xy in it is $−6$. Answer choice A is correct.

9. E — We can use the distributive property to answer the question. We need to distribute both the first term (x) and the second term ($−3$) in the first set of parentheses to each term in the second set of parentheses. The expression becomes:

$x(x^2 − 4x + 7) − 3(x^2 − 4x + 7)$

Now we distribute and the result is:

$x^3 − 4x^2 + 7x − 3x^2 + 12x − 21$

By applying the commutative property of addition, the expression can be rewritten as:

$x^3 − 4x^2 − 3x^2 + 7x + 12x − 21$

Combining like terms produces $x^3 − 7x^2 + 19x − 21$ and choice E is correct.

10. C — In order to answer this question, we need to begin by distributing the negative sign to all terms in the second set of parentheses and eliminating the parentheses. This results in:

$4x^3 − 2x + 6 − 2x^3 − 3x^2 + 3$

Using the commutative property of addition allows us to rewrite the expression as:

$4x^3 − 2x^3 − 3x^2 − 2x + 6 + 3$

This simplifies to $2x^3 − 3x^2 − 2x + 9$. Answer choice C is correct.

Workout #10

Words to Learn

Below are the words used in Workout 10. Refer back to this list as needed as you move through the lesson.

Time words

Defer:	delay
Impending:	imminent (about to happen)
Impromptu:	unplanned
Ensuing:	following
Antiquated:	outdated

Memory words

Commemorate:	remember
Momentous:	important
Reminiscent:	suggestive of
Memento:	souvenir

State of being words

Emaciated:	scrawny
Glower:	glare
Slovenly:	unclean
Supple:	flexible
Tepid:	lukewarm
Vibrant:	energetic
Disheveled:	untidy
Derelict:	abandoned
Fallow:	inactive
Inanimate:	lifeless
Decrepit:	weakened
Dilapidated:	crumbling

Synonyms Practice

1. AWRY:
   - (A) disdainful
   - (B) universal
   - (C) nonchalant
   - (D) questionable
   - (E) wrong

2. OBLITERATE:
   - (A) reap
   - (B) eradicate
   - (C) hush
   - (D) argue
   - (E) discredit

3. BEQUEATH:
   - (A) give
   - (B) threaten
   - (C) bind
   - (D) refute
   - (E) fasten

4. RUSE:
   - (A) scruple
   - (B) extravagance
   - (C) trick
   - (D) honor
   - (E) necessity

5. PILLAGE:
   - (A) lose
   - (B) flush
   - (C) applaud
   - (D) plunder
   - (E) warn

6. REPROOF:
   - (A) possibility
   - (B) ardor
   - (C) vanity
   - (D) fervor
   - (E) criticism

7. RESPLENDENT:
   - (A) wasted
   - (B) incandescent
   - (C) extreme
   - (D) courageous
   - (E) uncouth

8. IMPROMPTU:
   - (A) adulterated
   - (B) disputed
   - (C) strenuous
   - (D) perturbed
   - (E) unplanned

9. SOUVENIR:
   - (A) personnel
   - (B) behavior
   - (C) memento
   - (D) ascent
   - (E) extortion

10. INANIMATE:
    - (A) inert
    - (B) widespread
    - (C) broad
    - (D) tedious
    - (E) disheveled

Analogies Practice

1. Slovenly is to immaculate as

   (A) ambiguous is to steep
   (B) quick is to odious
   (C) congenial is to contemptuous
   (D) appreciated is to grateful
   (E) erratic is to unfounded

2. Fallow is to dormant as

   (A) superlative is to outstanding
   (B) vehement is to ensuing
   (C) similar is to deft
   (D) incredulous is to believable
   (E) reputable is to noticeable

3. Decrepit is to dilapidated as

   (A) apparent is to precarious
   (B) common is to rampant
   (C) polluted is to parochial
   (D) slothful is to genteel
   (E) vibrant is to momentous

4. Emaciated is to portly as

   (A) tepid is to burning
   (B) emphatic is to hapless
   (C) begrudging is to listless
   (D) incendiary is to impending
   (E) despondent is to joyful

5. Gods is to celestial as

   (A) gnomes is to rabid
   (B) fairies is to antiquated
   (C) warlocks is to dubious
   (D) trickster is to devious
   (E) mortals is to judicious

Reading Practice

     There is a radical error, I think, in the usual mode of constructing a story. Either history affords a thesis—or one is suggested by an incident of the day—or, at best, the author sets himself to work in the combination of striking events to form merely the basis of his narrative—designing, generally, to fill in with description, dialogue, or autorial comment, whatever crevices of fact, or action, may, from page to page, render themselves apparent.

     I prefer commencing with the consideration of an effect. Keeping originality always in view—for he is false to himself who ventures to dispense with so obvious and so easily attainable a source of interest—I say to myself, in the first place, "Of the innumerable effects, or impressions, of which the heart, the intellect, or (more generally) the soul is susceptible, what one shall I, on the present occasion, select?" Having chosen a novel, first, and secondly a vivid effect, I consider whether it can be best wrought by incident or tone—whether by ordinary incidents and peculiar tone, or the converse, or by peculiarity both of incident and tone—afterward looking about me (or rather within) for such combinations of event, or tone, as shall best aid me in the construction of the effect.

     I have often thought how interesting a magazine paper might be written by any author who would—that is to say, who could—detail, step by step, the processes by which any one of his compositions attained its ultimate point of completion. Why such a paper has never been given to the world, I am much at a loss to say—but, perhaps, the autorial vanity has had more to do with the omission than any one other cause.

Line 5, 10, 15

1. Based on information in the passage, the author believes that a frequently overlooked characteristic of good writing is

    (A) accuracy.
    (B) realistic action.
    (C) originality.
    (D) the validity of an argument.
    (E) a sense of suspense.

2. The primary purpose of this passage is to

    (A) discourage the reader from becoming a writer.
    (B) challenge a process that many writers use.
    (C) suggest a way that editors should evaluate written work.
    (D) describe the different effects that an author can create.
    (E) explain the process that most writers use to begin a work.

3. The author's attitude toward "the usual mode of constructing a story" (line 1) is one of

   (A) disdain.
   (B) respect.
   (C) curiosity.
   (D) nonchalance.
   (E) ambivalence.

4. As used in line 5, the word "render" means

   (A) sustain.
   (B) dismiss.
   (C) loosen.
   (D) make.
   (E) hinder.

5. The second paragraph (lines 6-14) employs which of the following literary devices?

   (A) allegory
   (B) figurative language
   (C) foreshadowing
   (D) irony
   (E) exemplification

Math Practice

In this workout, we will tackle questions that deal with functions and set theory.

We will start with a couple of questions that test the definition of a function.

1. Which graph represents a relationship that is NOT a function?

    (A)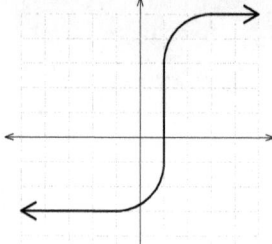

    (B)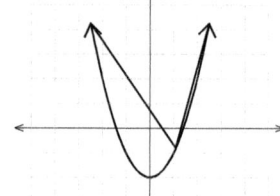

    (C)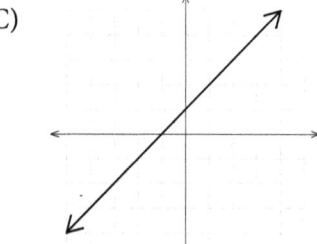

    (D)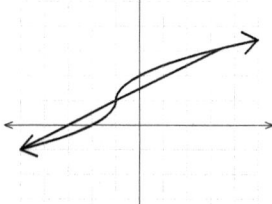

    (E)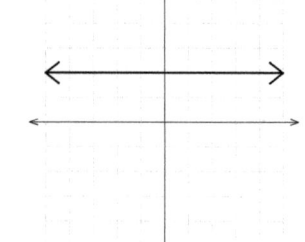

Workout #10

2. Shown below is a relationship between two variables, x and y.

x	y
10	5
12	m
15	10
q	11
20	15

Which of the following, if true, would prevent the relation in the table from being a function?

(A) $m = 7$
(B) $m = 8$
(C) $m = 9$
(D) $q = 15$
(E) $q = 16$

3. Which set gives the inputs of a function that consists of the ordered pairs (4, 5), (6, 10), and (9, 12)?

(A) {4}
(B) {4, 5}
(C) {4, 6, 9}
(D) {5, 10, 12}
(E) The empty set

Now we will answer some questions that require you to apply function notation.

4. What is the value of $f(-2)$ if $f(x) = 3x^2 - 2x + 7$?

(A) −30
(B) −23
(C) −9
(D) 23
(E) 40

153

5. Casey throws a baseball. The ball's height above the ground, $h(t)$, in inches, with respect to time, t, in seconds, is modeled by the function $h(t) = -3t^2 + 3t + 32$. Which best describes the meaning of $h(0) = 32$?

   (A) The ball will reach a maximum height of 32 inches.
   (B) The ball will reach a minimum height of 32 inches.
   (C) The ball will land on the ground after 32 seconds.
   (D) The ball drops 32 inches each second.
   (E) The ball was 32 inches above the ground when 0 seconds had elapsed.

6. Which statement describes the outputs of $f(x) = |x - 3| + 1$ if x is an integer less than 1?

   (A) All integers
   (B) All integers greater than or equal to 1
   (C) All integers greater than or equal to 4
   (D) All odd integers greater than 0
   (E) All odd integers greater than or equal to 5

Now we will work on some questions that test set theory. Keep in mind that the union of sets is ALL members of ALL sets. The intersection is only the elements that show up in all sets.

7. Use the Venn Diagram below to answer the question.

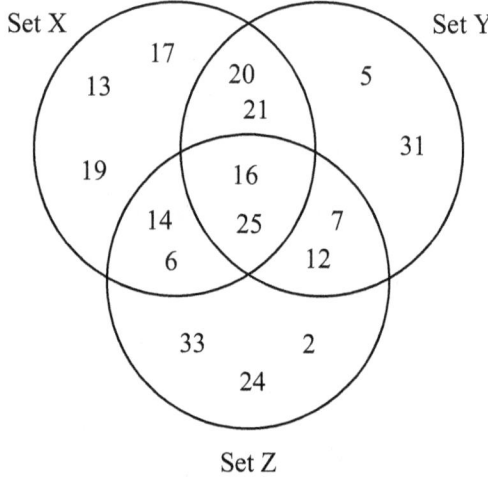

   Which set represents the intersection of sets X and Y?

   (A) {20, 21}
   (B) {16, 20, 21, 25}
   (C) {13, 17, 19, 31}
   (D) {16, 25}
   (E) {6, 7, 12, 14, 16, 20, 21, 25}

Workout #10

8. Set P contains 14 numbers and set S contains 12 numbers. If the intersection of sets P and S has 5 numbers in it, how many distinct numbers are in the union of sets P and S?

   (A) 16
   (B) 21
   (C) 26
   (D) 31
   (E) 36

9. Use the sets below to answer the question.

   $A = \{4, 5, 7, 9, 10, 12, 15\}$
   $B = \{2, 3, 4, 5, 6, 9, 11, 12\}$
   $C = \{4, 5, 7, 10, 13, 14\}$

   Which represents the intersection of set B with the intersection of sets A and C?

   (A) {4, 5}
   (B) {5}
   (C) {4, 5, 7}
   (D) {4, 5, 7, 9}
   (E) {4, 5, 7, 9, 12}

10. Set M has 16 elements and set N has 11 elements. If the union of sets M and N has 23 elements, how many elements are in the intersection of sets M and N?

    (A) 27
    (B) 23
    (C) 8
    (D) 5
    (E) 4

155

Workout #10 Answers

Synonyms Practice

1. E — The word list from workout #8 states that *awry* means "wrong." Choice E is correct. Choice D may be tempting but is not correct because the word *questionable* means that something might be wrong but not that something definitely is wrong.

2. B — The word list from workout #9 states that *obliterate* means "destroy." Another word for *destroy completely* is *eradicate*. Choice B is the correct answer.

3. A — The word list from workout #7 states that *bequeath* means "grant." If you grant someone something, you give it to that person. Therefore, to *bequeath* something is to give it, and choice A is correct.

4. C — The word list from workout #8 states that *ruse* means "trick." Choice C is correct.

5. D — The word list from workout #7 states that *pillage* means "plunder," so choice D is correct. Both words mean to totally destroy an area by looting, stealing, and general destruction.

6. E — The word list from workout #8 states that *reproof* means "criticism." Choice E is correct.

7. B — The word list from workout #9 states that *resplendent* means "gleaming." The word list from workout #3 states that *incandescent* means "glowing." Since *glowing* and *gleaming* are synonyms, *incandescent* and *resplendent* are also synonyms, and choice B is correct.

8. E — The word list states that *impromptu* means "unplanned," so choice E is correct. An impromptu gathering is one that is not planned in advance.

9. C — The word list states that a *memento* is a "souvenir." Therefore, the two words are synonyms, and choice C is correct.

10. A — The word list states that *inanimate* means "lifeless." The word list from workout #5 states that *inert* means "unmoving." Since *lifeless* and *unmoving* are synonyms, *inanimate* and *inert* are also synonyms, and choice A is correct. Notice that *inanimate* and *inert* start the same way (both have the *in-* prefix), so the odds are good that they are related.

Analogies

1. C — The relationship in this question is *opposites*: *slovenly* (unclean) is the opposite of *immaculate* (spotless). *Ambiguous* (unclear) is not related to *steep*, and *quick* is not related to *odious* (offensive), so choices A and B can be ruled out. *Congenial* (friendly) is the opposite of *contemptuous* (disdainful), so choice C is correct. *Appreciated* and *grateful* are similar in

Workout #10

meaning, not opposites, so we can eliminate choice D. *Erratic* (unpredictable) is not related to *unfounded* (without evidence), so choice E is not correct.

2. A — The relationship in this question is *synonyms*: *fallow* and *dormant* both mean "inactive." *Superlative* is a synonym for *outstanding*, so choice A is correct. *Vehement* (insistent) is not related to *ensuing* (following), and *similar* is not related to *deft* (nimble), so choices B and C are not correct. *Incredulous* (skeptical) is the opposite of *believable*, so choice D can be ruled out. *Reputable* (respectable) is not related to *noticeable* (able to be noticed), so choice E can also be eliminated.

3. B — The relationship in this question is *degree*: *decrepit* (weakened) is less extreme than *dilapidated* (crumbling). *Apparent* (obvious) is not related to *precarious* (insecure), so choice A can be ruled out. *Common* is a less extreme form of *rampant* (widespread), so choice B is the correct answer. *Polluted* is not related to *parochial* (unsophisticated), *slothful* (lazy) is not related to *genteel* (elegant), and *vibrant* (energetic) is not related to *momentous* (important), so answer choices C, D, and E are not correct.

4. E — The relationship in this question is *opposites*: *emaciated* (scrawny) is the opposite of *portly* (stout). *Tepid* (lukewarm) is less extreme than *burning*, but those words are not opposites, so choice A is not correct. *Emphatic* (definite) is not the opposite of *hapless* (unlucky), *begrudging* (envious) is not the opposite of *listless* (inactive), and *incendiary* (inflammatory) is not the opposite of *impending* (imminent or about to happen), so choices B, C, and D can be ruled out. *Despondent* (hopeless) is the opposite of *joyful*, so choice E is correct.

5. D — The relationship in this question is *characteristic of*: a characteristic of *gods* is that they are *celestial*. *Gnomes* are not *rabid*, *fairies* are not necessarily *antiquated* (outdated), and *warlocks* aren't always *dubious* (doubtful), so choices A, B, and C are not correct. A *trickster*, however, is always *devious* (deceitful), so choice D is the correct answer. *Mortals* are not necessarily *judicious* (responsible), so choice E can be eliminated.

Reading

1. C — The passage begins with describing how most authors start with a thesis and then try to fill in the details. In the second paragraph, the author contrasts this with how he works, "keeping originality always in view." Therefore, the author believes that most other authors focus too much on thesis and overlook originality. Choice C is correct.

2. B — The author begins by stating "there is a radical error, I think, in the usual mode of constructing a story." Therefore, he is challenging the usual mode (or a process that many writers use), and choice B is correct.

3. A — The author describes the usual mode as having a radical error, so his view of it is negative. We can eliminate choices B and C because *respect* and *curiosity* would be positive. We can also rule out choices D and E because *nonchalance* (lack of concern) and *ambivalence*

(being conflicted) are neither positive nor negative. *Disdain* is definitely *negative*, so choice A is the best answer.

4. D — The passage describes how some elements of a story written in the usual way will "render themselves apparent." Would it make sense to say *sustain* themselves apparent? *Dismiss* themselves apparent? *Loosen* themselves apparent? Or *hinder* themselves apparent? None of these make any sense, so we can rule out choices A, B, C, and E. However, it would make sense to say they *make* themselves apparent, so choice D is the correct answer.

5. E — In the second paragraph, there is no extended story based on another story, so it is not an allegory, and choice A is not correct. There is no figurative language, nothing is foreshadowed to happen in the future, and there is no irony, so choices B, C, and D can be ruled out. However, there is an extended example of how the author goes about his own process, so the paragraph contains exemplification, and choice E is correct.

Math Practice

1. A — In order for a graph to be a function, there cannot be more than 1 *y*-value for every *x*-value. The graph shown for choice A has multiple *y*-values for $x = 1$, so it is not a function. Choice A is correct.

2. D — In order for a relationship to be a function, there can only be one *y*-value for each *x*-value. There can be more than 1 *x*-value for each *y*-value, however. Therefore, there are no restrictions on *m* and choices A, B, and C can be ruled out. However, *q* cannot be equal to one of the *x*-values already given. If *q* was equal to 15 then there would be 2 points with the same *x*-value but a different *y*-value: (15, 10) and (15, 11). This would make the relationship not a function, so choice D is correct.

3. C — The inputs of a function are also the *x*-values. Since the *x*-values for the 3 points are 4, 6, and 9, answer choice C is correct.

4. D — The key to this question is keeping the function notation straight. To find the value of $f(-2)$, we have to substitute in -2 for *x* in the function given. Therefore:

$$f(-2) = 3(-2)^2 - 2(-2) + 7$$

Using the order of operations (and remembering that subtracting a negative number becomes adding the positive), this becomes:

$$f(-2) = 3(4) + 4 + 7 = 23$$

Answer choice D is correct.

Workout #10

5. E — This question is asking us to interpret function notation. The notation $h(0)$ means the value of the function (the height) when $t = 0$. Since this is equal to 32, the height of the ball when $t = 0$ is equal to 32 inches. Answer choice E is correct.

6. B — We can try plugging in some values and seeing what happens. The question says that x must be an integer less than 1. Since the greatest integer less than 1 is 0, we will first plug in 0 for *x*:

    $f(0) = |0 - 3| + 1 = |-3| + 1 = 3 + 1 = 4$

    Now let's try –1:

    $f(-1) = |-1 - 3| + 1 = |-4| + 1 = 4 + 1 = 5$

    Let's also try –2:

    $f(-2) = |-2 - 3| + 1 = |-5| + 1 = 5 + 1 = 6$

    We can see that because absolute value makes all negative values positive, if *x* is an integer less than 1 then the *f(x)* can be greater than or equal to 4. Answer choice C is correct.

7. B — The intersection of sets X and Y includes all numbers that are in both sets X and Y. The area where the circles for X and Y overlap includes 20 and 21 in the top part of the overlap as well as 16 and 25 in the bottom part of the overlap. The bottom 2 numbers are also in set Z, but for this problem that does not matter because set Z is not excluded. The numbers that are in both sets X and Y are 16, 20, 21, 25. Answer choice B is correct.

8. B — If we add together the number of elements in set P and the number of elements in set S, we get 14 + 12, or 26 elements in both sets. However, there are 5 numbers in both sets, so 5 numbers have been double counted. If we subtract 5 from 26, we find that there are 21 unique elements in sets P and S. Answer choice B is correct.

9. A — First we have to identify the intersection of sets A and C. The numbers 4, 5, 7, and 10 show up in both sets A and C. Of those numbers, only 4 and 5 also show up in set B. Answer choice A is correct.

10. E — If we add the number of elements in set M and the number of elements in set N, we get a total of 27 elements. However, the union has only 23 elements. Therefore, 4 elements must have been in both sets. Since the intersection is the number of elements that are in both sets, the intersection contains 4 elements and choice E is correct.

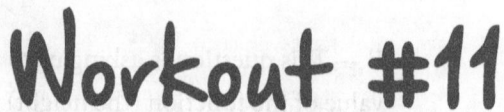

Words to Learn

Below are the words used in Workout 11. Refer back to this list as needed as you move through the lesson.

Celebrate good times

Carouse:	celebrate
Exultation:	rejoicing
Jocular:	joking
Raucous:	rowdy

Words you want to be

Candid:	honest
Debonair:	elegant
Peerless:	unrivaled
Virtuoso:	genius

Words you wouldn't want to be

Monotone:	droning
Complacent:	unconcerned
Deranged:	insane
Inane:	insignificant
Infamous:	notorious
Fastidious:	demanding
Pompous:	arrogant
Inept:	unskilled
Gullible:	naïve

Sad words

| Doleful: | sorrowful |
| Encumbered: | burdened |

Synonyms Practice

1. CONTORT:
   - (A) twist
   - (B) transplant
   - (C) dupe
   - (D) alienate
   - (E) lecture

2. DERANGED:
   - (A) affable
   - (B) disciplined
   - (C) erroneous
   - (D) random
   - (E) insane

3. NULLIFY:
   - (A) quell
   - (B) consolidate
   - (C) resolve
   - (D) invalidate
   - (E) propel

4. AFFECTATION:
   - (A) promotion
   - (B) pretension
   - (C) aversion
   - (D) hesitation
   - (E) tirade

5. ENCUMBERED:
   - (A) resistant
   - (B) deferred
   - (C) burdened
   - (D) tough
   - (E) contemptuous

6. DECREPIT:
   - (A) genteel
   - (B) tame
   - (C) impertinent
   - (D) sprained
   - (E) dilapidated

7. GLOWER:
   - (A) fabricate
   - (B) glare
   - (C) pout
   - (D) relinquish
   - (E) forbid

8. ENSUING:
   - (A) dominant
   - (B) transparent
   - (C) following
   - (D) yearning
   - (E) truthful

9. GULLIBLE:
   - (A) naïve
   - (B) humorous
   - (C) vehement
   - (D) benevolent
   - (E) beloved

10. MOMENTOUS:
    - (A) raucous
    - (B) anguished
    - (C) rabid
    - (D) important
    - (E) thrilling

Analogies Practice

1. Deft is to virtuoso as

    (A) fastidious is to scourge
    (B) derelict is to building
    (C) complacent is to renegade
    (D) overbearing is to guard
    (E) pompous is to snob

2. Eminent is to peerless as

    (A) terse is to congenial
    (B) doleful is to despondent
    (C) fallow is to listless
    (D) jocular is to serious
    (E) fervent is to inept

3. Monotone is to animated as

    (A) slovenly is to immaculate
    (B) tepid is to scalding
    (C) resplendent is to impromptu
    (D) pugnacious is to disagreeable
    (E) considerate is to withdrawn

4. Carousing is to revelry as

    (A) portrait is to reproof
    (B) burrow is to transportation
    (C) disagreement is to rift
    (D) commemoration is to power
    (E) youth is to banter

5. Candid is to furtive as

    (A) treasured is to disheveled
    (B) atrocious is to leisurely
    (C) devious is to ambitious
    (D) vibrant is to inert
    (E) obedient is to dogged

Reading Practice

THERE are wars and rumors of wars in a portion of the territory occupied by the doctrine of organic evolution. All is not working smoothly and well and according to formula. It begins to appear that those men of science who, having derived the doctrine of organic evolution in its modern form from observations on earthworms, on climbing-plants, and on brightly colored birds, and who then straightway applied it blithely to man and his affairs, have made enemies of no small part of the human race.

Line 5

It was all well enough to treat some earthworms, some climbing-plants, and some brightly colored birds as fit, and others as unfit, to survive; but when this distinction is extended over human beings and their economic, social, and political affairs, there is a general pricking-up of ears. The consciously fit look down on the resulting discussions with complacent scorn. The consciously unfit rage and roar loudly; while the unconsciously unfit bestir themselves mightily to overturn the whole theory upon which the distinction between fitness and unfitness rests. If any law of nature makes so absurd a distinction as that, then the offending and obnoxious law must be repealed, and that quickly.

10

The trouble appears to arise primarily from the fact that man does not like what may be termed his evolutionary poor relations. He is willing enough to read about earthworms and climbing-plants and brightly colored birds, but he does not want nature to be making leaps from any of these to him.

15

1. According to the passage, earthworms

    (A) do not follow the rules of fitness and unfitness.
    (B) are not comparable to humans.
    (C) are a reliable species to use in the study of evolution.
    (D) are viewed by some people as following different rules than those of humans.
    (E) have evolved bright colors in order to survive.

2. In the context of the passage, the word "blithely" (line 5) means

    (A) eagerly.
    (B) cautiously.
    (C) angrily.
    (D) respectfully.
    (E) forlornly.

3. Based on information, the author believes that some people do not agree with applying the principles of organic evolution to humans because

   (A) humans are vastly different organisms than earthworms and birds.
   (B) they do not want to admit to a connection between themselves and organisms they view as inferior.
   (C) they distrust the conclusions of scientists.
   (D) there is not enough evidence to prove whether the principles of organic evolution are true.
   (E) there is too much fighting among scientists for the average person to sort out the truth.

4. The author uses the term "evolutionary poor relations" to imply

   (A) that the consciously fit are superior to the unconsciously fit.
   (B) that some groups of people are of higher value than other groups of people.
   (C) that some people do not want to admit their connection to less advanced organisms.
   (D) that the author is better than some of the people he is related to.
   (E) evolution has made some organisms less worthy than other organisms.

5. The tone of the passage can best be described as

   (A) sarcastic.
   (B) informative.
   (C) optimistic.
   (D) informal.
   (E) opinionated.

Workout #11

Math Practice

In this workout, we will work on problems that use the concepts of proportions and ratios as well as questions that use mean, median, and mode.

First, we will try some ratio and proportion questions.

1. In a class, the ratio of girls to boys is 3 to 4. Among the girls, $\frac{1}{3}$ of the students have brown hair. Of these girls, 60% of them also have brown eyes. If there are 3 girls with brown hair and brown eyes, how many students are in the class?

    (A) 3
    (B) 5
    (C) 15
    (D) 20
    (E) 35

2. Everett drives 90 miles in 2 hours and then stops for 1 hour. He then drives another 100 miles in 3 hours. What was his average driving speed, in miles per hour, during his trip?

    (A) 32
    (B) 38
    (C) 40
    (D) 45
    (E) 52

3. The ratio of apples to oranges is $\frac{3}{7}$. If there are a total of 210 apples and oranges, how many oranges are there?

    (A) 30
    (B) 63
    (C) 147
    (D) 280
    (E) 490

4. A store lowers prices by 20% and then increases those prices by 30%. What is the ratio of the original prices to the prices after the increase?

   (A) $\dfrac{1}{10}$

   (B) $\dfrac{4}{5}$

   (C) $\dfrac{9}{10}$

   (D) $\dfrac{25}{26}$

   (E) $\dfrac{11}{10}$

5. The ratio of the length of a piece of rope to the length of a piece of string is 4:3. If 6 inches were cut off of the rope and then 1 inch was cut off of the piece of string, the ratio of their lengths would be 3:4. How much longer is the piece of rope than the piece of string?

   (A) 3 inches
   (B) 4 inches
   (C) 6 inches
   (D) 9 inches
   (E) 12 inches

Now we will work on mean, median, and mode questions. Keep in mind that mean is the average, median is the middle number when the numbers are put in order, and the mode is the number(s) that shows up most often.

6. Laverne has taken 4 tests and has a mean score of 88 on those 4 tests. She has 1 more test to take and this test will count as 2 test grades. She wants a total mean of at least 86 for her test grade. What is the lowest she can score on the last test and have a mean test grade of 86?

   (A) 78
   (B) 82
   (C) 84
   (D) 86
   (E) 88

7. Ms. Roy adds 5 points to each test grade in her class. Which measure of center would be least affected?

    (A) mean
    (B) mode
    (C) midrange
    (D) range
    (E) median

8. A survey was done, asking participants how many siblings they had. The chart below shows the results.

Number of siblings	Number of respondents
0	5
1	6
2	7
3	6
4	4
5	3

    What was the mode of this data?

    (A) 2
    (B) 3
    (C) 4
    (D) 6
    (E) 7

9. Guillermo records the inches of rainfall in his town every day for 1 week. The chart below displays his findings in inches.

Day	Inches of rainfall
Sunday	7.2
Monday	0
Tuesday	1.1
Wednesday	0.9
Thursday	1.2
Friday	0.8
Saturday	1.3

   Which measure of center best represents how many inches of rain fell in his town on 1 day in that week?

   (A) range
   (B) mode
   (C) median
   (D) mean
   (E) outlier

10. Curtis has played 9 basketball games and scored a mean of 12 points per game. If one game is disregarded when he figures out his mean number of points scored, the mean number of points scored rises to 13 points per game. How many points did he score in the game that he disregarded?

    (A) 1
    (B) 4
    (C) 5
    (D) 7
    (E) 8

Workout #11 Answers

Synonyms Practice

1. A — The word list for workout #9 states that *contort* means "twist." Answer choice A is correct. The word *contort* contains the root *con*, which means "with," and *tort*, which means "to twist."

2. E — The word list states that *deranged* means "insane." Answer choice E is correct.

3. D — The word list from workout #9 states that *nullify* means "invalidate." Answer choice D is correct.

4. B — The word list from workout #8 states that *affectation* means "pretension." Answer choice B is correct. Both words mean for a person to put themselves before (or make themselves more important) than other people — remember that *pretension* has the prefix *pre*, which means "before."

5. C — The word list states that *encumbered* means "burdened." Answer choice C is correct.

6. E — The word list from workout #10 states that *decrepit* means "weakened" and *dilapidated* means "crumbling." Since these words can have the same meaning, answer choice E is correct.

7. B — The word list from workout #10 states that *glower* means "glare." Answer choice B is correct.

8. C — The word list from workout #10 states that *ensuing* means "following." Answer choice C is correct.

9. A — The word list states that *gullible* means "naïve." Answer choice A is correct. Both words describe a person who will easily believe something that is not true or easily be tricked.

10. D — The word list from workout #10 states that *momentous* means "important." Answer choice D is correct. You can remember the meaning because something momentous is an important moment.

Analogies Practice

1. E — The relationship in this question is characteristic of: *deft* (skilled) is a characteristic of a *virtuoso* (genius). *Fastidious* (demanding) is not a characteristic of a scourge (plague) and choice A can be ruled out. *Derelict* (abandoned) could describe a building, but it does not describe every building and since *deft* describes every virtuoso, choice B is not correct. A *renegade* (dissenter or rebel) is the opposite of *complacent* (unconcerned), so choice C can be eliminated. *Overbearing* (domineering) could be a characteristic of a guard, but again not

every guard is overbearing, and choice D is not the best answer. Finally, *pompous* (arrogant) is a characteristic of a snob. Answer choice E is correct.

2. B — The relationship in this question is one of degree: *eminent* (distinguished) is less extreme than *peerless* (unrivaled). *Terse* (concise) is not related to *congenial* (friendly) and choice A is not correct. *Doleful* (sorrowful) is less extreme than *despondent* (hopeless) and choice B is the correct answer. *Fallow* and *listless* both mean "inactive," but *listless* is not more extreme than *fallow*, so choice C is not correct. *Jocular* (joking) is the opposite of *serious* and choice D can be eliminated. Finally, *fervent* (enthusiastic) is not related to *inept* (unskilled), so choice E can be ruled out.

3. A — The relationship in this question is opposites: *Monotone* (droning or boring) is the opposite of *animated* (lively). *Slovenly* (unclean) is the opposite of *immaculate* (spotless) and choice A is correct. The relationship in choice B is one of degree - *tepid* (lukewarm) is less extreme than *scalding* (burning hot), so choice B is not correct. *Resplendent* (gleaming) is not related to *impromptu* (unplanned), so choice C can be ruled out. *Pugnacious* is similar to *disagreeable*, only *pugnacious* is more extreme and choice D can be eliminated. Finally, *considerate* is not related to *withdrawn* and choice E is not correct.

4. C — The relationship in this question is synonyms: *carousing* and *revelry* both mean "merrymaking." *Portrait* (picture) is not related to *reproof* (criticism) and *burrow* (den) is not related to *transportation*, so choices A and B can be eliminated. A disagreement is a rift (division) and choice C is the correct answer. Finally, *commemoration* (remembrance) is not related to *power* and *youth* is not related to *banter* (light talk), so choices D and E can be ruled out.

5. D — The relationship in this question is opposites: *candid* (honest) is the opposite of *furtive* (stealthy). *Treasured* is not related to *disheveled* (untidy), *atrocious* (dreadful) is not related to *leisurely*, and *devious* (deceitful) is not related to *ambitious*, so choices A, B, and C are not correct. *Vibrant* (energetic) is the opposite of *inert* (unmoving) and choice D is the correct answer. *Obedient* is not the opposite of *dogged* (determined) and choice E can be ruled out.

Reading Practice

1. D — The last sentence of the passage states that some people are "willing enough to read about earthworms and climbing-plants and brightly colored birds, but he does not want nature to be making leaps from any of these to him." This states that some people don't see the connection between themselves and earthworms. In the context, this also implies that the rules established with earthworms are not applicable to humans. Answer choice D is correct.

2. A — The passage states that those who have made a conclusion from animals and "then straightaway applied it blithely to man and his affairs, have made enemies of no small part of the human race." If the conclusion were applied eagerly, would enemies be made? Yes, so choice A is the correct answer. If the conclusion were applied cautiously, angrily, respectfully,

or forlornly (sorrowfully), then it is less likely that enemies would be made and choices B, C, D, and E do not fit the context as well as choice A, so they are not correct.

3. B — In lines 15-16, the passage states, "the trouble appears to arise primarily from the fact that man does not like what may be termed his evolutionary poor relations." This implies that man does not want to be seen as related to his "poor relations," or organisms that are viewed as inferior. Choice B is correct.

4. C — This question is asking us why a piece of information is included. The main point of the last paragraph is that some people reject the theory of evolution simply because they don't want to admit to being related to some organisms. The term "evolutionary poor relations" is used to emphasize the condescending view that some people take, or that some people don't want to admit that they are related to the "lesser" organisms. Answer choice C best restates this and is the correct answer.

5. E — We can use the process of elimination to answer this question. The tone is definitely not optimistic or informal, so we can rule out choices C and D. Now we have to decide between *sarcastic*, *informative*, and *opinionated*. The author definitely takes a stance rather than just conveying information, so *informative* (choice B) can be eliminated. In deciding between *sarcastic* and *opinionated*, they are similar only opinionated is less extreme. Since this test prefers the less extreme choice, *opinionated* is the better option and choice E is correct.

Math Practice

1. E — We can use the trick of using the last information given first. The question tells us that 3 girls have both brown hair and brown eyes, and this represents 60% of the girls with brown hair. If 3 girls represent 60%, or $\frac{3}{5}$, of the girls with brown hair, then there must be 5 girls with brown hair. The question also tells us that $\frac{1}{3}$ of the girls have brown hair. Therefore, 5 girls represents $\frac{1}{3}$ of the total girls and there must be 15 total girls. Finally, the question first tells us that the ratio of girls to boys is 3 to 4. If there are 15 total girls, then we must multiply each ratio part by 5 to find the actual quantities. Since 4×5 is 20, there must be 20 boys. Since the question asks for the total number of students, we add 15 and 20 to find that there are 35 children in the class. Answer choice E is correct.

2. A — The key to this question is that we have to add up the total miles driven in the trip and then divide it by the total time that the trip took, including the stop. If we add 90 + 100, we find that he drove 190 miles. If we add 2 + 1 + 3, we know that his trip took a total of 6 hours.

Finally, we divide 190 ÷ 6. The answer is $31\frac{2}{3}$ miles per hour. This is not an answer choice, however. We need to round off to 32 and answer choice A is correct.

3. C — The problem states that the ratio of apples to oranges is 3 to 7. However, the problem gives us the total number of apples and oranges. Therefore, we need to convert the part-to-part ratio into a part-to-whole fraction. If we add 3 and 7, we know that there is a total of 10 parts, the fraction of the total that is apples is $\frac{3}{10}$, and the fraction of the total that is oranges is $\frac{7}{10}$. Since the question asks how many oranges there are, we need to find $\frac{7}{10}$ of 210. Remembering that the word *of* signals multiplication, we can perform $\frac{7}{10} \times 210$ to find that there are 147 oranges. Answer choice C is correct.

4. D — One approach is to choose an imaginary item and then figure out the change in price. Let's make the original price of the item $100. If that price was reduced by 20% then the new price would be $80. Now we have to find 30% of $80 and add that in (the trick here is that we find 30% of the new price — $80 — and not 30% of the original price). Since 10% of 80 is 8, 30% of 80 is 24. If we add $24 to $80, the new price is $104. The ratio of the original price to the price after the increase is $\frac{100}{104}$. That is not an answer choice, however, so we have to simplify the fraction. We can do this by dividing both the numerator and denominator by 4, which results in $\frac{25}{26}$. Answer choice D is correct.

5. A — In a ratio, each part of the ratio is multiplied by the same number in order to yield the actual numbers. Therefore, if the ratio of rope to string is 4:3, the actual lengths are $4x$ inches and $3x$ inches, where x is the multiplier. If 6 inches were cut off the rope, the new length is $4x - 6$, and if 1 inch was cut off the string, the new length is $3x - 1$. The next piece of information is that the new ratio of the lengths is 3:4. We can use a fraction to represent this ratio:

$$\frac{4x-6}{3x-1} = \frac{3}{4}$$

We can cross-multiply and the result is $4(4x - 6) = 3(3x - 1)$. Using the distributive property results in $16x - 24 = 9x - 3$. If we subtract $9x$ from each side and add 24, we now have $7x = 21$ and $x = 3$. We have to remember that x was simply the multiplier, however. Therefore, since the length of the rope is $4x$, the actual length is 4(3) or 12 inches. Since the length of the string is $3x$, the actual length is 3(3), or 9 inches. Since the difference between 12 and 9 is 3 inches, answer choice A is correct.

6. B — This is a weighted mean problem. In this type of problem, we use the fact that if mean = sum of numbers ÷ number of numbers, then mean × number of numbers = sum of numbers. There will be a total of 6 test scores since the last test counts twice and she has already taken four tests. If she wants a mean test grade of 86, the sum of her scores needs to be 86 × 6, or 516. She has already taken 4 tests and her mean score on those tests is 88, so the total sum of her scores must be 4 × 88, or 352. If her current total is 352 points and she wants a total of 516 points, she needs 516 − 352, or 164 points from the last test. Since the test counts twice, we divide 164 by 2 and find that she must score an 82 on the final test. Answer choice B is correct.

7. D — This is a conceptual question that does not require calculating. If 5 points are added to each test grade, the mean, mode, midrange, and median would all increase by 5. However, since both the least and the greatest number would both increase by 5, the range would remain unchanged. Answer choice D is correct.

8. A — To answer this question, we have to remember that the chart is not telling us individual data points, but rather how many of each data point there are. If we were to list out the data points used to create this chart, they are 0, 0, 0, 0, 0, 1, 1, 1, 1, 1, 1, and so on. There would be 7 twos in the list of data points and this is more than any other number, so the mode of the data is 2. Answer choice A is correct.

9. C — If we look at the data, most of the data points are clustered around 1 inch of rain. There is an outlier (7.2 inches), however, that would have an outsized effect on the range and mean, causing them to be much higher than the rain on $\frac{6}{7}$ of the days. We can eliminate choices A and D. We can also eliminate choice E because the outlier by definition does not accurately represent most of the data. The mode only tells us the number that shows up most frequently and there are no numbers that show up more than once in this data set, so we can easily rule out choice B. The median best represents the data because it falls in the middle of most of the data points and is not greatly increased by one outlier. Choice C is correct.

10. B — This is a weighted mean question. In this type of problem, we use the fact that if mean = sum of numbers ÷ number of numbers, then mean × number of numbers = sum of numbers. In the original calculation, there were 9 scores and the mean of them was 12 points, so the sum must have been 12 × 9, or 108 points. When one game was disregarded, there were 8 games with a mean score of 13 points. We can multiply 8 × 13 and find that there would then be a total of 104 points. Since the difference in the sum of scores is 108 − 104 or 4 points when the game is removed, 4 points must have been scored in that game. Answer choice B is correct.

Workout #12

Words to Learn

Below are the words used in Workout 12. Refer back to this list as needed as you move through the lesson.

How many?

Devoid:	without
Influx:	inpouring
Myriad:	many
Negligible:	paltry
Permeate:	saturate
Glut:	overfill

Things that go together

Affix:	attach
Assimilate:	conform
Composite:	combined
Converse:	discuss
Discourse:	conversation
Kindred:	related
Liaison:	contact

Go off course

Diffuse:	spread
Disperse:	spread
Meander:	wander
Vagrant:	wandering

Smart folks

Adroit:	skillful
Astute:	perceptive (smart, but not necessarily book smart)
Preeminent:	superior (better than anyone else)

Synonyms Practice

1. VIRTUOSO:
   - (A) vocation
   - (B) memento
   - (C) arrangement
   - (D) scruple
   - (E) genius

2. CONVERSE:
   - (A) fetter
   - (B) discuss
   - (C) breach
   - (D) sway
   - (E) accost

3. LIAISON:
   - (A) contact
   - (B) theme
   - (C) fervor
   - (D) pardon
   - (E) apex

4. DOLEFUL:
   - (A) slovenly
   - (B) adulterated
   - (C) depressed
   - (D) joking
   - (E) vague

5. ANTIQUATED:
   - (A) precarious
   - (B) parched
   - (C) invigorating
   - (D) outdated
   - (E) ignorant

6. ACQUISITION:
   - (A) possession
   - (B) knowledge
   - (C) bolster
   - (D) hurdle
   - (E) burden

7. ABRIDGE:
   - (A) obliterate
   - (B) shorten
   - (C) layer
   - (D) affix
   - (E) concoct

8. SATURATE:
   - (A) defer
   - (B) install
   - (C) permeate
   - (D) dream
   - (E) refute

9. ASSAIL:
   - (A) deplete
   - (B) narrate
   - (C) incriminate
   - (D) vary
   - (E) berate

10. MEANDER:
    - (A) vibrate
    - (B) allay
    - (C) note
    - (D) wander
    - (E) taint

Analogies Practice

1. Myriad is to negligible as
   - (A) thorough is to tepid
   - (B) debonair is to clumsy
   - (C) vibrant is to hurried
   - (D) inanimate is to inert
   - (E) dreadful is to responsive

2. Proficient is to adroit as
   - (A) supple is to flexible
   - (B) dizzy is to swift
   - (C) good is to preeminent
   - (D) fallow is to raucous
   - (E) emphatic is to covetous

3. Devoid is to glut as
   - (A) tangible is to economical
   - (B) candid is to honesty
   - (C) whimsical is to forbearance
   - (D) condescending is to revulsion
   - (E) dispersed is to consolidation

4. Unfounded is to rumor as
   - (A) complacent is to exultation
   - (B) pleasant is to influx
   - (C) kindred is to drift
   - (D) radical is to renegade
   - (E) astute is to track

5. Tawdry is to uncouth as
   - (A) pompous is to overconfident
   - (B) streaked is to refuted
   - (C) organized is to fastidious
   - (D) drowsy is to contemptible
   - (E) visible is to eradicated

Reading Practice

> All the perceptions of the human mind resolve themselves into two distinct kinds, which I shall call IMPRESSIONS and IDEAS. The difference betwixt these consists in the degrees of force and liveliness, with which they strike upon the mind, and make their way into our thought or consciousness. Those perceptions, which enter with most force and violence, we may name
>
> Line 5 impressions: and under this name I comprehend all our sensations, passions and emotions, as they make their first appearance in the soul. By ideas I mean the faint images of these in thinking and reasoning; such as, for instance, are all the perceptions excited by the present discourse, excepting only those which arise from the sight and touch, and excepting the immediate pleasure or uneasiness it may occasion. I believe it will not be very necessary to employ many words in
>
> 10 explaining this distinction. Every one of himself will readily perceive the difference betwixt feeling and thinking. The common degrees of these are easily distinguished; though it is not impossible but in particular instances they may very nearly approach to each other. Thus in sleep, in a fever, in madness, or in any very violent emotions of soul, our ideas may approach to our impressions, as on the other hand it sometimes happens, that our impressions are so faint and low, that we cannot
>
> 15 distinguish them from our ideas. But notwithstanding this near resemblance in a few instances, they are in general so very different, that no-one can make a scruple to rank them under distinct heads, and assign to each a peculiar name to mark the difference.

1. The author's primary purpose in writing this passage is to describe

    (A) how emotions affect intellectual decisions.
    (B) the different categories of human perception.
    (C) how similar thinking and feeling can often be.
    (D) how impressions are informed.
    (E) a common error that is made when considering the differences between thinking and feeling.

2. According to the passage, a main difference between impressions and ideas is that impressions are

    (A) more likely to be inaccurate than ideas.
    (B) received in a subtler manner than ideas.
    (C) frequently brought about by a fever or madness.
    (D) ideas that have had time to develop more fully.
    (E) perceived with a much greater force than ideas.

3. The author suggests that most people understand that
   (A) thinking and feeling often overlap.
   (B) impressions are frequently formed from an emotional response.
   (C) it is not necessary to differentiate between impressions and ideas.
   (D) there are very few occasions in which thinking and feeling are tough to differentiate.
   (E) ideas can easily be changed by impressions.

4. The author uses the phrase, "in sleep, in madness, or in any very violent emotions of our soul," in order to emphasize
   (A) that only in extreme cases are ideas similar to impressions.
   (B) the exceptional nature of impressions.
   (C) how strong emotion generally forms impressions.
   (D) the importance of differentiating between ideas and impressions.
   (E) how similar ideas and impressions can be.

5. As used in line 16, the word "scruple" most nearly means
   (A) impression.
   (B) support.
   (C) hesitation.
   (D) deceit.
   (E) suddenness.

Math Practice

1. A teacher is lining up 6 students in the hallway. If there are 2 students who cannot stand next to each other in line, in how many different orders can the teacher line up the students?

    (A) 24
    (B) 48
    (C) 360
    (D) 480
    (E) 720

2. A cone has a radius that is the same length as its height. If the volume of this cone is 9π inches^3, what is the diameter of the cone?

    $$V = \frac{1}{3}\pi r^2 h$$

    (A) 3 cm
    (B) 3π cm
    (C) 6 cm
    (D) 6π cm
    (E) 9 cm

3. In the addition problem shown below, the triangle and square represent unique single digits.

    ```
        3 2 7
    +   1 4 △
    ─────────
        4 □ 3
    ```

    What digit does the square represent?

    (A) 6
    (B) 7
    (C) 8
    (D) 9
    (E) 0

4. How many times larger is the number 5^4 than the number 5^{-2}?

    (A) 2
    (B) 4
    (C) 6
    (D) 5^2
    (E) 5^6

5. The midpoint of line segment $\overline{BC}$ is (–4, 2). If the coordinates of point B are (–5, 6), what are the coordinates of point C?

   (A) (–6, 10)
   (B) (–4, –3)
   (C) (–3, –2)
   (D) (–3, 2)
   (E) (–2, –2)

6. Ramona sold 3 candy bars on her first day. On her second day, she sold 6 candy bars and on her third day she sold 9 candy bars. If this pattern continues and she makes $0.60 per candy bar, how much money will she have made after 30 days?

   (A) $418.50
   (B) $837
   (C) $1,255.50
   (D) $1,395
   (E) $2,790

7. In the 6-digit number 61X,90Y, X and Y represent digits. If 61X,90Y is divisible by 15, which could NOT be the value of the sum X + Y?

   (A) 2
   (B) 5
   (C) 8
   (D) 10
   (E) 11

8. Raul hits a baseball and the height of the ball, y, in cm, is related to the time, x, in seconds, after Raul has hit the ball. It is modeled by the function $y = -9x^2 + 27x + 36$. After how many seconds will the ball hit the ground?

   (A) 1
   (B) 2
   (C) 4
   (D) 8
   (E) 12

9. Which expression is equivalent to $\frac{x-3}{2} - \left(x - \frac{1}{4}\right)$?

   (A) $\frac{-5-2x}{4}$

   (B) $\frac{-1}{2}$

   (C) $\frac{x-2}{4}$

   (D) $\frac{-2-x}{4}$

   (E) $\frac{2x-4}{4}$

10. A relation is defined by the ordered pairs $(3, b)$, $(8, 16)$, $(m, 10)$, and $(7, 14)$. Which value would prevent the relation from being a function?

    (A) $m = 10$
    (B) $m = 8$
    (C) $b = 16$
    (D) $b = 6$
    (E) $b = 3$

11. The mean height of a group of 3 students is 52 inches. The mean height of another group of 5 students is 48 inches. What is the mean height of all 8 students, in inches?

    (A) 48
    (B) 49.5
    (C) 50
    (D) 50.5
    (E) 52

Workout #12 Answers

Synonyms Practice

1. E — The word list from workout #11 states that *virtuoso* means "genius." Answer choice E is correct.

2. B — The word list states that *converse* means "discuss." Choice B is correct. To help remember this meaning, remember that the meaning of the prefix *con-* is "together" or "with" and to *converse* is to discuss with someone.

3. A — The word list states that *liaison* means "contact." Answer choice A is correct.

4. C — The word list from workout #11 states that *doleful* means "sorrowful." Since *depressed* is a synonym for *sorrowful*, answer choice C is correct.

5. D — The word list from workout #10 states that *antiquated* means "outdated" and choice D is correct. You can remember this meaning because the word *antiquated* is similar to *antique*, which describes something that is old, or outdated.

6. A — The word list from workout #7 states that *acquisition* means "possession." Answer choice A is correct. The word *acquisition* is related to the word *acquire*, which means "to get something," so an acquisition is something you have gotten.

7. B — The word list from workout #6 states that *abridge* means "shorten." Answer choice B is correct.

8. C — The word list states that *permeate* means "saturate." This question asks for the meaning of *saturate* and *permeate* (choice C) is the correct answer. This question is a reminder that as you learn words, you have to know them backward and forward! The actual test could ask for the word you have learned or the definition of the word you have learned.

9. E — The word list from workout #6 states that *assail* means "attack." *Berate* means "to verbally attack a person," so choice E is the best answer and is correct.

10. D — The word list states that *meander* means "wander." Choice D is correct.

Analogies Practice

1. B — The relationship in this question is one of opposites: *myriad* (many) is the opposite of *negligible* (paltry or a small amount). *Thorough* is not related to *tepid* (lukewarm) and choice A is not correct. *Debonair* (elegant) is the opposite of *clumsy* and choice B is the correct answer. *Vibrant* (energetic) is not the opposite of *hurried*, *inanimate* (lifeless) is similar in meaning to

inert (unmoving), and *dreadful* (horrific) is not related to *responsive*. Since choices C, D, and E do not have words that are opposite in meaning, they can be eliminated.

2. C — The relationship in this question is one of degree: *proficient* (able to do something) is less extreme than *adroit* (skilled at doing something). Answer choice A gives two words that are similar in meaning, but since *flexible* is not more extreme than *supple*, answer choice A can be eliminated. *Dizzy* and *swift* are not related, so choice B can also be ruled out. If we look at choice C, an extreme form of *good* is *preeminent* (superior to others) and choice C is correct. *Fallow* (inactive) is the opposite of *raucous* (rowdy) and choice D can be eliminated. *Emphatic* (definite) is not related to *covetous* (desiring something) and choice E is not correct.

3. E — The relationship here is one where the first word describes the opposite of the second word: *devoid* (lacking) is the opposite of a *glut* (overfill or too much of something). *Tangible* (able to be touched) is not related to *economical* (frugal), *candid* (honest) would describe *honesty*, *whimsical* (fanciful) is not related to *forbearance* (self-control), and *condescending* (patronizing) is a less extreme form of *revulsion* (dislike). Since answer choices A, B, C, and D do not contain words where the first word describes the opposite of the second word, they are not correct. *Dispersed* (spread out) does describe the opposite of *consolidation* (combination) and choice E is the correct answer.

4. D — The relationship in this question is characteristic of: *unfounded* (unjustified) is a characteristic of a *rumor*. *Complacent* (uncaring) is not a characteristic of *exultation* (extreme joy), *pleasant* is unrelated to *influx* (flowing in), and *kindred* (related) is not related to *drift*. Choices A, B, and C can be ruled out. *Radical* (extreme) is a characteristic of a *renegade* (dissenter or rebel) and choice D is the correct answer. *Astute* (perceptive) is not related to *track* and choice E can be ruled out.

5. A – The relationship in this question is synonyms: *tawdry* and *uncouth* both mean "cheap" or "tasteless." *Pompous* and *overconfident* are also synonyms, so choice A is the correct answer. *Streaked* (having streaks) and *refuted* (proven false) are not related so we can eliminate choice B. Choice C is tempting because the words are similar in meaning. However, *fastidious* is a more extreme form of *organized* and *uncouth* is not more extreme than *tawdry*, so choice C can be ruled out. *Drowsy* (sleepy) is not related to *contemptible* (shameful) and *visible* (can be seen) is not related to *eradicated* (eliminated), so choices D and E are not correct.

Reading Practice

1. B — The passage begins by stating that there are two types of perceptions: impressions and ideas. The passage then goes on to describe what makes the two types of perceptions unique and the rare times that they overlap. The primary purpose is therefore to describe the different categories of human perception and choice B is correct.

2. E — The passage states, "the difference betwixt these consists in the degrees of force and liveliness… Those perceptions, which enter with most force and violence, we may name impressions." This is best restated by choice E, so it is the correct answer.

3. D — In lines 10-12, the author discusses most people: "Every one of himself will readily perceive the difference betwixt feeling and thinking. The common degrees of these are easily distinguished; though it is not impossible but in particular instance they may very nearly approach to each other." This is suggesting that most people can differentiate between thinking and feeling but also that it is not impossible that the two may nearly approach each other. The statement, "it is not impossible," suggests that the occurrence is rare where thinking and feeling can't be differentiated between. Answer choice D best restates this and is correct.

4. A — The author states that usually people can differentiate between thoughts (ideas) and feelings (impressions) except for in particular instances. The author then lists "in sleep, in madness, or in any very violent emotions of our soul" as examples. Therefore, he is showing that it is only in rare, or extreme, cases that the two cannot be differentiated between. Answer choice A best restates this and is correct.

5. C — In lines 15-16, the passage states, "no-one can make a scruple to rank them under distinct heads." He is saying that no one would have any doubt or hesitation about considering ideas and impressions as distinct categories. Scruple must therefore mean support and choice B is correct.

Math Practice

1. D — This is a very hard probability question. Let's start by figuring out how many possibilities there are if there were no restrictions on who could stand next to whom. There are 6 possibilities for which child is first in line, and then 5 possibilities for which child is second (we already chose 1 child to go first), and then 4 possibilities for which child is third (we already chose children to go in first and second place), and so on. Therefore, we multiply the possibilities for each spot in line, or $6 \times 5 \times 4 \times 3 \times 2 \times 1$, and find that there are 720 possible combinations if there are no restrictions. Now we will randomly assign the students who cannot stand next to each other. Let's say our students are A, B, C, D, E, and F and students A and B cannot be next to each other. We need to figure out how many of our total combinations have A and B next to each other. Let's say A is first in line and B is second in line. There would be 4 spots left and 4 students, so the number of combinations that have A, B, and then some other students are $4 \times 3 \times 2 \times 1$ or 24 combinations. There are 24 combinations we can take out that include A first and B second. Now let's think about the combinations to be eliminated if A is second in line. In this case, we have to rule out combinations that have B first and A second as well as combinations that have A second and B third. If B is first and A is second, then we have $4 \times 3 \times 2 \times 1$, or 24, combinations for the remaining spots. If B is second and A is third, then we also have 24 combinations to be eliminated.

This pattern continues:

    If A is first, there are 24 combinations that can be eliminated.

    If A is second, there are 48 combinations that either have B right before or right after A.

    If A is third, there are 48 combinations that either have B right before or right after A.

    If A is fourth, there are 48 combinations that either have B right before or right after A.

    If A is fifth, there are 48 combinations that either have B right before or right after A.

    If A is sixth, there are 24 combinations that have B right before A (it can't come after A if A is last in line).

If we add these together, we find that there are 240 combinations out of a total of 720 that have A and B together. If we subtract these combinations that are not allowed (240) from the total number of combinations (720), we find that there are 480 combinations that work. Choice D is correct.

2.   C — The volume of a cone is $\frac{1}{3}\pi r^2 h$, where r is the radius and h is the height. However, the problem tells us that the height is the same as the radius, so we can substitute in r for h and the formula becomes $\frac{1}{3}\pi r^2(r)$ or $\frac{1}{3}\pi r^3$. Now we can set this equal to 9π: $\frac{1}{3}\pi r^3 = 9\pi$. If we multiply both sides by 3 the equation becomes $\pi r^3 = 27\pi$. We can divide both sides by π and the result is $r^3 = 27$. Since $3^3 = 27$, the radius is equal to 3. To find the diameter, we simply double the radius and find that the diameter is equal to 6. Choice C is correct.

3.   B — This is a reasoning problem. We can see from the first column on the left that 7 plus some number has an answer with 3 as the units digit. Since we can't add something to 7 and get just 3 as an answer, we know that 7 must add with some number to get 13. Since 7 + 6 is equal to 13, we know that the triangle is 6 and we would write a 3 under the digits 7 and 6 and then carry the 1 to the next column. If we add the 1 that was carried, 2, and 4, then the total for that column is 7. The square must be equal to 7 and choice B is correct.

4.   E — The question is asking us to identify what we need to multiply 5^{-2} by in order for the result to be 5^4. We can represent this as $5^{-2} \times$ ____ $= 5^4$. If we remember that when we multiply 2 numbers with the same base, we add the exponents (and notice that 5^{-2} and 5^4 have the same base), then our problem becomes $5^{-2} \times 5^x = 5^4$. Since $-2 + 6 = 4$, we know that x must be equal to 6 and 5^{-2} is multiplied by 5^6 in order to produce 5^4. Answer choice E is correct.

5. C — To find the midpoint of a segment, the general formula is:

$$\left(\frac{x_1+x_2}{2}, \frac{y_1+y_2}{2}\right)$$

where (x_1, y_1) and (x_2, y_2) are the endpoints. Essentially, we take the mean of the x-coordinates and the mean of the y-coordinates to find the midpoint. This problem is tricky because we have the midpoint and one endpoint and need to solve for the other endpoint. We can substitute in the coordinates given for point B and the midpoints:

$$\frac{-5+x}{2} = -4$$

$$-5 + x = -8$$

$$x = -3$$

$$\frac{6+y}{2} = 2$$

$$6 + y = 4$$

$$y = -2$$

The coordinates of the other endpoint (or point C) are (–3, –2). Answer choice C is correct.

6. B — This question requires us to use the formula for sum of a sequence:

$$S_n = \frac{n(a_1 + a_n)}{2}$$

where s_n is the sum of n terms, a_1 is the first term in the sequence and a_n is the last term in the sequence. (This formula comes from the formula for mean. In a sequence, the mean of all the terms is the same as the mean of the first and last term. Therefore, if we multiply the mean of the first and last terms by the number of terms, we will get the sum of the terms.) In this sequence, there are 30 terms. The first term is 3 and the pattern is that we multiply the ordinal number of the term by 3 to get the value of that term. Therefore, on Day 30, we multiply 3 × 30 and find that 90 candy bars are sold. If we substitute into the formula,

$$S_n = \frac{30(3+90)}{2}$$

Workout #12

dividing both the top and the bottom by 2 results in $s_n = 15(93)$. Since $15 \times 93 = 1{,}395$, Ramona sold 1,395 candy bars. However, she makes only $0.60 from each candy bar, so we need to multiply 1,395 by $0.60 to find out how much money she makes. Since $1{,}395 \times \$0.60$ is $837, answer choice B is correct.

7. D — The key to this question is that if a number is divisible by 15, it is also divisible by its factors — 3 and 5. If a number is divisible by 3, the sum of the digits is also divisible by 3. If we add the digits in this case, the sum is $6 + 1 + X + 9 + 0 + Y$, which combines to $16 + X + Y$. Therefore $16 + X + Y$ must be divisible by 3. If $X + Y$ was equal to 2, $16 + 2$ is equal to 18, which is divisible by 3, and the whole thing could be divisible by 15, so choice A is not correct (note: in order to be divisible by 5, the number simply must end in 0 or 5 and since Y could be 0 in any combination of X and Y, we can ignore whether or not the number is divisible by 5 as well). If we continue with choice B, $16 + 5 = 21$, which is divisible by 3 and we can rule out choice B. If we look at choice C, $16 + 8 = 24$, which is divisible by 3 and we can eliminate choice C. If we substitute in 10 for the sum of $X + Y$, we get $16 + 10$, which is equal to 26. Since 26 is not divisible by 3, the whole number cannot be divisible by 15 and answer choice D is the correct answer. Finally, $16 + 11 = 27$, which is divisible by 3, so the whole number could be divisible by 15 and choice E is not correct.

8. C — When the ball hits the ground, the height will be 0. We can substitute in 0 for the height and our equation becomes $0 = -9x^2 + 27x + 36$. We can divide both sides by -9 and the equation becomes $0 = x^2 - 3x - 4$. We can factor this to $(x - 4)(x + 1) = 0$. Both 4 and -1 would make this equation true. However, we have to remember that x represents time and we cannot have a negative amount of time. Therefore, 4 is the only possible answer. Answer choice C is correct.

9. A — In order to combine the terms in the expression given, we need to find a common denominator. First, however, we need to get rid of the parentheses. We can do this by distributing the negative sign and the expression is now:

$$\frac{x-3}{2} - x + \frac{1}{4}$$

Now we can establish a common denominator. In this case, the common denominator is 4. We can multiply both the numerator and denominator of the first term by 2/2, the numerator and denominator of the second term by 4, and we don't have to do anything to the last term. We can do this because if we multiply both the numerator and denominator by the same number, we don't change the value of the term.

Our expression is now:

$$\frac{2}{2}\left(\frac{x-3}{2}\right) - \frac{4x}{4} + \frac{1}{4}$$

If we distribute, the expression becomes:

$$\frac{2x-6}{4} - \frac{4x}{4} + \frac{1}{4}$$

Now we combine the numerators since the denominator is 4 for all of the terms:

$$\frac{2x-6-4x+1}{4}$$

Finally, we combine like terms and the result is:

$$\frac{-5-2x}{4}$$

Answer choice A is correct.

10. B — In order for a set of points not to be a function, there has to be more than one *y*-value for a single *x*-value. If $m = 8$, then there would be the ordered pair (8, 16) as well as the ordered pair (8, 10). In this scenario, a single *x*-coordinate (8) would have two *y*-values (16 and 10), so the points would not be a function. Choice B is correct.

11. B — This question is asking us to find a weighted mean. In order to do this, we find the sum of each group, add them together to find the sum of the entire group, and divide by the total number of numbers. To find the sum of each group, we multiply the mean by the number of numbers. Therefore, the sum of the heights of the 3 students with a mean height of 52 inches is 3×52, or 156 inches. The sum of the heights of the 5 students with a mean height of 48 inches is 5×48 or 240 inches. If we add these together, the sum is $156 + 240$, or 396 inches. Since there are 8 students, we divide 396 by 8 and find a total mean of 49.5 inches for all 8 students. Answer choice B is correct.

Workout #13

Words to Learn

Below are the words used in Workout 13. Refer back to this list as needed as you move through the lesson.

Nice people

Altruistic:	generous
Amicable:	friendly
Credulous:	trusting
Amenable:	willing
Deference:	respect
Laudable:	praiseworthy

Just boring

Banal:	unoriginal
Insipid:	bland
Mundane:	ordinary
Prosaic:	dull
Vapid:	uninteresting

To make less

Debase:	devalue (to reduce the value of)
Relegate:	demote (to put in a lesser position)
Impasse:	deadlock
Impede:	obstruct

Doesn't play well

Beguile:	trick
Crass:	gross
Coerce:	force
Connive:	conspire
Flippant:	disrespectful
Animosity:	hatred

Synonyms Practice

1. COERCE:
   - (A) force
   - (B) humiliate
   - (C) obliterate
   - (D) trample
   - (E) banter

2. KINDRED:
   - (A) flawed
   - (B) bare
   - (C) related
   - (D) inanimate
   - (E) slovenly

3. INSIPID:
   - (A) adulterated
   - (B) vapid
   - (C) quaint
   - (D) wan
   - (E) meager

4. EMACIATED:
   - (A) inane
   - (B) mortified
   - (C) gullible
   - (D) scrawny
   - (E) automatic

5. VIBRANT:
   - (A) gullible
   - (B) ragged
   - (C) deft
   - (D) rapid
   - (E) invigorated

6. BEGUILE:
   - (A) trick
   - (B) apologize
   - (C) triumph
   - (D) glower
   - (E) concoct

7. IMPASSE:
   - (A) myriad
   - (B) satire
   - (C) gauntlet
   - (D) bargain
   - (E) standoff

8. DEFERENCE:
   - (A) liaison
   - (B) banner
   - (C) cooperation
   - (D) respect
   - (E) victory

9. RAMPANT:
   - (A) impending
   - (B) complex
   - (C) prevalent
   - (D) overbearing
   - (E) gracious

10. CAROUSE:
    - (A) gaze
    - (B) celebrate
    - (C) serve
    - (D) prosper
    - (E) incriminate

Analogies Practice

Workout #13

1. Debase is to depreciate as

    (A) deranged is to debonair
    (B) disheveled is to decrepit
    (C) disperse is to diffuse
    (D) derelict is to dubious
    (E) doleful is to devious

2. Affable is to amicable as

    (A) jocular is to morbid
    (B) negligible is to paltry
    (C) terse is to frosty
    (D) spectacular is to pugnacious
    (E) playful is to robust

3. Flippant is to contemptuous as

    (A) dubious is to erroneous
    (B) peerless is to nondescript
    (C) ponderous is to candid
    (D) equivalent is to virtual
    (E) erratic is to celestial

4. Altruistic is to benefactor as

    (A) vagrant is to youngster
    (B) prosaic is to scourge
    (C) superlative is to athlete
    (D) conniving is to schemer
    (E) brawny is to kindred

5. Assimilate is to rebel as

    (A) refute is to judge
    (B) resort is to sanction
    (C) mystify is to perplex
    (D) converse is to pillage
    (E) reminisce is to forget

Reading Practice

Some men are like the twang of a bow-string. Hardy was like that—short, lithe, sunburned, vivid. Into the lives of Jarrick, Hill, and myself, old classmates of his, he came and went in the fashion of one of those queer winds that on a sultry day in summer blow unexpectedly up a city street out of nowhere. His comings excited us; his goings left us refreshed and a little vaguely
Line 5   discontented. So many people are gray. Hardy gave one a shock of color, as do the deserts and the mountains he inhabited. It was not particularly what he said—he didn't talk much—it was his appearance, his direct, a trifle fierce, gestures, the sense of mysterious lands that pervaded him. One never knew when he was coming to New York and one never knew how long he was going to stay; he just appeared, was very busy with mining companies for a while, sat about clubs in the late
10   afternoon, and then, one day, he was gone.

Sometimes he came twice in a year; oftener, not for two or three years at a stretch. When he did come we gave him a dinner—that is, Jarrick, Hill, and myself. And it was rather an occasion. We would procure a table in the gayest restaurant we could find, near, but not too near, the music—Hill it was who first suggested this as a dramatic bit of incongruity between Hardy and the frequenters
15   of Broadway—and the most exotic food obtainable, for a good part of his time Hardy, we knew, lived upon camp fare. Then we would try to make him tell about his experiences. Usually he wouldn't. Impersonally, he was entertaining about South Africa, about the Caucasus, about Alaska, Mexico, anywhere you care to think; but concretely he might have been an illustrated lecture for all he mentioned himself. He was passionately fond of abstract argument. "Y' see," he would explain,
20   "I don't get half as much of this sort of thing as I want. Of course, one does run across remarkable people—now, I met a cow-puncher once who knew Keats by heart—but as a rule I deal only with material things, mines and prospects and assays and that sort of thing."

1. Based on the passage, Hardy's personality can best be characterized as

    (A) aloof and condescending.
    (B) reserved and observant.
    (C) unpredictable and jovial.
    (D) mysterious and adventurous.
    (E) refined and demanding.

2. According to the passage, the narrator knows Hardy because they

    (A) met while traveling.
    (B) attended school together.
    (C) frequently dined at the same restaurants.
    (D) worked together in the past.
    (E) were raised in the same town.

3. The narrator describes Hardy as "like the twang of a bow-string," because Hardy

    (A) brought an energy with him that stood out from the narrator's normal surroundings.
    (B) was given to sudden outbursts.
    (C) was frequently loud and gregarious when out in public.
    (D) had musical talent.
    (E) talked in a manner that reminded the narrator of a bow-string.

4. The narrator describes Hardy's stories as

    (A) entertaining but sometimes exaggerating the truth.
    (B) hard to understand.
    (C) vaguely unsettling.
    (D) full of conflicting information.
    (E) factual but impersonal in nature.

5. When describing Hardy, the narrator uses as tone that can best be described as

    (A) irritated.
    (B) appreciative.
    (C) humorous.
    (D) sullen.
    (E) reverent.

Math Practice

1. Peter is flipping a coin 3 times. It can land on either heads or tails each time. If it lands on heads the first 2 times that Peter tosses the coin, what is the probability that it will land on heads the third time that Peter tosses the coin?

    (A) $\dfrac{1}{9}$

    (B) $\dfrac{1}{6}$

    (C) $\dfrac{1}{3}$

    (D) $\dfrac{1}{4}$

    (E) $\dfrac{1}{2}$

2. If h represents the height of a triangle, and the base is 4 cm less than the height, which expression represents the area of the triangle, in cm²?

    (A) $\dfrac{1}{2}h^2 - 2h$

    (B) $\dfrac{1}{2}h^2 - 4h$

    (C) $h^2 - 2h$

    (D) $h^2 - 4h$

    (E) $2h^2 - 4h$

3. If the product of $3h$ and the sum of h and 5 is equal to -12, which of the following could be the value of h?

    (A) -3
    (B) -1
    (C) 1
    (D) 3
    (E) 4

4. $\sqrt[3]{x^{12}y^{10}}$

   (A) $360xy$
   (B) x^6y^5
   (C) x^9y^7
   (D) $x^4y^3\sqrt[3]{y}$
   (E) y^4y^3

5. The rectangle PQRS, in the coordinate grid below, is rotated 180° about the origin and then translated down 2 units to form rectangle P'Q'R'S'.

   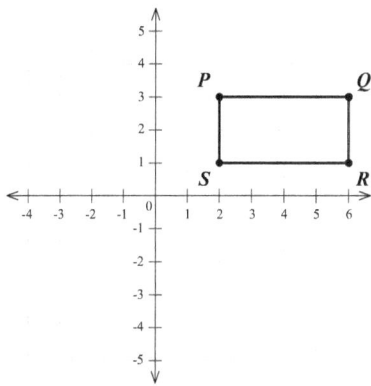

   What are the coordinates of Q'?

   (A) (−6, −5)
   (B) (−6, −3)
   (C) (−6, −1)
   (D) (−6, 1)
   (E) (−6, 5)

6. 4, 2, −4, −2, 4, 2, −4, −2, …

   If the pattern above continues indefinitely and 4 is the first term in the sequence, which of the following terms would have a value of −4?

   (A) 41st
   (B) 42nd
   (C) 43rd
   (D) 44th
   (E) 45th

7. In the inequality $nx - 3 < -12$, which value of n will result in the solution $x < -3$?

   (A) -3

   (B) $-\dfrac{1}{3}$

   (C) $\dfrac{1}{3}$

   (D) 3

   (E) 9

8. Which expression is equivalent to $-10x^2 + x + 3$?

   (A) $(2x + 1)(5x - 3)$
   (B) $(2x - 1)(5x - 3)$
   (C) $(2x - 1)(5x + 3)$
   (D) $-(2x - 1)(5x + 3)$
   (E) $-(2x + 1)(5x - 3)$

9. Simplify: $(6x^3 - 3x^2 + 2) - (3x^3 + 2x + 5)$

   (A) $3x^3 - 3x^2 + 2x - 3$
   (B) $3x^3 - 3x^2 - 2x - 3$
   (C) $3x^3 - 6x^2 + 2x - 3$
   (D) $3x^3 - 6x^2 - 2x - 3$
   (E) $3x^3 - 3x^2 - 2x + 7$

10. What is the value of $f(-4)$ if $f(x) = -2x^2 - 3x - 2$?

    (A) -46
    (B) -22
    (C) 18
    (D) 42
    (E) 46

11. The ratio of red marbles to green marbles in a bag is 3:5. If 2 red marbles were removed from the bag and 10 green marbles were added, the ratio of red to green marbles would become 5:11. How many marbles are in the bag?

    (A) 27
    (B) 45
    (C) 65
    (D) 72
    (E) 80

Workout #13 Answers

Synonyms Practice

1. A — The word list states that *coerce* means "force." Answer choice A is correct.

2. C — The word list states from workout #12 that *kindred* means "related." Answer choice C is correct. You can use a related word to remember this — perhaps you have heard family members referred to as *kin*.

3. B — The word list states that *insipid* means "bland" and *vapid* means "uninteresting." Since *bland* and *uninteresting* are synonyms, *insipid* and *vapid* have the same meaning, and choice B is correct.

4. D — The word list from workout #10 states that *emaciated* means "scrawny," so choice B is correct. Both words describe someone who is severely underweight.

5. E — The word list from workout #10 states that *vibrant* means "energetic." The word list from workout #5 states that *invigorating* means "energizing." Since *invigorated* is another form of the same word, we know that *energetic*, *vibrant*, and *invigorated* are synonyms. Answer choice E is correct.

6. A — The word list states that *beguile* means "trick." Answer choice A is correct.

7. E — The word list states that *impasse* means "deadlock." A *deadlock* describes a situation where no agreement can be reached. A *standoff* also describes this type of situation, so choice E is the correct answer.

8. D — The word list states that *deference* means "respect." Answer choice D is correct.

9. C — The word list from workout #9 states that *rampant* means "widespread." *Prevalent* also means "widespread," so choice C is the correct answer.

10. B — The word list from workout #11 states that *carouse* means "celebrate," so choice B is correct.

Analogies Practice

1. C — The relationship in this question is synonyms: *debase* and *depreciate* both mean "to reduce in value." *Deranged* (insane) is unrelated to *debonair* (elegant), so choice A can be ruled out. *Disheveled* (untidy) and *decrepit* (weakened) have a degree relationship — they are similar in meaning, only *decrepit* is more extreme than *disheveled*. *Disperse* and *diffuse* both mean "to spread out," so choice C is correct. *Derelict* (abandoned) is unrelated to *dubious*

(doubtful), and *doleful* (sorrowful) is unrelated to *devious* (deceitful), so choices D and E can be eliminated.

2. B — The relationship in this question is synonyms: *affable* and *amicable* both mean friendly. *Jocular* (joking) is unrelated to *morbid* (gruesome), so choice A can be ruled out. *Negligible* and *paltry* both refer to a small amount of something and are synonyms, so choice B is correct. *Terse* (concise) and *frosty* have a degree relationship; they both can describe behavior that is less than welcoming, only *frosty* is more extreme than *terse*. They are not synonyms, so choice C is not correct. *Spectacular* is not related to *pugnacious* (quarrelsome), and *playful* is not related to *robust*, so choices D and E are not correct.

3. A — The relationship in this question is one of degree: a more extreme version of *flippant* (disrespectful) is *contemptuous* (disdainful). *Dubious* (doubtful) is also less extreme than *erroneous* (wrong), so answer choice A is correct. *Peerless* (unrivaled) is not related to *nondescript*, *ponderous* (thinking about something) is not related to *candid* (honest), *equivalent* is not related to *virtual*, and *erratic* (unpredictable) is not related to *celestial* (heavenly), so choices B, C, D, and E are not correct.

4. D — The relationship in this question is characteristic of: *altruistic* (generous) is a characteristic of a *benefactor*. *Vagrant* (wandering) is not necessarily a characteristic of a youngster, *prosaic* (dull) is definitely not a characteristic of a scourge (plague), and *superlative* (superior) may or may not describe an athlete, so answer choices A, B, and C are not correct. *Conniving* (plotting) is a characteristic of a *schemer*, so choice D is correct. *Brawny* (strong) is not related to *kindred* (related), so choice E can be ruled out.

5. E — The relationship in this question is opposites: *assimilate* (conform) is the opposite of *rebel* (refuse to obey). *Refute* (disprove) is not the opposite of *judge*, so choice A is not correct. *Resort* (utilize) is not related to *sanction* (approve), *mystify* and *perplex* are similar (and not opposite), and *converse* (discuss) is not related to *pillage* (plunder), so choices B, C, and D are not correct. *Reminisce* (remember) is the opposite of *forget*, so choice E is the correct answer.

Reading Practice

1. D — We can use the process of elimination on this question. If we look at answer choice A, the description of Hardy fits with the word *aloof* but not *condescending* — the passage does not imply that Hardy looks down on other people. Choice A is not correct. The passage does not describe Hardy as reserved, but rather as "vivid" (line 2). Choice B can be eliminated. While the passage does describe Hardy as unpredictable, it does not describe him as jovial. Rather, the passage describes that "he didn't talk much" (line 6). Answer choice C can be ruled out. The passage does describe him as both mysterious (they never know when he will come) and adventurous (he travels to distant lands), so choice D is the correct answer. The passage does

Workout #13

not describe Hardy as refined (he dines mostly on camp fare) or as demanding, so choice E is not the correct answer.

2. B — In line 2 the author lists "Jarrick, Hill, and myself, old classmates of his," implying that they all attended school together. Choice B is correct.

3. A — The passage describes that Hardy "came and went in the fashion of one of those queer winds" and "so many people are gray. Hardy gave one shock of color." This implies that Hardy has an energy about him that the narrator is not used to in his ordinary life. Choice A is correct.

4. E — In lines 17-19, the passage states, "Impersonally, he was entertaining about South Africa, about the Caucasus, about Alaska, Mexico, anywhere you care to think; but concretely he might have been an illustrated lecture for all he mentioned himself." The narrator compares Hardy to an illustrated lecture, which is both factual and impersonal in nature. Answer choice E is correct.

5. B — The narrator's tone is positive when he discusses Hardy, so we can eliminate choices A and D. Now we have to choose between *appreciative*, *humorous*, or *reverent*. *Reverent* implies a quiet respectfulness for an authority, and since the narrator does not see Hardy as an authority, choice E can also be eliminated. While the narrator seems amused by Hardy, the overall tone of the passage is not humorous, so choice C can be ruled out. Finally, the narrator does seem to appreciate Hardy with all his peculiarities, so choice B is the correct answer.

Math Practice

1. E — This is kind of a trick question. The probability that the coin will land heads up is the same for each time the coin is tossed: $\frac{1}{2}$. The fact that the first 2 tosses landed on heads does not affect the probability that the coin will land heads up the third time the coin is tossed. Choice E is the correct answer.

2. A — We can begin with the formula for the area of a triangle: $\frac{1}{2}(b \times h)$, where b represents the length of the base and h represents the height of the triangle. In this case, we can represent the height of the triangle as h. Since the base is 4 cm less than the height, we can represent the base as $h - 4$. If we substitute into the formula, the area of the triangle can be found using the expression $\frac{1}{2}((h - 4) \times h)$. If we first distribute within the parentheses, the expression becomes $\frac{1}{2}(h^2 - 4h)$. Now we can distribute $\frac{1}{2}$ and the expression becomes $\frac{1}{2}h^2 - 2h$. Answer choice A is correct.

3. B — We can begin by translating the words "the product of 3h and the sum of h and 5 is equal to –12" into the equation $3h(h + 5) = -12$. At this stage, we could factor, but since it is a multiple-choice test, we will simply plug in answer choices for h until we find the one where $3h(h + 5) = -12$. Let's start with choice A. If h is equal to –3, then the expression $3h(h + 5)$ becomes $(3 \times -3)(-3 + 5)$ or $-9(2)$. Since this simplifies to –18, not –12, answer choice A is not correct. Now we can try choice B and substitute in –1 for h: $3h(h + 5)$ becomes $(3 \times -1)(-1 + 5) = -3(4) = -12$. Since the expression $3h(h + 5)$ is equal to –12 when we substitute in –1 for h, answer choice B is correct. Since we have found an answer choice that works, we can stop there.

4. D — We can use fractional exponents to answer this question. We can rewrite the expression given as:

$$\left(x^{12} y^{10}\right)^{\frac{1}{3}}$$

Now we can distribute the $\frac{1}{3}$ exponent to each of the exponents in parentheses and our expression becomes:

$$x^{\frac{12}{3}} y^{\frac{10}{3}}$$

Since $\frac{12}{3}$ is equal to 4, our expression becomes:

$$x^4 y^{\frac{10}{3}}$$

Now we have to break apart the y exponent so that we have a whole number and a remaining fractional exponent:

$$x^4 y^{\frac{9}{3}} y^{\frac{1}{3}} = x^4 y^3 y^{\frac{1}{3}}$$

Finally, we can rewrite the fractional exponent of y as a cube root:

$$x^4 y^3 \sqrt[3]{y}$$

Answer choice D is correct.

5. A — To answer this question, we really only need to perform the transformation on point Q since that is the only point the question asks about. We can imagine drawing an arm from the origin to point Q. The arm would go over 6 units and up 3 units. If we rotate this arm 180°, it

now goes to the left 6 units and down 3 units. Point Q would then be located at (–6, –3). If we move that point down 2 units, the point Q' is located at (–6, –5). Answer choice A is correct.

6. C — If we look at the sequence, there are 4 terms in the sequence and –4 is the third term in the sequence. Therefore, if we divide the ordinal number (1st, 2nd, 3rd, etc.) by 4 (the number of terms in the sequence), the term will be –4 if the remainder is 3 since –4 is the third term in the sequence. Basically, if we divide the ordinal number of a term by the number of terms in the sequence and the remainder is 1, then the term will be the first term in the sequence. If we divide the ordinal number of the term by the number of terms in the sequence and the remainder is 2, then the term is the second term in the sequence, and so on. If there is no remainder, then the term is the last term in the sequence. In this case, we want the third term in the sequence, so the remainder should be 3 when we divide the ordinal number of the term by 4 (number of terms in the sequence). If we divide 41 by 4, the result is 10 with a remainder of 1, so choice A is not correct. If we divide 42 by 4, the result is 10 with a remainder of 2, so choice B can be ruled out. If we divide 43 by 4, the result is 10 with a remainder of 3. Therefore, the 43rd term would be –4, and choice C is correct.

7. D — We can begin by adding 3 to both sides. This results in:

$$nx < -9$$

Now we have to divide both sides by n in order to isolate x and the result is:

$$x < \frac{-9}{n}$$

In order for this inequality to yield the solution $x < -3$, n must equal 3. Answer choice D is correct.

8. E — We could factor the expression, but since this is a multiple-choice test, we can also use the process of elimination. The expression begins with $-10x^2$, but choices A, B, and C have neither a negative number first nor a negative sign in front of the expression. Choice D or E must be correct. If we use FOIL, choice D becomes $-(10x^2 + 6x - 5x - 3)$, which simplifies to $-(10x^2 + x - 3)$ or $-10x^2 - x + 3$. Since we need the middle term to be $+x$ (and not $-x$), choice D is not correct. Let's look at choice E. If we use FOIL, choice E becomes $-(10x^2 - 6x + 5x - 3)$, which simplifies to $-(10x^2 - x - 3)$ or $-10x^2 + x + 3$. Since this is the expression we are looking for, choice E is correct.

9. B — We can begin by eliminating the parentheses (remembering to distribute the negative sign to terms in the second set of parentheses): $6x^3 - 3x^2 + 2 - 3x^3 - 2x - 5$. Now we can use the commutative property to line up the terms in descending order (remembering that each term takes the +/– sign in front of it when it moves): $6x^3 - 3x^3 - 3x^2 - 2x - 5 + 2$. Now we combine like terms and the final expression is $3x^3 - 3x^2 - 2x - 3$. Answer choice B is correct.

10. B — To find $f(-4)$, we simply substitute in -4 for x in the function given:

$$f(-4) = -2(-4)^2 - 3(-4) - 2$$

If we start with parentheses, this simplifies to:

$$f(-4) = -2(16) - 3(-4) - 2$$

Now we perform multiplication and the function becomes:

$$f(-4) = -32 + 12 - 2$$

Finally, we perform addition/subtraction from left to right and the final answer is $f(-4) = -22$. Choice B is correct.

11. D — We can begin by representing the original ratio of red to green marbles as $3x:5x$. We can do this since in a ratio, the ratio parts are multiplied by the same number (in this case x) to find the actual number. If we remove 2 red marbles, then our new number of red marbles is $3x - 2$. If we add 10 green numbers, then the new number of green marbles is $5x + 10$. These numbers are in the ratio of 5:11, which can also be written as $\frac{5}{11}$. We can set up a proportion:

$$\frac{3x-2}{5x+10} = \frac{5}{11}$$

Now we cross-multiply and solve:

$$11(3x - 2) = 5(5x + 10)$$

$$33x - 22 = 25x + 50$$

$$8x - 22 = 50$$

$$8x = 72$$

$$x = 9$$

The next step is to remember what x represents: the multiplier in the original ratio to find the actual number of marbles. Since the original ratio was $3x:5x$, if we substitute in 9 for x, it becomes $3(9):5(9)$ or 27:45. If we add these together, we find a total of 72 marbles. Answer choice D is correct.

Workout #14

Words to Learn

Below are the words used in Workout 14. Refer back to this list as needed as you move through the lesson.

Getting in trouble

Censure:	criticize
Chastise:	discipline
Decry:	condemn

When will this end?

Culminate:	to complete
Definitive:	ultimate (final answer)
Incessant:	unending

Being mean

Caustic:	bitter
Deride:	mock
Disparage:	belittle (to put down)
Harangue:	scold

Broken

Defunct:	non-functioning
Erode:	deteriorate
Fiasco:	failure

Enthusiastic bunch

Avid:	enthusiastic
Effervescence:	enthusiasm
Vociferous:	noisy

Person you want to know

Discreet:	prudent (respectful of privacy)
Ingenuous:	honest
Intrepid:	fearless
Paragon:	a model (a perfect example)
Solicitous:	attentive

Synonyms Practice

1. DIATRIBE:
   - (A) discourse
   - (B) transaction
   - (C) tirade
   - (D) etiquette
   - (E) aversion

2. FETTER:
   - (A) restrain
   - (B) submerge
   - (C) grimace
   - (D) disperse
   - (E) consecrate

3. APEX:
   - (A) banter
   - (B) pinnacle
   - (C) legend
   - (D) skirmish
   - (E) draft

4. CREDULOUS:
   - (A) banal
   - (B) mediocre
   - (C) resplendent
   - (D) gullible
   - (E) wretched

5. DOLEFUL:
   - (A) laudable
   - (B) conniving
   - (C) mystical
   - (D) vigilant
   - (E) somber

6. PRUDENT:
   - (A) vehement
   - (B) exhausted
   - (C) discreet
   - (D) prosaic
   - (E) impending

7. EXUBERANT:
   - (A) effervescent
   - (B) eccentric
   - (C) emaciated
   - (D) enviable
   - (E) ethical

8. DERIDE:
   - (A) demure
   - (B) disparage
   - (C) deft
   - (D) dormant
   - (E) diligent

9. PUGNACIOUS:
   - (A) enraptured
   - (B) tolerable
   - (C) proficient
   - (D) squeaky
   - (E) belligerent

10. SOLICITOUS:
    - (A) encumbered
    - (B) noncommittal
    - (C) flawed
    - (D) attentive
    - (E) complacent

Workout #14

Analogies Practice

1. Displeased is to caustic as

    (A) vapid is to flexible
    (B) selfish is to decrepit
    (C) momentous is to civil
    (D) fallow is to messy
    (E) negligible is to devoid

2. Candid is to ingenuous as

    (A) victorious is to flippant
    (B) notorious is to infamous
    (C) defunct is to particular
    (D) adroit is to inept
    (E) glamorous is to composite

3. Incessant is to finite as

    (A) supple is to perishable
    (B) erroneous is to disheveled
    (C) petrified is to intrepid
    (D) available is to youthful
    (E) crass is to disgusting

4. Vociferous is to raucous as

    (A) cooperative is to amenable
    (B) kindred is to putrid
    (C) immaculate is to belittling
    (D) spiritual is to popular
    (E) calm is to precarious

5. Mundane is to chores as

    (A) incendiary is to deference
    (B) definitive is to influx
    (C) furtive is to zenith
    (D) annoying is to nuisance
    (E) ruthless is to fervor

Reading Practice

> There were four of us—George, and William Samuel Harris, and myself, and Montmorency. We were sitting in my room, smoking, and talking about how bad we were—bad from a medical point of view I mean, of course.
>
> We were all feeling seedy, and we were getting quite nervous about it. Harris said he felt such extraordinary fits of giddiness come over him at times, that he hardly knew what he was doing; and then George said that he had fits of giddiness too, and hardly knew what he was doing. With me, it was my liver that was out of order. I knew it was my liver that was out of order, because I had just been reading a patent liver-pill circular, in which were detailed the various symptoms by which a man could tell when his liver was out of order. I had them all.
>
> It is a most extraordinary thing, but I never read a patent medicine advertisement without being impelled to the conclusion that I am suffering from the particular disease therein dealt with in its most virulent form. The diagnosis seems in every case to correspond exactly with all the sensations that I have ever felt.
>
> I remember going to the British Museum one day to read up the treatment for some slight ailment of which I had a touch—hay fever, I fancy it was. I got down the book, and read all I came to read; and then, in an unthinking moment, I idly turned the leaves, and began to indolently study diseases, generally. I forget which was the first distemper I plunged into—some fearful, devastating scourge, I know—and, before I had glanced half down the list of "premonitory symptoms," it was borne in upon me that I had fairly got it.

Line 5 ... *10* ... *15*

1. The narrator of this passage can best be described as

    (A) well-informed.
    (B) easily distracted.
    (C) anxious.
    (D) uncomfortable.
    (E) impulsive.

2. The author's main purpose in this passage is to

    (A) introduce a sense of suspense.
    (B) give insight into a character.
    (C) inform the reader about the symptoms of a disease.
    (D) warn the reader about patent medicine advertisements.
    (E) describe a place.

3. The author includes the descriptions of the narrator's friends in order to show that the narrator

    (A) is social.
    (B) spends time with people who are unhealthy.
    (C) is experiencing something that is common.
    (D) is less healthy than his peers.
    (E) is easily influenced by the opinion of others.

4. As used in line 4, the word "seedy" most nearly means

    (A) unkempt.
    (B) energetic.
    (C) apathetic.
    (D) overlooked.
    (E) crummy.

5. The author uses the word "impelled" in line 11 in order to emphasize that the author

    (A) feels forced into one interpretation.
    (B) is made nervous by the information in the advertisements.
    (C) doubts the truth of the advertisements.
    (D) is frequently ill.
    (E) doesn't want to believe what the advertisements say.

Math Practice

1. A librarian is creating book bags. Each bag is to contain 2 non-fiction books, 3 fiction books, and 1 book of poetry. If he can choose between 5 non-fiction books, 6 fiction books, and 2 poetry books, how many unique combinations can he create?

    (A) 400
    (B) 800
    (C) 1,200
    (D) 2,400
    (E) 4,800

2. In the figure shown, what is the value of x?

    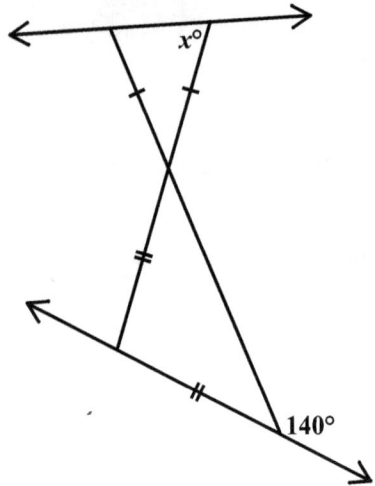

    (A) 55°
    (B) 70°
    (C) 75°
    (D) 105°
    (E) 110°

3. At a movie theater, matinée tickets are one price and evening tickets are another. On a day when 50 people attended a matinée and 75 people attended an evening show, the theater collected $525 in ticket sales. On another day, 30 people attended a matinée and 20 people came to the evening show and the theater collected $190 in ticket sales. What was the price of an evening ticket?

    (A) $3
    (B) $4
    (C) $5
    (D) $6
    (E) $7

4. Which is equivalent to $\sqrt{18}+\sqrt{27}$?
   - (A) $\sqrt{45}$
   - (B) $3\sqrt{5}$
   - (C) $5\sqrt{3}$
   - (D) $9\sqrt{3}$
   - (E) $3\sqrt{2}+3\sqrt{3}$

5. Line p is perpendicular to the graph of $3x + 5y = 4$. If the points $(-1, q)$ and $(5, 12)$ are on line p, what is the value of q?
   - (A) 2
   - (B) 5
   - (C) $\dfrac{48}{5}$
   - (D) $\dfrac{78}{5}$
   - (E) 12

6. The price of a sweater was decreased by 20% and then that price was increased by 25%. The final price is what percent of the original price?
   - (A) 90%
   - (B) 95%
   - (C) 100%
   - (D) 105%
   - (E) 110%

7. Which inequality represents all possible solutions to $2x + 5 < 9$ and $3x + 1 < 10$?
   - (A) $x > -2$
   - (B) $x < 9$
   - (C) $x < 2$
   - (D) $x < 2$ and $x < 9$
   - (E) all real numbers

8. What is the greatest common factor of $3(16x^2 - 4)$ and $3(4x^2 + 6x + 2)$?
   - (A) x^2
   - (B) $x + 1$
   - (C) $4x + 2$
   - (D) $12x + 6$
   - (E) $12x - 6$

9. When $(x + 3)(x^2 + 5x - 4)$ is expanded and like terms are combined, what is the coefficient of the term that contains x^2?

   (A) 5
   (B) 8
   (C) 9
   (D) 12
   (E) 15

10. Set X has 13 distinct elements and the union of set X and set Y has 20 distinct elements and the intersection has 4 distinct elements. How many distinct elements are there in set Y?

    (A) 11
    (B) 12
    (C) 13
    (D) 16
    (E) 33

11. The entrants in a race were asked for their age, in years. The histogram below represents their responses.

    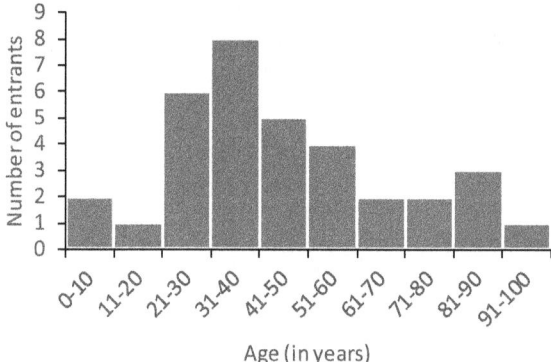

    Which of the following could NOT be equal to the median?

    (A) interquartile range
    (B) mean
    (C) mode
    (D) weighted average
    (E) range

Workout #14 Answers

Synonyms practice

1. C — The word list from workout #6 states that *tirade* means "diatribe." Answer choice C is correct. Remember, when you learn the vocabulary words, don't just learn the word given and its synonym; make sure that if the definition is given, you could provide the original word from the list. (In this question, *tirade* was the word in the word list but *diatribe* was the question word.)

2. A — The word list from workout #7 states that *fetter* means "restrain." Answer choice A is correct.

3. B — The word list from workout #5 states that *apex* and *pinnacle* both mean "peak." Therefore, they are synonyms, and choice B is correct.

4. D — The word list from workout #13 states that *credulous* means "trusting." The word includes the root *cred*, which means to believe, so a credulous person is someone who believes others easily. The word list from workout #11 states that *gullible* means "naïve," which also describes someone who believes easily. Answer choice D is correct.

5. E — The word list from workout #11 states that *doleful* means "sorrowful." Since *somber* is a synonym for *sorrowful*, answer choice E is correct.

6. C — The word list states that *discreet* means "prudent." Therefore, choice C is correct. Remember, when you study vocabulary, make sure you know the definition of the word in the list, but also that if you are given one of the definitions, you can come up with the word from the list. Learn the words forward and back.

7. A — The word list from workout #1 states that *exuberant* means "enthusiastic." *Effervescent* can also mean "enthusiastic." Choice A is correct.

8. B — The word list states that *deride* means "mock" and *disparage* means "belittle." Since *mock* and *belittle* are very close in meaning, *deride* and *disparage* can be considered synonyms. Answer choice B is correct.

9. E — The word list from workout #6 states that *pugnacious* means "quarrelsome," describing a person who is looking to start a fight. The word *belligerent* also describes someone looking to start a fight, so choice E is correct. You can remember the meaning of *belligerent* because the root *bell* means war.

10. D — The word list states that *solicitous* means "attentive." Answer choice D is correct.

Analogies

1. E — The relationship in this question is *degree*: *displeased* is less extreme than *caustic* (bitter). *Vapid* (uninteresting) is not related to *flexible*, *selfish* is unrelated to *decrepit* (weakened), *momentous* (important) is unrelated to *civil*, and *fallow* (inactive) is unrelated to *messy*, so answer choices A, B, C, and D can be ruled out. *Negligible* (paltry or a small amount) is less extreme than *devoid* (without), so answer choice E is correct.

2. B — The relationship in this question is *synonyms*: *candid* and *ingenuous* both mean "honest." *Victorious* is not related to *flippant* (disrespectful) and answer choice A is not correct. *Notorious* and *infamous* are synonyms, both mean "famous" in a bad way, and answer choice B is correct. *Defunct* (nonfunctioning) is not related to *particular*, *adroit* (skillful) and *inept* (unskilled) are opposite in meaning, and *glamorous* is unrelated to *composite* (combined). Since answer choices C, D, and E do not contain words that are synonyms, they are not correct.

3. C — The relationship in this question is *opposites*: *incessant* (unending) is the opposite of *finite* (limited). *Supple* (flexible) is not related to *perishable* (capable of spoiling) and *erroneous* (wrong) is not related to *disheveled* (messy), so choices A and B are not correct. *Petrified* (scared) is the opposite of *intrepid* (brave), so choice C is correct. *Available* is unrelated to *youthful*, so choice D can be ruled out. *Crass* and *disgusting* are synonyms (and not opposites), so choice E is not correct.

4. A — The relationship in this question is *synonyms*: *vociferous* and *raucous* both mean "noisy." *Cooperative* and *amenable* (willing) are also synonyms, so answer choice A is correct. *Kindred* (related) is not related to *putrid* (decaying), *immaculate* (spotless) is not related to *belittling* (criticizing), *spiritual* is not related to *popular*, and *calm* is not related to *precarious* (insecure), so choices B, C, D, and E can be eliminated.

5. D — The relationship in this question is *characteristic of*: *mundane* (boring) is a characteristic of *chores* (duties). *Incendiary* (inflammatory) is not a characteristic of *deference* (respect), *definitive* (ultimate) is not a characteristic of an *influx* (inpouring), and *furtive* (secretive) is not a characteristic of a *zenith* (peak). *Annoying* is a characteristic of a *nuisance* (something that is irritating), so answer choice D is correct. *Ruthless* (heartless) is not a characteristic of *fervor* (enthusiasm), so answer choice E can be eliminated.

Reading Practice

1. C — The passage states, "We were all feeling seedy, and we were getting quite nervous about it," (line 4). This shows that the narrator is nervous, or anxious, so choice C is correct.

2. B — We can think about genre with this question. It is in the style of a narrative passage from a book or story. This allows us to eliminate choices C and D since informing the reader

about the symptoms of a disease or warning the reader about patent medicine advertisements would belong in an informative passage and not a narrative passage. There is not a sense of suspense in the passage, so choice A is not correct. Choices B and E remain. Since the passage is primarily about a person, and not a place, choice B is the best answer and is correct.

3. C — The question is asking specifically why a piece of information is included. It doesn't show that the narrator is less healthy than his peers or is easily influenced by the opinions of others, so choices D and E can easily be eliminated. The descriptions of the narrator's friends do show that he is social and that he spends time with people who are unhealthy, but these ideas do not advance the main idea of the passage. The main idea of the passage is that when people read patent medicine advertisements or research diseases, they often convince themselves that they have the disease in question. In this case, showing that both the narrator and his friends have the same reaction show that it is a common reaction. Answer choice C best supports this main idea and is the correct answer.

4. E — In line 4, the narrator says that he and his friends were all feeling "seedy." He then describes the various physical ailments that they are experiencing. Therefore, *seedy* has to do with the physical effects of not feeling well. Since a person would not feel *unkempt* (messy), *energetic*, *apathetic* (uncaring), or *overlooked* because of physical ailments, we can rule out choices A, B, C and D. However, a person would feel *crummy*, so choice E is correct.

5. A — This question is asking why the word *impelled* is used in the passage. The word *impel* means to force, so using this word shows that the narrator felt forced to conclude that he was suffering from whatever disease the medicine advertised is supposed to cure.

Math Practice

1. A — To answer this question, we can draw out lines for each book that will be chosen:

$$\underline{} \ \underline{} \ \underline{} \ \underline{} \ \underline{} \ \underline{}$$
NF NF   F   F   F   P

Now we can fill in the number of options we have for each book chosen. For the fist nonfiction book there are 5 options. However, since we have already picked 1 book, there are only 4 choices for the second nonfiction book. For the first fiction book, there are 6 choices, but only 5 choices remain for the second fiction book, and only 4 choices remain for the third fiction book. There are 2 choices for the poetry book.

If we fill in the choices in our diagram, it now looks like:

$$\frac{5}{NF} \ \frac{4}{NF} \ \frac{6}{F} \ \frac{5}{F} \ \frac{4}{F} \ \frac{2}{P}$$

We now have to multiply the number of options for each book chosen by each other to find the total combinations. However, we also need to account for the fact that some options are repeats. Essentially, let's say we chose a book about Einstein as the first non-fiction selection and a book about Amelia Earhart for the second nonfiction selection. The problem is that if we chose the Amelia Earhart book for the first non-fiction book and the Einstein book for the second non-fiction book, that would be the same combination, but we will have counted it twice since the order that the books are chosen in does not matter. To remove the repeats, we need to divide by 2!3!. The 2! accounts for the 2 non-fiction choices that could be repeats. The 3! accounts for the 3 fiction choices that could be repeats. (2! means 2×1, 3! means $3 \times 2 \times 1$.)

Our problem now looks like this:

$$\frac{5 \times 4 \times 6 \times 5 \times 4 \times 2}{2!3!} = \frac{5 \times 4 \times 6 \times 5 \times 4 \times 2}{2 \times 1 \times 3 \times 2 \times 1}$$

If we do the math, simplifying first where we can, we find that there are 400 unique combinations for the book bags. Choice A is correct.

2. B — We start with the angle measure we are given, which is 140°. The angle adjacent to it is supplementary to 140°, so it must be equal to 40° (as shown in figure below).

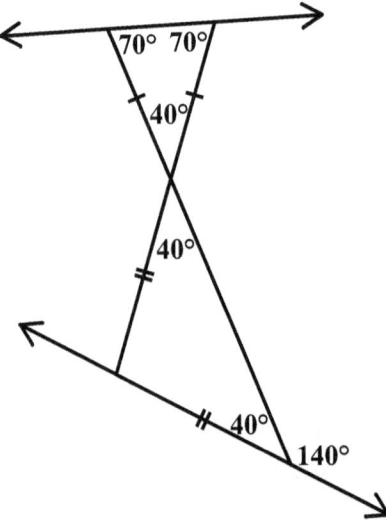

Since the triangle that the 40° is in is isosceles (two sides are the same length), we know that the angle opposite the other congruent side (the top angle of this triangle) is also 40°. Since opposite angles are equal in measure, the bottom angle of the top triangle must be 40° as well. The top triangle is also isosceles. The two congruent sides are opposite the top angles, so the top angles must be the same. The sum of the top angles and 40° must also be equal to 180°. Therefore, the sum of the top angles is 140°. Since the angles are equal in measure, we divide

140 by 2 and find that the measure of each top angle is 70°. The top right angle is marked as $x°$, so x must be equal to 70. Choice B is correct.

3. C — We can begin by setting up two equations. We can represent the cost of each matinée ticket as M and the cost of each evening ticket as E. To find the amount of money earned from each ticket type, we multiply the cost of each ticket by the number of that type of ticket sold. Therefore, the equation representing the sales from the first show is $50M + 75E = 525$, and the equation representing the sales from the second show is $30M + 20E = 190$. We now have 2 equations and can use the substitution method. We will isolate M in the first equation so that we can substitute in to the second equation to solve for E. If we begin by subtracting $75E$ from both sides in the first equation it becomes:

$$50M = 525 - 75E$$

Now we divide both sides by 50 and simplify, which results in:

$$M = \frac{525}{50} - \frac{75}{50}E = \frac{21}{2} - \frac{3}{2}E$$

We can substitute this for M in the second equation:

$$30M + 20E = 30\left(\frac{21}{2} - \frac{3}{2}E\right) + 20E = 190$$

Distributing the 30 results in $315 - 45E + 20E = 190$, which simplifies to $315 - 25E = 190$ if we combine like terms. If we subtract 315 from both sides, the equation becomes $-25E = -125$, so E must be equal to $5. Answer choice C is correct.

4. E — The first step is to simplify $\sqrt{18}$ and $\sqrt{27}$. We can factor $\sqrt{18}$ into $\sqrt{9} \times \sqrt{2}$ and $\sqrt{27}$ into $\sqrt{9} \times \sqrt{3}$. Since 9 is a perfect square, we can then rewrite $\sqrt{9}$ as simply 3 and our terms become $3\sqrt{2}$ and $3\sqrt{3}$. In this case, both terms have a 3 in front. However, the numbers under the radicals are different, and since the operation between them is addition, we cannot combine them since they are not like terms. Our final expression is $3\sqrt{2} + 3\sqrt{3}$. Answer choice E is correct.

5. A — When we see the word "perpendicular" on the SSAT, it almost always indicates that we are supposed to apply the fact that the slopes of perpendicular lines are negative reciprocals of each other. We can find the slope of the line given by rearranging the equation $3x + 5y = 4$ into slope-intercept ($y = mx + b$) form. We first subtract $3x$ from both sides, and the result is:

$$5y = -3x + 4$$

Now we divide both sides by 5, which produces:

$$y = -\frac{3}{5}x + \frac{4}{5}$$

Now that we have the equation in $y = mx + b$ form, we know that the slope is the coefficient of x, which in this case is $-\frac{3}{5}$. Therefore, the slope of the perpendicular line is the negative reciprocal of $-\frac{3}{5}$, or $\frac{5}{3}$. Now we can apply the equation for finding slope when we have 2 points:

$$m = \frac{y_1 - y_2}{x_1 - x_2}$$

$$\frac{5}{3} = \frac{q - 12}{-1 - 5} = \frac{q - 12}{-6}$$

Now we can use cross-multiplying to solve. This produces $5 \times -6 = 3(q - 12)$. If we combine like terms on the left and distribute the 3 on the right, the equation becomes $-30 = 3q - 36$. Now we add 36 to both sides and have $6 = 3q$. Finally, we divide both sides by 3 and the answer is $q = 2$. Answer choice A is correct.

6. C — To answer this question, we can make up a beginning price. We will say that the sweater was $100 to being with since that makes percent problems easier. If the sweater was $100 to begin, a 20% price decrease would be $20 and the new price would be $80. Now we have to increase $80 by 25%. Since 25% is equal to $\frac{1}{4}$ and $\frac{1}{4}$ of 80 is 20, the price would be increased by $20. The final price is $100. Since $100 is 100% of $100, answer choice C is correct.

7. C — We can start by solving each inequality. If we begin with the first one, $2x + 5 < 9$, we can first subtract 5 from each side and the result is $2x < 4$. Now we divide by 2 and find the solution set for the first inequality is $x < 2$. Now we find the solution for the second inequality, $3x + 1 < 10$. We begin by subtracting 1 from each side and the result is $3x < 9$. If we divide both sides by 3, the final solution set is $x < 3$. Now we have to combine the 2 solutions sets. Since the word "and" is used, the solution set includes numbers that show up in the solution set of both inequalities. Since the first solution set is $x < 2$ and the second solution set is $x < 3$, the area of overlap is numbers that are less than 2, or $x < 2$. Answer choice C is correct.

8. D — In order to find the greatest common factor, we need to factor each term into its prime factors. If we look at the first term, $3(16x^2 - 4)$, we might notice that we can factor a 4 from the expression in parentheses. The expression becomes $3 \times 4(4x^2 - 1)$ if we do this. We can also factor 4 into 2×2 and the expression is now $3 \times 2 \times 2 \times (4x^2 - 1)$. Now, we might notice

that $4x^2 - 1$ is a difference of the squares expression and can be factored to $(2x + 1)(2x - 1)$. Therefore, the prime factors of the first expression are 3, 2, 2, and $2x + 1$, and $2x - 1$. Now we factor the second expression: $3(4x^2 + 6x + 2)$. We can begin by noticing that a 2 can be factored from the expression in parentheses. The expression becomes $3 \times 2(2x^2 + 3x + 1)$. The expression $2x^2 + 3x + 1$ can be factored into $(2x + 1)(2x + 1)$. The prime factors of $3(4x^2 + 6x + 2)$ are therefore, 3, 2, $(2x + 1)$, $(2x + 1)$. The factors that the 2 expressions have in common are therefore 3, 2, and $2x + 1$. If we multiply these factors together to get the greatest common factor, the result is $6(2x + 1)$, which simplifies to $12x + 6$. Answer choice D is correct.

9. B — We can set up a chart in order to solve. We do this to make sure that each term in the first set of parentheses is multiplied by each number in the second set of parentheses.

	x^2	$+5x$	-4
x	x^3	$+5x^2$	$-4x$
$+3$	$+3x^2$	$+15x$	-12

If we then combine like terms, the final expression is $x^3 + 8x^2 + 11x - 12$. Since the coefficient of x^2 is 8 in the final expression, the correct answer is choice B.

10. A — The question states that set X has 13 distinct elements, and the union of sets X and Y has 20 distinct elements. If we subtract 13 from 20, we find that there are 7 new distinct elements that set Y adds to the union of sets X and Y. However, the intersection of the 2 sets contains 4 elements. Therefore, there were elements of set Y that were already included in the union of sets X and Y since they were in set X. Therefore, to find the total number of elements in set Y, we add the 4 elements that were also in set X with the 7 new distinct elements that set Y added to the union, and we find that there are a total of 11 elements in set Y.

11. E — This question requires applying theory instead of calculating specific values. Since a histogram does not give individual data points, we can't know what the mean, median, and mode are exactly. We can figure out an age range for the median, however. If we add up the height of the bars, $2 + 1 + 6 + 8 + 5 + 4 + 2 + 2 + 3 + 1 = 34$, we find that there were 34 survey respondents. Therefore, the median must be between the 17th and 18th survey respondents. Since the 17th survey respondent fell within the 31-40 age range and the 18th respondent fell within the 41-50 age range, we know the median age must be somewhere between 31 and 50. The smallest possible range would exist if the youngest respondent was 10 and the oldest respondent was 91. Since the difference between these 2 numbers is 81, the smallest possible range is 81, which is larger than the largest possible median age. Therefore, the median age range cannot be the same number and choice E is correct.

Workout #15

Words to Learn

Below are the words used in Workout 15. Refer back to this list as needed as you move through the lesson.

Wouldn't want to be this

Pungent:	strong smelling
Fetid:	smelly
Hackneyed:	stale (or overdone)
Ignominious:	disgraceful
Indolent:	lazy
Pariah:	outcast
Supercilious:	haughty (or snobby)

What's the truth?

Candor:	honesty
Guile:	deception
Conjecture:	speculate (make an assumption without the facts)
Incognito:	disguised
Indeterminate:	vague
Inexplicable:	mystifying
Nebulous:	vague
Overt:	obvious
Innuendo:	insinuation

Sure of itself

Adamant:	uncompromising
Inalienable:	absolute
Incorrigible:	unchangeable
Indomitable:	unconquerable

Synonyms Practice

1. RELEGATE:
   - (A) contort
   - (B) divert
   - (C) obliterate
   - (D) resist
   - (E) demote

2. CENSURE:
   - (A) commemorate
   - (B) corrupt
   - (C) compact
   - (D) chastise
   - (E) carouse

3. IMPEDE:
   - (A) contend
   - (B) waddle
   - (C) obstruct
   - (D) omit
   - (E) injure

4. VAGRANT:
   - (A) meandering
   - (B) ragged
   - (C) kindred
   - (D) husky
   - (E) slovenly

5. AFFIX:
   - (A) transcribe
   - (B) attach
   - (C) reveal
   - (D) culminate
   - (E) ascend

6. ERODE:
   - (A) return
   - (B) deteriorate
   - (C) embarrass
   - (D) verify
   - (E) coerce

7. JOCULAR:
   - (A) awry
   - (B) trivial
   - (C) devious
   - (D) sarcastic
   - (E) joking

8. PARIAH:
   - (A) outcast
   - (B) reputation
   - (C) innuendo
   - (D) shock
   - (E) oath

9. IMPROMPTU:
   - (A) emphatic
   - (B) disdainful
   - (C) positive
   - (D) unplanned
   - (E) collapsed

10. PERMEATE:
    - (A) ratify
    - (B) trade
    - (C) saturate
    - (D) foretell
    - (E) affront

Analogies Practice

1. Nebulous is to definitive as
   - (A) adamant is to vehement
   - (B) thankful is to grateful
   - (C) novel is to hackneyed
   - (D) subordinate is to overt
   - (E) avid is to perturbed

2. Supercilious is to pompous as
   - (A) ominous is to incredulous
   - (B) incandescent is to wise
   - (C) tangent is to fundamental
   - (D) humane is to morbid
   - (E) fetid is to pungent

3. Candor is to guile as
   - (A) animosity is to affection
   - (B) impurity is to buttress
   - (C) example is to paragon
   - (D) regret is to marvel
   - (E) liaison is to cushion

4. Inexplicable is to reason as
   - (A) altruistic is to generosity
   - (B) indeterminate is to gesture
   - (C) amicable is to plunge
   - (D) vapid is to interest
   - (E) judicious is to understanding

5. Indolent is to slothful as
   - (A) worrisome is to debonair
   - (B) astute is to perceptive
   - (C) energetic is to improved
   - (D) mundane is to responsible
   - (E) fastidious is to dreadful

Reading Practice

Of course there are disadvantages of suburban life. In the fourth act of the play there may be a moment when the fate of the erring wife hangs in the balance, and utterly regardless of this the last train starts from Victoria at 11.15. It must be annoying to have to leave her at such a crisis; it must be annoying too to have to preface the curtailed pleasures of the play with a meat tea and a hasty dressing in the afternoon. But, after all, one cannot judge life from its facilities for playgoing. It would be absurd to condemn the suburbs because of the 11.15.

There is a road eight miles from London up which I have walked sometimes on my way to golf. I think it is called Acacia Road; some pretty name like that. It may rain in Acacia Road, but never when I am there. The sun shines on Laburnum Lodge with its pink may tree, on the Cedars with its two clean limes, it casts its shadow on the ivy of Holly House, and upon the whole road there rests a pleasant afternoon peace. I cannot walk along Acacia Road without feeling that life could be very happy in it—when the sun is shining. It must be jolly, for instance, to live in Laburnum Lodge with its pink may tree. Sometimes I fancy that a suburban home is the true home after all.

When I pass Laburnum Lodge I think of Him saying good-bye to Her at the gate, as he takes the air each morning on his way to the station. What if the train is crowded? He has his newspaper. That will see him safely to the City. And then how interesting will be everything which happens to him there, since he has Her to tell it to when he comes home. The most ordinary street accident becomes exciting if a story has to be made of it. Happy the man who can say of each little incident, "I must remember to tell Her when I get home." And it is only in the suburbs that one "gets home." One does not "get home" to Grosvenor Square; one is simply "in" or "out."

1. The author's attitude toward the suburbs can best be described as

   (A) skeptical.
   (B) disdainful.
   (C) enchanted.
   (D) envious.
   (E) admiring.

2. The first paragraph suggests that a disadvantage of the suburbs is that

   (A) there are few cultural events in the suburbs.
   (B) a person may find their lives interrupted by the need to stick to a train schedule.
   (C) wives are sometimes left unhappy in the suburbs.
   (D) if a crisis arises, it can be difficult to get home.
   (E) the weather is unpredictable in the suburbs.

3. As used in line 4, the word "curtailed" most nearly means

   (A) shortened.
   (B) annoyed.
   (C) pleased.
   (D) worn out.
   (E) simulated.

4. The passage describes the author's view of Acacia Road as

   (A) pragmatic.
   (B) scornful.
   (C) uninformed.
   (D) idealistic.
   (E) insincere.

5. In the last paragraph, the author implies that living in the suburbs

   (A) does not feel like home.
   (B) requires more advanced planning.
   (C) makes daily events that occur in the city seem more notable.
   (D) makes marriage more difficult.
   (E) is less exciting than living in the city.

Math Practice

1. Samara draws a marble from a bag, replaces the marble in the bag, and then draws another marble. If $P(\text{red}) = 0.3$, $P(\text{green}) = 0.5$ and $P(\text{blue}) = 0.2$, what is the probability Samara will draw a red or green marble the first time and a blue marble the second time?

    (A) 0.16
    (B) 0.2
    (C) 0.5
    (D) 0.8
    (E) 1

2. If the area of the figure shown is $4\sqrt{3}$ cm², what is its perimeter?

    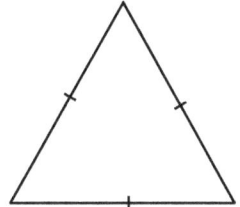

    (A) 4 cm
    (B) $4\sqrt{3}$
    (C) 8 cm
    (D) $8\sqrt{3}$
    (E) 12 cm

3. If twice the smallest of 4 consecutive numbers is equal to the largest number, what is the largest number?

    (A) −1
    (B) 3
    (C) 4
    (D) 5
    (E) 6

4. The atomic radius of hydrogen is approximately 2.5×10^{-11} meters. The atomic radius of mercury is approximately 1.5×10^{-10} meters. The atomic radius of mercury is about how many meters bigger than the atomic radius of hydrogen?

    (A) 10
    (B) 100
    (C) 1×10^{-1}
    (D) 1.25×10^{-10}
    (E) 1.25×10^{-12}

5. The distance between point A (−4, 3) and point B (8, m) is 13 units. What is one possible value for m?

   (A) −2
   (B) −1
   (C) 0
   (D) 1
   (E) 2

6. If a car is driving at 30 miles per hour, about how many feet does it travel in 1 second? (5,280 feet = 1 mile)

   (A) 4.4
   (B) 44
   (C) 88
   (D) 264
   (E) 2,640

7. If g is divisible by 9, then $4(g + 3)$ is divisible by what number?

   (A) 6
   (B) 9
   (C) 14
   (D) 15
   (E) 21

8. What are the solutions to $2x^2 + 11x - 6$?

   (A) 1, −6
   (B) $-\dfrac{11}{2}, 6$
   (C) −1, 6
   (D) $-\dfrac{1}{2}, 6$
   (E) $-6, \dfrac{1}{2}$

9. If $\frac{x-3}{x} = 0.625$, then what is the value of $\frac{x+3}{x+2}$?
   (A) 0.625
   (B) 0.875
   (C) 1.0
   (D) 1.1
   (E) 1.125

10. Use the sets below to answer the question.

    Set L = {5, 6, 7, 9, 12, 14, 15}
    Set M = {6, 8, 10, 14, 16}
    Set N = {8, 10, 12, 14, 16, 18}

    What is the intersection of sets L, M, and N?

    (A) {14}
    (B) {6, 14}
    (C) {6, 14, 16}
    (D) {14, 16}
    (E) {10, 14, 16}

11. A bus route is 140 miles long. The drive takes between 2.5 and 3 hours. What is the range of average driving speeds, in mph?

    (A) between 42 and 47
    (B) between 47 and 56
    (C) between 56 and 60
    (D) between 60 and 66
    (E) between 66 and 70

Workout #15 Answers

Synonyms Practice

1. E — The word list from workout #13 states that *relegate* means "demote." Answer choice E is correct.

2. D — The word list from workout #14 states that *censure* means "criticize." It also states that *chastise* means "discipline." Since being criticized and being disciplined can mean the same thing, *censure* and *chastise* are synonyms, and choice D is correct.

3. C — The word list from workout #13 states that *impede* means "obstruct." Choice C is correct.

4. A — The word list from workout #12 states that *vagrant* means "wandering." It also states that *meander* means "wander." Therefore, *vagrant* and *meandering* are synonyms.

5. B — The word list from workout #12 states that *affix* means "attach." Answer choice B is correct. Notice that *affix* and *attach* begin with the same letter, which is a clue that they might have a prefix in common and are therefore related in meaning.

6. B — The word list from workout #14 states that *erode* means "deteriorate." Answer choice B is correct.

7. E — The word list from workout #11 states that *jocular* means "joking." Answer choice E is correct.

8. A — The word list from workout #15 states that *pariah* means "outcast." Answer choice A is correct.

9. D — The word list from workout #10 states that *impromptu* means "unplanned." Answer choice D is correct.

10. C — The word list from workout #12 states that *permeate* means "saturate." Answer choice C is correct.

Analogies Practice

1. C — The relationship in this question is *opposites*: *nebulous* (vague) is the opposite of *definitive* (ultimate or final answer). *Adamant* (uncompromising) and *vehement* (insistent) are synonyms, and *thankful* and *grateful* are synonyms, so answer choices A and B are not correct. *Novel* (original) is the opposite of *hackneyed* (stale or overdone), so answer choice C is correct. *Subordinate* (lesser) is not related to *overt* (obvious), and *avid* (enthusiastic) is not related to *perturbed* (troubled), so answer choices D and E can be ruled out.

2. E — The relationship in this question is *synonyms*: *supercilious* (haughty or snobby) is a synonym for *pompous* (arrogant). *Ominous* (threatening) is not related to *incredulous* (skeptical), *incandescent* (glowing) is not related to *wise*, *tangent* (loosely related) is the opposite of *fundamental* (essential part of something), and *humane* is not related to *morbid* (gruesome), so answer choices A, B, C, and D are not correct. *Fetid* (smelly) and *pungent* are synonyms, so choice E is correct.

3. A — The relationship in this question is *means without*: *candor* (honesty) means without *guile* (deception). *Animosity* (hatred) means without *affection* (fondness), so answer choice A is correct. *Impurity* is not related to *buttress* (support), so choice B can be ruled out. Answer choice C shows a different type of relationship — a *paragon* is a perfect *example* — so choice C can be eliminated. *Regret* is not related to *marvel*, and *liaison* (contact) is not related to *cushion*, so answer choices D and E are not correct.

4. D — The relationship in this question is *means without*: *inexplicable* (mystifying) means without *reason*. *Altruistic* means to have *generosity*, not to be without it, so answer choice A is not correct. *Indeterminate* (vague) is not related to *gesture*, and *amicable* (friendly) is not related to *plunge*, so choices B and C are not correct. *Vapid* (uninteresting) means without *interest*, so answer choice D is the correct answer. *Judicious* (responsible) is not related to *understanding*, so answer choice E is not the correct answer.

5. B — The relationship in this question is *synonyms*: *indolent* (lazy) is a synonym for *slothful*. *Worrisome* (troublesome) is not related to *debonair* (charming), so choice A can be eliminated. *Astute* and *perceptive* are synonyms, so choice B is correct. *Energetic* is not related to *improved*, *mundane* (ordinary) is not related to *responsible*, and *fastidious* (demanding) is not related to *dreadful*. Answer choices C, D, and E are not correct.

Reading Practice

1. E — The author speaks of the suburbs in a positive manner. We can eliminate choices A, B, and D because the words *skeptical*, *disdainful*, and *envious* are negative. We have to decide whether the author's attitude toward the suburbs is *enchanted* or *admiring*. On this test, the more moderate answer tends to be correct, so *admiring* is a better answer, and choice E is correct.

2. B — The first paragraph describes a play that someone must leave early because of the train schedule. This implies that a person who lives in the suburbs must stick to a train schedule and that is a disadvantage. Answer choice B is correct. There is simply not evidence for the other answer choices.

3. A — The sentence containing the word *curtailed* discusses having to leave a play before it is over. Therefore, the experience of the play is shortened and choice A is correct.

4. D — In the second paragraph, the author describes Acacia Road. It describes a place where he never witnesses it raining, the sun shines, and "upon the whole road there rests a pleasant afternoon peace." This describes a place that is unrealistically perfect, or idealistic. Answer choice D is correct.

5. C — The key to this question is that we have to look for the answer with the most direct evidence. The paragraph describes a man who walks about the city, having experiences, and remembering them because there is someone at home he wishes to tell about these experiences. This implies that daily events in the city are more memorable (or notable) if a person is returning to the suburbs at the end of the day. Answer choice C best restates this and is the correct answer.

Math Practice

1. A — In order to find the probability that two events will both occur, we multiply the probabilities that each individual event will occur. The first event is that a red or green marble will be selected. Since drawing either a red or a green marble will work, we add the probability of selecting a red marble (0.3) to the probability of selecting a green marble (0.5) and find that the probability of selecting a red or green marble is 0.8. The probability of the second desired event (selecting a blue marble) occurring is 0.2. Therefore, we multiply 0.8 by 0.2 to find that the probability of both events occurring is 0.16. Answer choice A is correct.

2. E — (Note: if you haven't learned the rules for 30-60-90 triangles, don't worry about this problem — these rules are rarely tested on the SSAT. Remember, this book is only for the very hardest questions.) In order to find area, we need to multiply $\frac{1}{2}$ × base × height. This triangle, however, is not a right triangle, so the height is not a side of the triangle. Our first step is to draw in the height as a line down the middle of the triangle. Since this is an equilateral triangle, the height drawn in divides the triangle in half, creating two triangles with angle measures of 30°, 60°, and 90°, as shown:

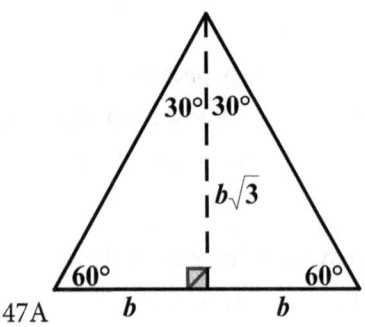

We can name half of the base b (for the base of the smaller triangle we created). Since this is opposite the 30° angle, the side opposite the 60° angle is $b\sqrt{3}$. If we substitute into the formula for area of a triangle, it becomes:

$$\text{area} = \frac{1}{2} \times b \times b\sqrt{3}$$

The area is given as $4\sqrt{3}$, but we cut that larger triangle in half, so the area of each smaller triangle is $2\sqrt{3}$. If we substitute that in, the equation becomes:

$$2\sqrt{3} = \frac{1}{2} \times b \times b\sqrt{3}$$

If we divide both sides by $\sqrt{3}$, the result is:

$$2 = \frac{1}{2} \times b \times b = \frac{1}{2}b^2$$

Multiplying both sides by 2 and then taking the square root of both sides produces $b = 2$. We have to remember that b was only half of the bottom side, however, so the whole side length is 4 cm. Since it is an equilateral triangle, we can multiply the bottom side length (4) by 3 and find that the perimeter is 12 cm. Answer choice E is correct.

3. E — This is a consecutive number problem. The question asks for the largest number, so we will represent the numbers as $x - 3$, $x - 2$, $x - 1$, and x, where x is the largest number. The question states that twice the smallest number is equal to the largest number. We can represent this as $2(x - 3) = x$. If we distribute the 2, the result is $2x - 6 = x$. If we subtract x from both sides and then add 6 to both sides, the result is $x = 6$. Since we defined x as the largest number, answer choice E is correct.

4. D — This question is asking us to find the difference between 2.5×10^{-11} and 1.5×10^{-10}. Since the exponents for the 10 in each expression are different, we have to first put them into the same place value before subtracting. One way to do this is to convert 1.5×10^{-10} into 15×10^{-11}. Now we subtract 2.5×10^{-11} from 15×10^{-11}, and the result is 12.5×10^{-11}. In order to write this in correct scientific notation, we need to move the decimal one place to the left and change the exponent for 10 to −10. The expression becomes 1.25×10^{-10}. Answer choice D is correct.

5. A — We can use the distance formula for this question:

$$\text{distance} = \sqrt{(x_1 - x_2)^2 + (y_1 - y_2)^2}$$

Now we can substitute in 13 for the distance and the coordinates for points *A* and *B*. The equation becomes:

$$13 = \sqrt{(-4-8)^2 + (3-m)^2}$$

If we square both sides and combine like terms in the first set of parentheses, the result is $169 = (-12)^2 + (3 - m)^2$, which can be rewritten as $169 = 144 + (3 - m)^2$. Now we subtract 144 from both sides and the equation becomes $25 = (3 - m)^2$. If we take the square root of both sides, we find that 3 − m can be equal to either 5 or −5, since taking the square root of a number produces both a positive and a negative number. This means that *m* can be equal to either −2 or 8. The question only asks for a possible value of *m*, and since *m* can be equal to −2, choice A is correct.

6. B — Our first step is to set up a series of proportions using conversion factors. We start with what we are given (the car drives 30 miles in 1 hour) and then set up the proportions so that the units we do not want cancel out:

$$\frac{30 \text{ miles}}{1 \text{ hr}} \times \frac{5{,}280 \text{ feet}}{1 \text{ mile}} \times \frac{1 \text{ hr}}{60 \text{ min}} \times \frac{1 \text{ min}}{60 \text{ sec}}$$

We are left with feet per second, so we know that we set up the problem correctly.

Now we can ignore the units and simplify before solving:

$$\frac{30 \times 5{,}280}{60 \times 60}$$

$$\frac{30}{60} \times \frac{5{,}280}{60}$$

$$\frac{1}{2} \times 88$$

Since $\frac{1}{2}$ of 88 is 44, answer choice B is correct.

7. A — One approach for this question is to plug in a number and see if we can rule out any answer choices (if *g* is divisible by 9, then any number divisible by 9 must follow the rule). Let's say that *g* is equal to 9. If we substitute in 9 for *g*, then 4(*g* + 3) is equal to 4(9 + 3), or 48. Since 48 is divisible by 6, we can keep choice A. However, 48 is not divisible by 9, 14, 15, or 21, so we can rule out choices B, C, D, and E. Since only choice A works with the number we chose, answer choice A is correct.

Workout #15

8. E — One approach to this question is to factor $2x^2 + 11x - 6$. If we use FOIL (first outer inner last), the only positive factors of 2 are 2 and 1, so we know that the 2 first terms of the factors must be $2x$ and x, and we have the general form $(2x + \_\_)(x + \_\_)$. Now we must try out factor pairs of –6 and multiply to see what would give us $+11x$ as the middle term. If we do this, we find that $2x^2 + 11x - 6$ factors to $(2x - 1)(x + 6)$. To find the solutions, we set each pair of parentheses equal to zero and solve for x. If $2x - 1 = 0$, then x must be equal to $\frac{1}{2}$ and if $x + 6 = 0$, then x must be equal to –6. Therefore, the possible solutions are $\frac{1}{2}$ and –6 and answer choice E is correct.

9. D — One way to solve this problem is to first solve for x. We can do this by multiplying both sides of the first equation by x. This results in $x - 3 = 0.625x$. If we subtract $0.625x$ from both sides, then add 3 to both sides, the result is $0.375x = 3$. Next, we divide both sides by 0.375, which produces $x = 8$. We can substitute 8 in for x in the expression $\frac{x+3}{x+2}$ and the result is $\frac{11}{10}$. If we divide 11 by 10, the result is 1.1, so answer choice D is correct.

10. A — The intersection of the sets includes numbers that show up in all 3 sets. Since 14 is the only number that shows up in all 3 sets, answer choice A is correct.

11. B — We can start this question by dividing 140 miles by 2.5 to find the speed in miles per hour (the word "per" tells us to divide) when the drive took 2.5 hours. Since $140 \div 2.5 = 56$, we know that one end of our range is 56 miles per hour. Choice B or C must be correct. Instead of calculating the second speed, we can use reasoning. If the speed was 56 miles per hour when the drive took 2.5 hours, the speed would have to be less than 56 miles per hour when the drive took 3 hours. Since 47 is less than 56, answer choice B is correct.

Appendix – Tips for the Writing Sample

When you take the SSAT, you will be asked to complete a writing sample. You will be given 25 minutes and two pages to write your response. You will be given a choice between an essay topic and a creative topic. The questions are relatively open-ended, giving you a lot of room to show your creativity – even if you choose the essay prompt.

So what kind of questions can you expect to see? For the essay prompt, you might see questions like:

- What would you change about your school and why?

- If you could relive one day, what day would it be and what would you change?

For the creative prompts, they might look like "story starters" that a teacher may have used in your school. The test writers will give you a starting sentence and you take it from there. Here are some examples of what these questions could look like:

- A strange wind blew through town on that Thursday night.

- He thought long and hard before slowly opening the door.

- She had never been in an experience quite like this before.

To approach the writing sample, follow this four-step plan:

Step 1: Choose topic

- There is no "right" choice when deciding between an essay or fiction prompt.

- If you are extremely creative and love playing with language, the fiction prompt is a great way to showcase this talent. This talent may not appear elsewhere on your application, so here is your chance.

- If you are great at organizing ideas and developing examples, then the essay prompt may be for you.

- If you do decide ahead of time whether to write about the creative or essay prompt, be flexible. You may get to the test, read the creative prompt and just take off with it. Alternatively, you may read the creative prompt and have nothing, but the essay prompt looks intriguing.

Appendix – Tips for the Writing Sample

Step 2: Plan

- Take just a couple of minutes and plan. It will be time well spent.

- If you are writing an essay, plan out what your main point (thesis) will be and what examples you are going to use.

- If you are writing from the creative prompt, decide where your story is going. You want to build to a climax, so decide ahead of time what that will be. You don't want lots of descriptive language that goes nowhere. Decide what your problem will be and how you intend to resolve it.

Step 3: Write

- Break your writing into paragraphs – don't create a two-page blob with no structure.

- If you are writing an essay topic, aim for 4-5 paragraphs (introduction, 2-3 body paragraphs, and a conclusion).

- If you choose a creative topic, remember to start new paragraphs for dialogue and to break up long descriptions.

- Write legibly. It does not have to be perfect and schools know that you are writing with a time limit, but if the admissions officers can't read what you wrote, they can't judge it.

Step 4: Edit / proofread

- Save a couple of minutes for the end to look over your work.

- You won't be able to do a major editing job where you move around sentences and rewrite portions.

- Look for where you may have left out a word or misspelled something. If a word is not legible, fix that.

- Make your marks simple and clear. If you need to take something out, just put a single line through it. Use a carat to insert words that you forgot.

The writing sample is not graded, but the schools that you apply to do receive a copy.

So, what are schools looking for?

Organization

Schools want to see that you can organize your thoughts before writing.

If you choose the essay topic, shoot for a 4-5 paragraph essay. There should be an introductory paragraph with a clear thesis, or main point. There should then be 2-3 body, or example, paragraphs. Each of these paragraphs should have its own, distinct theme. There should then be a concluding paragraph that ties up your ideas and then suggests what comes next. For example, if you wrote about how to improve your school, maybe you could finish up by describing how these changes could help other schools as well.

If you choose the creative topic, there should also be structure to your story. There needs to be a problem, which builds to a climax, and then a resolution. Since you only have two pages and 25 minutes to get this done, you should know your problem before you begin to write.

Word choice

Use descriptive language. Don't describe anything as "nice" or "good." Tell us specifically why something is nice or good. Better yet, show us and don't tell us. For example, don't just say that you would make the cafeteria nicer in your school. Tell us how you would rearrange the tables to create greater class unity and improve nutritional selections in order to improve students' academic achievement.

Use transitions. When you switch ideas, use words such as "however," "but," "although," and "in contrast to." When you are continuing with an idea, use words such as "furthermore," "in addition," and "in summation." Writing without transition words is one of the biggest complaints of English teachers, so show the reader that you know how to use them.

Creativity and development of ideas

It is not enough just to be able to fit your writing into the form that you were taught in school. These prompts are designed for you to show how you think. This is your chance to shine! For the creative prompts, this is your chance to come up with unique ideas. If you choose the essay topic, the readers will be looking more at how well you develop your ideas. Can you see the outcome of actions? Can you provide details that are both relevant to the essay and supportive of your thesis or main idea?

The writing sample is a place for you to showcase your writing skills. It is one more piece of information that the admissions committee will use in making their decisions.

Looking for more instruction and practice?

Check out these other titles for the Upper Level SSAT:

Success on the Upper Level SSAT: A Complete Course

- ✓ Strategies to use for each section of the Upper Level SSAT
- ✓ Reading and vocabulary drills
- ✓ In-depth math content instruction with practice sets
- ✓ 1 full-length practice test (different from the practice tests in *The Best Unofficial Practice Tests for the Upper Level SSAT*)

The Best Unofficial Practice Tests for the Upper Level SSAT

- ✓ 2 full-length practice tests (different from the practice test in *Success on the Upper Level SSAT*)

Books by Test Prep Works

	Content instruction	Test-taking strategies	Practice problems	Full-length practice tests
ISEE				
Lower Level (for students applying for admission to grades 5-6)				
Success on the Lower Level ISEE	✓	✓	✓	✓ (1)
30 Days to Acing the Lower Level ISEE		✓	✓	
The Best Unofficial Practice Tests for the Lower Level ISEE				✓ (2)
Middle Level (for students applying for admission to grades 7-8)				
Success on the Middle Level ISEE	✓	✓	✓	✓ (1)
The Best Unofficial Practice Tests for the Middle Level ISEE				✓ (2)
Upper Level (for students applying for admission to grades 9-12)				
Success on the Upper Level ISEE	✓	✓	✓	✓ (1)
The Best Unofficial Practice Tests for the Upper Level ISEE				✓ (2)
SSAT				
Middle Level (for students applying for admission to grades 6-8)				
Success on the Middle Level SSAT	✓	✓	✓	✓ (1)
The Best Unofficial Practice Tests for the Middle Level SSAT				✓ (2)
Upper Level (for students applying for admission to grades 9-12)				
Success on the Upper Level SSAT	✓	✓	✓	✓ (1)
30 Days to Acing the Upper Level SSAT		✓	✓	
30 More Days to Acing the Upper Level SSAT			✓	
The Best Unofficial Practice Tests for the Upper Level SSAT				✓ (2)

www.ingramcontent.com/pod-product-compliance
Lightning Source LLC
Chambersburg PA
CBHW081833170426
43199CB00017B/2722